THE TOP 10 AS WE HIT BOTTOM

WHAT GLOBAL WARMING, NUCLEAR WAR, CYBERWAR, PANDEMICS, SUPERVOLCANOES, ASTEROID STRIKES, OUT-OF-CONTROL A.I. AND OTHER UNPLEASANTRIES COULD DO TO US.

RESEARCH AND REALLY SCARY TEXT BY **JIM PARRY** HEARTWARMING ILLUSTRATIONS BY **RON BARRETT**

COMPILED BY THE CENTER FOR IMPENDING DOOM

SKYHORSE PUBLISHING

Skyhorse Publishing books may be purchased in bulk at special discounts for sales promotion, corporate gifts, fund-raising, or educational purposes. Special editions can also be created to specifications. For details, contact the Special Sales Department, Skyhorse Publishing, 307 West 36th Street, 11th Floor, New York, NY 10018 or info@skyhorsepublishing.com.

Skyhorse® and Skyhorse Publishing® are registered trademarks of Skyhorse Publishing, Inc.®, a Delaware corporation.

Visit our website at www.skyhorsepublishing.com.

10 9 8 7 6 5 4 3 2 1

Interior illustrations by Ron Barrett
Cover design by Daniel Brount

Library of Congress Cataloging-in-Publication Data is available on file.

ISBN: 978-1-5107-4647-3
eBook ISBN: 978-1-5107-4648-0

Printed in China

TABLE OF CONTENTS

GLOBAL

WARMING

GLOBAL WARMING: WHAT'S CAUSING IT.

THE TOP 10 CAUSES OF CLIMATE CHANGE

By percent of global greenhouse gas emissions.

1. Electricity and heat: 30.6%
    Burning fossil fuels.

2. Transportation: 14.8%
    Driving, flying, etc.

3. Manufacturing and construction: 13.3%
    Making things and building things.

4. Agriculture: 11.1%
    Especially to produce meat,
    particularly beef.

5. Other fuel combustion: 8.2%
    Wood, fuels to heat buildings, etc.

6. Industrial processes: 5.8%
    Especially cement and aluminum production.

7. Deforestation and land use changes: 5.7%
    Chopping down rain forests.

8. Fugitive emissions: 5.3%
    Gas flares and other emissions
    associated with energy production.

9. Waste: 3.1%
    Landfills produce methane.

10. Bunker fuels: 2.2%
    Ships in international waters
    and international flights.

Beef (verb): *to complain that people are complicit in destroying the planet,*
especially to complain while eating Angus steak

THE TOP 10 COUNTRIES CONTRIBUTING TO GLOBAL WARMING

The top 10 since pre-industrial times. Of the .7°C increase since then, the contribution of each country:

	°C
1. United States	.151
2. China	.063
3. Russia	.059
4. Brazil	.049
5. India	.047
6. Germany	.033
7. United Kingdom	.032
8. France	.016
9. Indonesia	.013
10. Canada	.013
10. Japan	.013

The top 10 emitting CO_2 today. Percent of world CO_2 emissions in 2015:

	percent
1. China	29.51
2. United States	14.34
3. European Union	9.62
4. India	6.81
5. Russia	4.88
6. Japan	3.47
7. Germany	2.16
8. Iran	1.76
9. South Korea	2.16
10. Canada	1.54

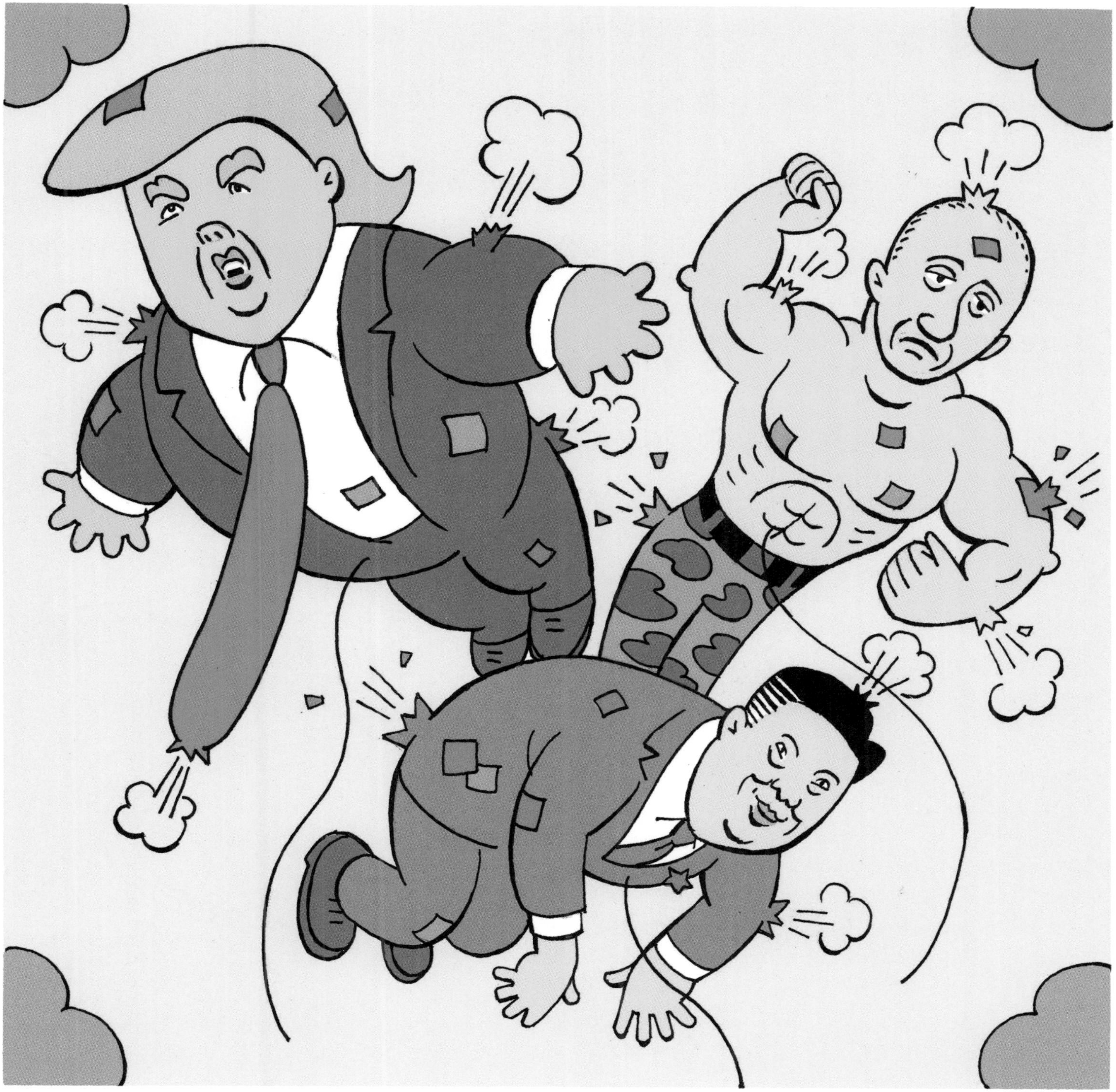

THE TOP 10 SOURCES OF METHANE, INCLUDING FARTING CLAMS

CO_2 gets the most attention but, molecule for molecule, methane traps more heat—depending on the time frame, about 30 times more. Here are the top sources of methane released into the atmosphere.

1. Wetlands — 22%
2. Coal mining, oil and gas production — 19%
3. Enteric fermentation (in the digestive process of animals such as cattle)* — 16%
4. Rice cultivation — 12%
5. Biomass burning — 8%
6. Landfills — 6%
6. Sewage treatment — 6%
6. Animal waste* — 6%
9. Termites — 4%
10. CH4 hydrates (frozen methane) on the sea floor — 3%

* In addition to CO_2, every cow releases between 70 and 120 kilotons of methane per year. Clams, oysters and mussels also give off methane; for example, 10% of the methane emissions from the Baltic Sea comes from "farting" clams.

GLOBAL WARMING: THE GOOD THINGS WE'RE PROBABLY GOING TO LOSE.

THE TOP 10 SPECIES WE'LL LOSE TO CLIMATE CHANGE

The polar bear is the poster-creature of climate-change victims, but these ten are actually closer to extinction. One of them—a mosaic-tailed rat—is already gone. Oh, we don't care about losing a rat? Hey, rats leaving a sinking ship is a warning . . . maybe we should be warned.

1. **Staghorn coral and other corals—bleached to death**
   Itself a living species, coral forms reefs that house a greater diversity of animal and plant life than even rain forests. Rising sea temperatures force coral to expel their algae. This bleaches the coral and can kill it. By 2050, more than 98% of the world's coral reefs will be afflicted by bleaching-level thermal stress. Goodbye, coral reefs.

2. **Ringed seal—less shelter for the pups**
   These Arctic seals need sea ice. After they give birth, they build snow dens on it to shelter their pups. But in warm spring temperatures, these dens collapse, exposing the newborns to cold, predators and pathogens. And now the ice is breaking up early, separating the newborns from their mothers. Goodbye, ringed seal.

3. **White lemuroid ringtail possum—dying in the heat**
   This timid, furry creature lives only in the high-altitude cloud forest of Australia's Mount Lewis. Above 86 degrees Fahrenheit, it can survive only a few hours. Mount Lewis's climate is rapidly changing. A severe 2005 heat wave killed most of these cool-loving possums; a 2014 survey spotted only four or five adults. Goodbye, white lemuroid ringtail possum.

4. **Adélie penguin—not enough fish and not enough ice**
   Warmer seas mean less fish, so these Antarctic penguins have to eat more krill—which is less nutritious. Melting ice turns these penguins' nest sites into puddles—in which their eggs can't survive. Since the 1970s, their colonies on the West Antarctic Peninsula have dropped at least 80%. Goodbye, Adélie penguin.

5. **Sea turtles—hardly any males left**
   They lay their eggs on sandy beaches, and hotter sands cause more of them to be born female. Already, 99% of immature green turtles born in the northern part of the Great Barrier Reef are female. If sand temperature tops 84.7 degrees during incubation . . .100% females. Goodbye, sea turtles.

6. **Sierra Nevada blue—driven up, into oblivion**
   This small butterfly, brilliant blue (the male) and dark black-brown (the female), lives only in the peaks of Spain's Sierra Nevadas and another small mountainous area further north. Drought, rising

temperatures, and reduced snow coverage are set to drive it even higher, into extinction. Goodbye, Sierra Nevada blue.

7. **Bramble Cay melomys—lost to higher high tide**
   Bramble Cay is part of the Great Barrier Reef. Since 1998, the cay's area above high tide has shrunk—and this mosaic-tailed rat lost 97% of its habitat. Last seen by a fisherman in 2009, it's been judged the first mammal to go extinct due to human-induced climate change. Goodbye, Bramble Cay melomys.

8. **Giant mountain lobelia—running out of mountain**
   A native of mountains in eastern Africa, this spectacular plant looks like a spiky tropical palm, but it shoots up a huge woolly top sometimes more than 30 feet tall. As the world warms, mountains are warming even

faster. By 2080, only 3.4% of its habitat will be left. Soon after . . . ? Goodbye, giant mountain lobelia.

9. **Baird's sandpiper—not enough insects for the chicks**
   These birds live in the high Arctic where rising temperatures are making them breed earlier in the season. This means more chicks are emerging before the peak abundance of the insects they feed on. Goodbye, Baird's sandpiper.

10. **Hawaiian honeycreepers—dying from malaria**
    These small, often brightly colored birds tend to live in higher elevations, such as the Kauai Mountains. As the world warms, mosquitos move into higher elevations, often carrying malaria. Honeycreepers are particularly susceptible to avian malaria. Goodbye, Hawaiian honeycreepers.

THE TOP 10 FOODS WE'LL LOSE TO CLIMATE CHANGE

1. Guacamole
2. Apples
3. Beer
4. Rice and Beans
5. Seafood
6. Chocolate
7. Coffee
8. Peanut Butter
9. Wine
10. French Fries

— *EcoWatch*

1. Coffee
2. Chocolate
3. Tea
4. Honey
5. Seafood
6. Rice
7. Wheat
8. Orchard Fruits
9. Maple Syrup
10. Peanuts

— *Thought.com*

"U.N. experts are saying that climate change could start threatening the world's supply of fruits and vegetables. Then Americans said, 'OK, let us know when it starts affecting Twinkies and Hot Pockets.'"

— Jimmy Fallon

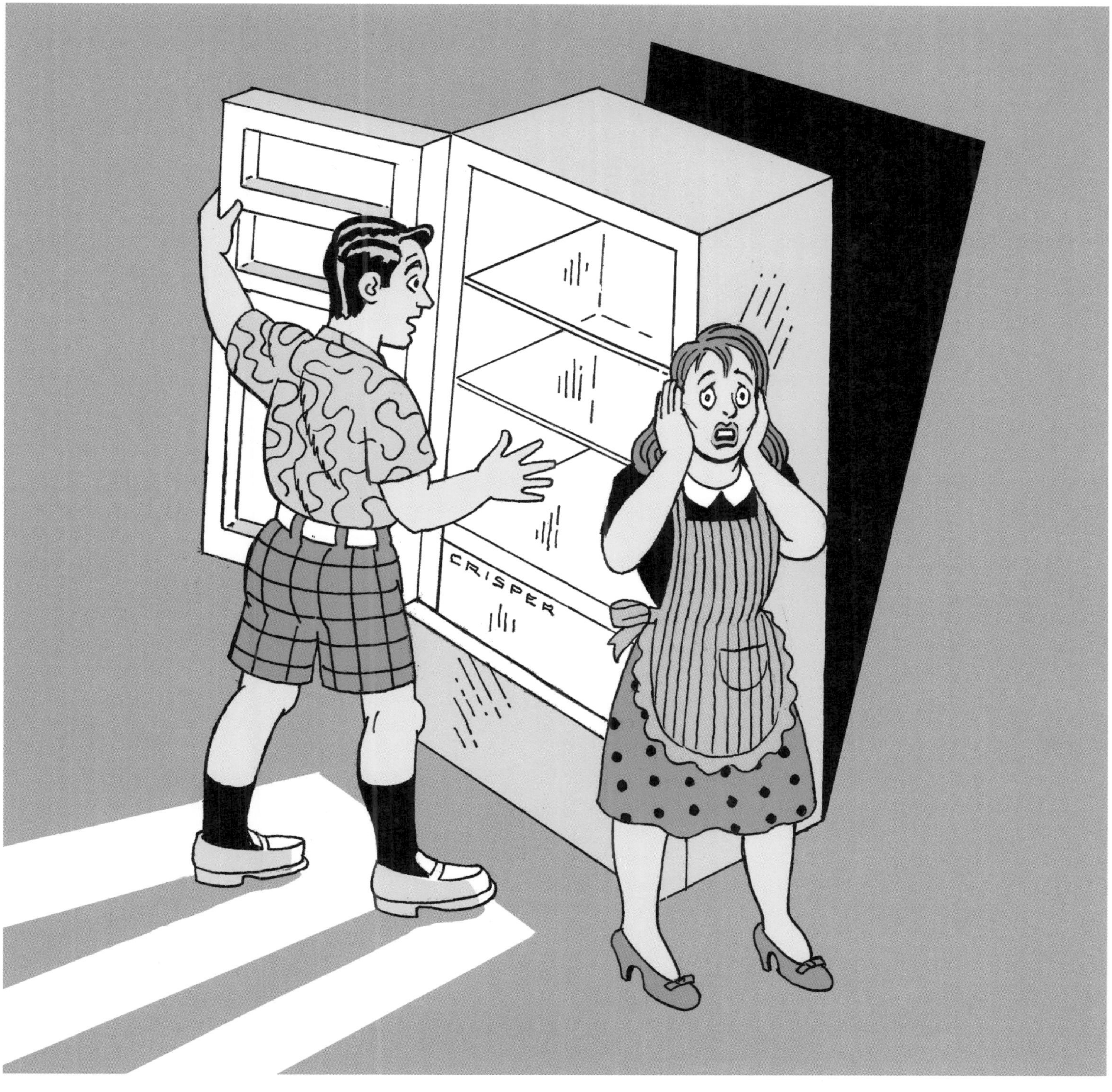
CRISPER

THE TOP 10 CITIES THAT WON'T BE 100% GUARANTEED COLD ENOUGH TO HOST THE WINTER OLYMPICS

Chance that daily minimum temperature in February is at or below freezing, 2041-2070:

1. Sochi, Russia 2014	36%
2. Gamisch-Parten, Germany 1936	56%
3. Vancouver, Canada 2010	63%
4. Oslo, Norway 1952	76%
5. Chamonix, France 1924	77%
6. Innsbruck, Austria 1964, 1976	79%
7. Sarajevo, Yugoslavia 1984	80%
8. Grenoble, France 1968	81%
9. Squaw Valley, California 1960	83%
10. Turin, Italy 2006	90%

Double black diamonds (noun): Symbol indicating that just beneath the few inches of snow on the ski slope are many large, sharp, black rocks

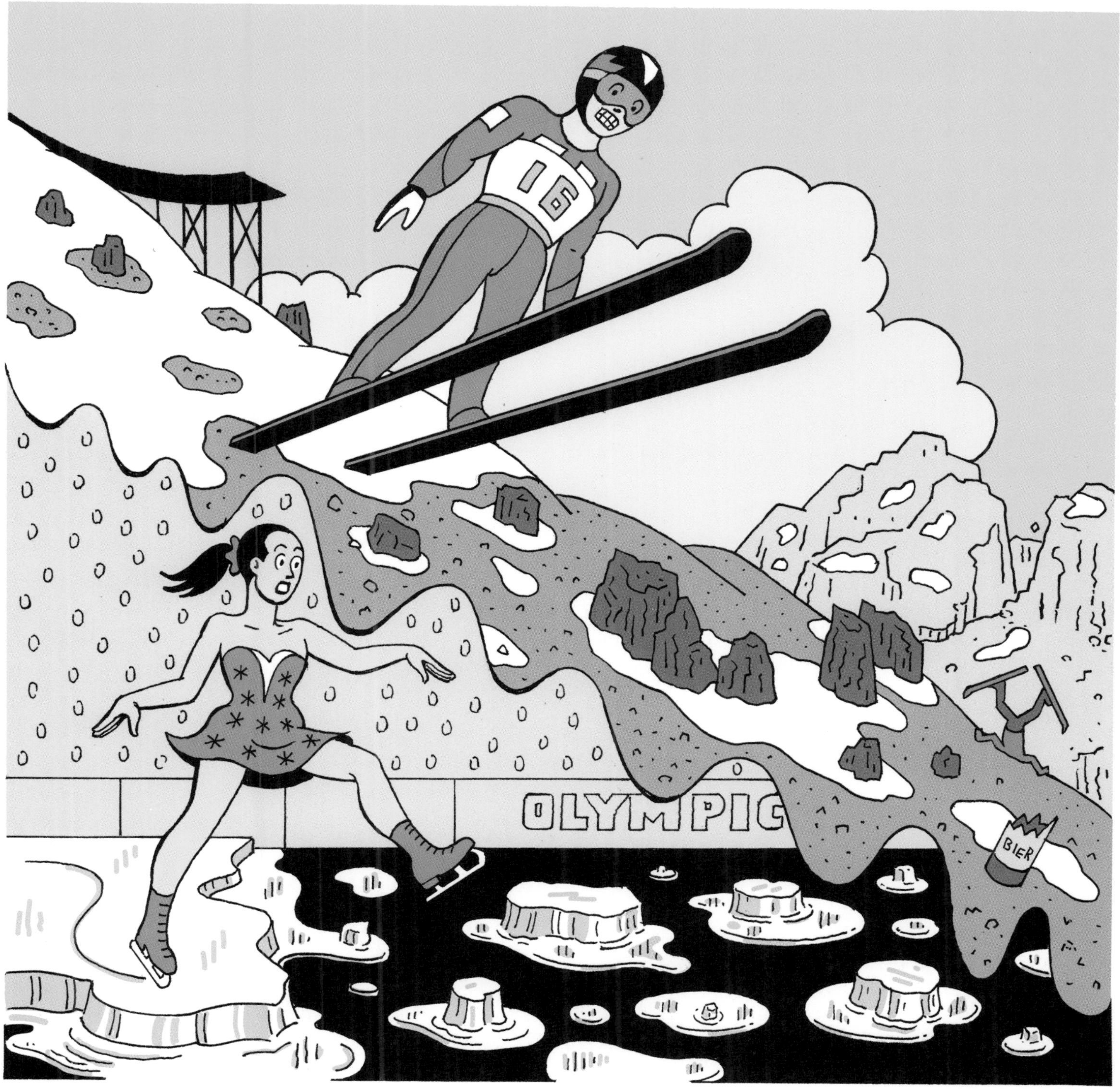
16
OLYMPIC
BIER

THE TOP 10 SHRINKING GLACIERS IN GLACIER NATIONAL PARK

Ice lost between 1966 and 2015:

1. Agassiz   lost 213 acres   (54%)

2. Sperry   lost 133 acres   (40%)

3. Jackson   lost 129 acres   (41%)

4. Grinnell   lost 113 acres   (45%)

5. Kintla   lost 107 acres   (33%)

6. Harrison   lost 98 acres   (19%)

7. Rainbow   lost 93 acres   (26%)

8. Two Ocean   lost 87 acres   (82%)

9. Blackfoot   lost 83 acres   (18%)

10. Logan   lost 70 acres   (56%)

Gravel National Park (noun): *What was Glacier National Park*

THE TOP 10 SPECIES SHRINKING IN SIZE BECAUSE OF GLOBAL WARMING

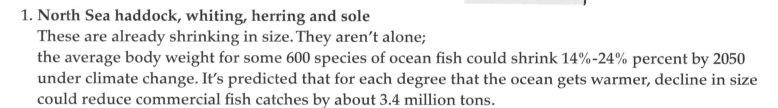

Marine life is most affected. Warmer seas speed up fish's metabolism, so fish need to draw more oxygen from the ocean. Yet global warming is reducing oxygen in some parts of the sea. Body size of fish decreases 20%-30% for every 1 degree Celsius increase in water temperature.

1. **North Sea haddock, whiting, herring and sole**
   These are already shrinking in size. They aren't alone; the average body weight for some 600 species of ocean fish could shrink 14%-24% percent by 2050 under climate change. It's predicted that for each degree that the ocean gets warmer, decline in size could reduce commercial fish catches by about 3.4 million tons.

2. **Copepods**
   These crustaceans are zooplankton, a key component of the ocean food web. Perhaps the most abundant multicellular animals on Earth, they are one to two millimeters long. As temperatures rise, they shrink: 2.5% for every 1 degree of Celsius. As they shrink, the fish that eat them will have to spend more time searching for more of them.

3. **Polar bears**
   Polar bear skulls collected in East Greenland in 1961-2002 are 2% to 9% smaller than polar bear skulls collected there in 1892-1938. Why? As the East Greenland coast has been losing sea ice, it takes bears more time and energy to hunt seals—so the bears have less energy that can go into their own growth.

4. Musk oxen

A musk ox can usually nuzzle snow out of the way to find foliage beneath. But as Arctic winters get warmer, there are more times when rain falls on accumulated snow. This coats the snowpack in ice—which a musk ox can't get through. If a pregnant musk ox has less to eat, her newborn is undernourished, born small, and grows up smaller.

5. Chamois goats in the Italian Alps

Young goats now weigh 25% less than young goats did 30 years ago. During this time, temperatures where the goats live have risen 3° to 4°C. Scientists think that to avoid overheating, the goats spend more time resting and less time foraging. Being smaller may help them; smaller animals shed heat faster than larger ones.

6. Soay sheep on the Scottish islands of St. Kilda

Today they weigh about 6.6 pounds less than Soay sheep in 1986. Why? Since 1980, winters here have become warmer and shorter; grass grows for more of the year. In this climate, there's less need to pile on pounds in the first years of life. Lambs grow more slowly, become smaller adults and are capable of raising only smaller lambs.

7. Salamanders

Six species in the Appalachians have been growing shorter over the last 50 years, each generation shrinking by one percent. Salamanders in the southernmost sites, where temperatures rose the most, shrank the most.

8. Beetles

In the wild, the four largest species have shrunk 20% in the past 45 years. This echoes the findings that, when raised in the lab, ground beetles shrank by 1% of their body weight for every 1°C increase in temperature.

9. Oysters and sea scallops

More CO_2 in the atmosphere, less carbonate in sea water. As shellfish need it to grow their shells, they become smaller.

10. Red deer, snakes, toads, tortoises and blue tits

All these have shrunk in size over the last century—because of global warming, say scientists.

Will humans also shrink? The 2017 movie *Downsizing* imagines that scientists have discovered how to shrink humans to five inches tall. And the movie says that Arctic methane emissions threaten the extinction of the human race. But perhaps inside a vault inside a mountain, these small humans will survive. The movie doesn't make clear what happens to the small fish, small copepods, small polar bears, etc.

THE TOP 10 CULTURAL UNESCO WORLD HERITAGE SITES THREATENED BY CLIMATE CHANGE

(listed alphabetically)

1. **Chan Chan Archaeological Zone, Peru**
   A vast adobe complex including temples, citadels and palaces, Chan Chan is the largest city in pre-Columbian America and the seat of the ancient Chimu civilization, reaching its peak in the 15th century.

2. **Chavin Archaeological Site, Peru**
   At 10,430 feet in a valley in the Andes, this complex of terraces and squares began to be built around 1200 BC and was occupied until around 400-500 BC by the Chavin, a major pre-Inca culture.

3. **Historic Center of Cesky Krumlov, Czech Republic**
   Built around a 13th-century castle with Gothic, Renaissance, and Baroque elements, this is a small medieval town whose architectural heritage, including burgher houses, has remained intact.

4. **Historic Center of Prague, Czech Republic**
   Built between the 11th and 18th centuries and saved from any large-scale urban renewal, its magnificent monuments include Hradcani Castle, St. Vitus Cathedral, Charles Bridge and many churches and palaces.

5. **Hoi An Ancient Town, Vietnam**
   Cut through with canals, this town has wooden Chinese shophouses and temples, colorful French colonial buildings, ornate Vietnamese "tube" houses and the iconic Japanese Covered Bridge with its pagoda.

6. **Port, Fortresses and Group of Monuments, Cartagena, Colombia**
   An eminent example of military architecture of the 16th, 17th, and 18th centuries, this is the most extensive systems of fortifications in South America. Within the colonial walled city are beautiful civil, religious and residential monuments.

7. **Rapa Nui National Park, Easter Island, Chile**

   On the most remote inhabited island on the planet, from the 10th through the 16th century the Rapa Nui people built carved about 900 *moai*—colossal statues representing ancestors.

8. **Timbuktu, Mali**

   In the 15th and 16th centuries, Timbuktu was an intellectual and spiritual capital of Islam. Its three great mosques—Djingareyber, Sankore, and Sidi Yahi—recall the city's golden age.

9. **Tower of London; Palace of Westminster and Westminster Abbey including Saint Margaret's Church; Maritime Greenwich, United Kingdom**

   The Tower was built by William the Conqueror; the Westminster site is a symbol of royal power; the buildings at Greenwich reflect English artistic and scientific endeavor in the 17th and 18th centuries.

10. **Venice and its Lagoon, Italy**

    The entire city is an extraordinary architectural masterpiece. Even the smallest building is apt to contains works by some of the world's greatest artists: Giorgione, Titian, Tintoretto, Veronese, etc.

"General Grant seriously remarked to a particularly bright young woman that Venice would be a fine city if it were drained."

Henry Adams, *The Education of Henry Adams*

THE TOP 10 NATURAL UNESCO WORLD HERITAGE SITES THREATENED BY CLIMATE CHANGE

Listed by the date each was designated a World Heritage Site, the earliest first.

1. **Sagarmatha National Park, Nepal, 1979**
   With dramatic mountains, glaciers, and deep valleys, this area of the Himalayas is dominated by Mt. Everest and is home to rare species such as the snow leopard.

2. **Ichkeul National Park, Tunisia, 1980**
   Ichkeul Lake is the last remaining lake in a chain that once extended across North Africa. Today the lake and wetlands are an important stopover for migrating birds such as storks and pink flamingos.

3. **Great Barrier Reef, Australia, 1981**
   Its 1,430 miles of coral make it the largest living thing on earth. Comprised of thousands of reefs and hundreds of islands, this ecosystem is home to countless species of fish and other aquatic life.

4. **Huascaran National Park, Peru, 1985**
   In the world's highest tropical mountain range, its deep ravines, glacial lakes and rich vegetation make it spectacularly beautiful. It is home to creatures such as the Andean condor.

5. **Kilimanjaro National Park, Tanzania, 1987**
   Looming over the savannah and encircled by mountain forest, the snowy peak of Kilimanjaro is the highest point in Africa. Many endangered species such as rhinos, lions, and elephants live in the park.

5. **Sundarbans National Park, India and Bangladesh, 1987**
   Covering 3,900 square miles of land and water in the Ganges delta, it contains the world's largest mangrove forests and is home to many rare or endangered species, including tigers.

7. **Wet Tropics of Queensland, Australia, 1988**
   Its rainforest with wild rivers, waterfalls, and rugged gorges holds an unmatched record of the evolution of land plants over the last 200 million years, and is home to many marsupials and songbirds.

8. **Komodo National Park, Indonesia, 1991**
   These volcanic islands are home to about 5,700 giant lizards, the "Komodo dragons" which, existing nowhere else in the world, are of great interest to scientists studying evolution.

9. **The Sundarbans, Bangladesh, 1997**
   Adjacent to the Sundarbans National Park, this is one of the world's largest mangrove forests. It is home to 260 species of birds and to tigers, crocodiles and pythons.

10. **Golden Mountains of Altai, Russia, 1998**
    Ranging from steppe to forest to alpine vegetation, this site of more than 6,220 square miles in central Siberia is an important habitat for endangered species such as the snow leopard.

10. **Ouadi Qadisha (the Holy Valley) and Horsh Arz el-Rab (the Forest of the Cedars of God), Lebanon, 1998**
    In the rocky cliffs of the Qadisha Valley are some of the world's earliest Christian monasteries and hermitages. Nearby are vestiges of the vast cedar forests prized, in ancient times, for wood for major religious buildings.

In total, there are 16 such World Heritage sites threatened by climate change.
The above list omits sites in Costa Rica, Australia, Greenland, South Africa
and Switzerland, all of which were designated later.

GLOBAL WARMING: THE BAD THINGS IT'S ALREADY GIVEN US.

THE TOP 10 WARMEST YEARS EVER

(1880-2018)

	Anomaly °C	Anomaly °F
1. 2016	.94	1.69
2. 2015	.90	1.62
3. 2017	.84	1.51
4. 2018	.77	1.39
5. 2014	.74	1.33
6. 2010	.70	1.26
7. 2013	.66	1.19
8. 2005	.65	1.17
9. 2009	.64	1.15
10. 1998	.63	1.13

July 2019 was the warmest month on record since 1880. In July, NOAA (National Oceanic and Atmospheric Administration) said that, so far, 2019 was tied for the second warmest year on record, behind only 2016—and had a 100% chance of ending up as one of the five warmest years on record.

Actual church sign: "Too hot to change sign. Message inside."

THE TOP 10 DEADLY HEAT WAVES

**Note that nine of these ten occurred since 1970,
when global temperatures began their uninterrupted rise.**

1. Europe 2003	70,000 killed
2. Russia 2010	56,000 killed
3. Eastern United States 1901	9,500 killed
4. United States 1988	5,000-10,000 killed
5. Europe 2006	3,418 killed
6. India 1998	2,541 killed
7. India 2015	2,500 killed
8. Pakistan 2015	2,000 killed
9. United States 1980	1,700-5,000 killed
10. Japan 2019	1,718 killed

THE TOP 10 CONFLICTS THAT CLIMATE CHANGE HAS HELPED FOMENT

The U.S. military calls climate change a "threat multiplier." A 2014 Department of Defense report identifies it as "the root of government instability [which] can create an avenue for extremist ideologies and conditions that foster terrorism."

1. Genocide in Darfur

It's been called the first climate war in modern times. From 1967 to 2007, the desert in northern Sudan advanced 60 miles south and rainfall dropped 16%-30%. Disappearing pasture and evaporating water holes raised tensions between farmers and herders as, for example, when Arab nomads, pushed south, cut down trees to feed their camels. Killings—including genocide—began in 2003. As of today, 480,000 people have been killed and 2.8 million have been displaced.

2. Insurgencies from Boko Haram, spreading from Nigeria

Since the 1970s, the number of rainy days in northeastern Nigeria has dropped 53%. Southward desertification of the Sahara of 1-10 kilometer per year has reduced arable land. Over the past 50 years, Lake Chad has shrunk 90%, with half of the decrease being due to climate change. The area around the lake is experiencing food and water shortages and economic near-collapse—an ideal breeding ground for recruitment by Boko Haram. Its violence now spreads into Cameroon, Niger and Chad.

3. The Syrian civil war and the rise of ISIS

In the last three decades, average rainfall has hit new record lows. Since the 1990s, droughts have increased in frequency and intensity—and human activity has made severe drought two to three times more likely than natural variability. The extreme drought of 2006-2011 helped displace two million people within Syria and drove many into extreme poverty and food insecurity; this fueled social unrest which precipitated the civil war and made room for ISIS.

4. **Afghanistan heats up, literally and figuratively**
   Since 1960, the mean annual temperature has risen .6°C and there are now an additional 25 hot days per year. Rainfall has decreased 2% per decade. Desertification is advancing. The country has been hit by devastating droughts, floods and landslides—a fertile environment for insurgents and for networks thriving on drug trafficking, kidnapping, extortion and contraband. Temperatures are projected to keep increasing—as much as another 4°C by the 2060s—as are droughts and floods.

5. **Somalia: drought makes famine makes conflict**
   Over the past decade, climate change-related desertification has expanded in Somalia. A mutually reinforcing cycle of drought, famine and conflict has internally displaced 750,000 Somalis; 1.5 million people—17% of the population—desperately need humanitarian relief. Amid this chaos, rival clan violence has emerged as the norm . . . a violence that has spilled over into Kenya.

6. **Terror spreading to Europe**
   Across the Middle East and Africa, agricultural land is turning to desert and heat waves are killing off crops and grazing animals. Farmers, fishermen and herders are being forced into cities—and they and city dwellers have often become prey to violence exacerbated by diminishing resources. This has diminished security and heightened fear. Fleeing their countries, some people succeed in reaching Europe. And some—angry at what has happened to them and prey to terrorist ideologies—carry the violence with them.

7. **Venezuela is losing its last glacier and social stability**
   Until 1991, Venezuela had five glaciers. Now there's just one. Its meltwater provides much of the country's drinking water. But this glacier is only 10% of what it was 30 years ago, and in ten or twenty years it will be gone. Climate change is also increasing the torrential rains, massive flooding, droughts and hurricanes that hit Venezuela. And more and more of its urban slums are on unstable terrain prone to mudslides. No surprise if the country slides into more violence.

8. **Guatemala's urban violence and organized crime**
   In 2008, Guatemala was hit by a severe tropical storm with mudslides. Then came a prolonged drought. In 2010 came a cyclone which destroyed a large part of the country's infrastructure. Food production for domestic consumption was hurt as were coffee and sugar exports. People's basic livelihoods are shaky, the government can't provide security. In parts of the country, criminal gangs are taking over, providing state-like services but also spreading violence.

9. **Bangladeshis trying to flee into India**

Bangladesh's vulnerability to climate change is second only to India's; it has already suffered some of the fastest sea level rises in the world. Bangladesh's prime minister has told the UN that a further one-meter rise would submerge a fifth of the country and turn 30 million people into "climate refugees." Up to 20 million Bangladeshis are already living illegally in India. India has a militarized fence along 70% of a 2500-mile border to keep Bangladeshis out. As water rises, so will violence on that border.

10. **Mekong Delta: too much salt water**

The Mekong River Delta is shared by Thailand, Laos, Cambodia and Vietnam. Sea level rise is wiping out 23 square miles of rice fields per year. At the projected rate, 40% of the delta will be gone by 2100. Already, nearly half its population has no access to fresh water. And erratic rainfall patterns have made floods worse during the wet season. China is building more dams on the Upper Mekong, and Thailand, Laos, Cambodia and Vietnam are planning more of their own dams—exacerbating climate-caused water tensions.

THE TOP 10 INVASIVE SPECIES MADE MORE INVASIVE BY CLIMATE CHANGE

They're taking over!

1. Burmese pythons in the Everglades

2. Lung worms in Alaskan musk ox

3. Argentine ants in California

4. Zebra mussels in the Great Lakes

5. Yellow toadflax in Colorado

6. Asian carp in the Great Lakes

7. Killer bees everywhere

8. Northern snakeheads everywhere

9. Spruce budworms everywhere

10. Kudzu everywhere

If you plant a kudzu in your back yard, it will beat you to your back door.

– rumor in the American South

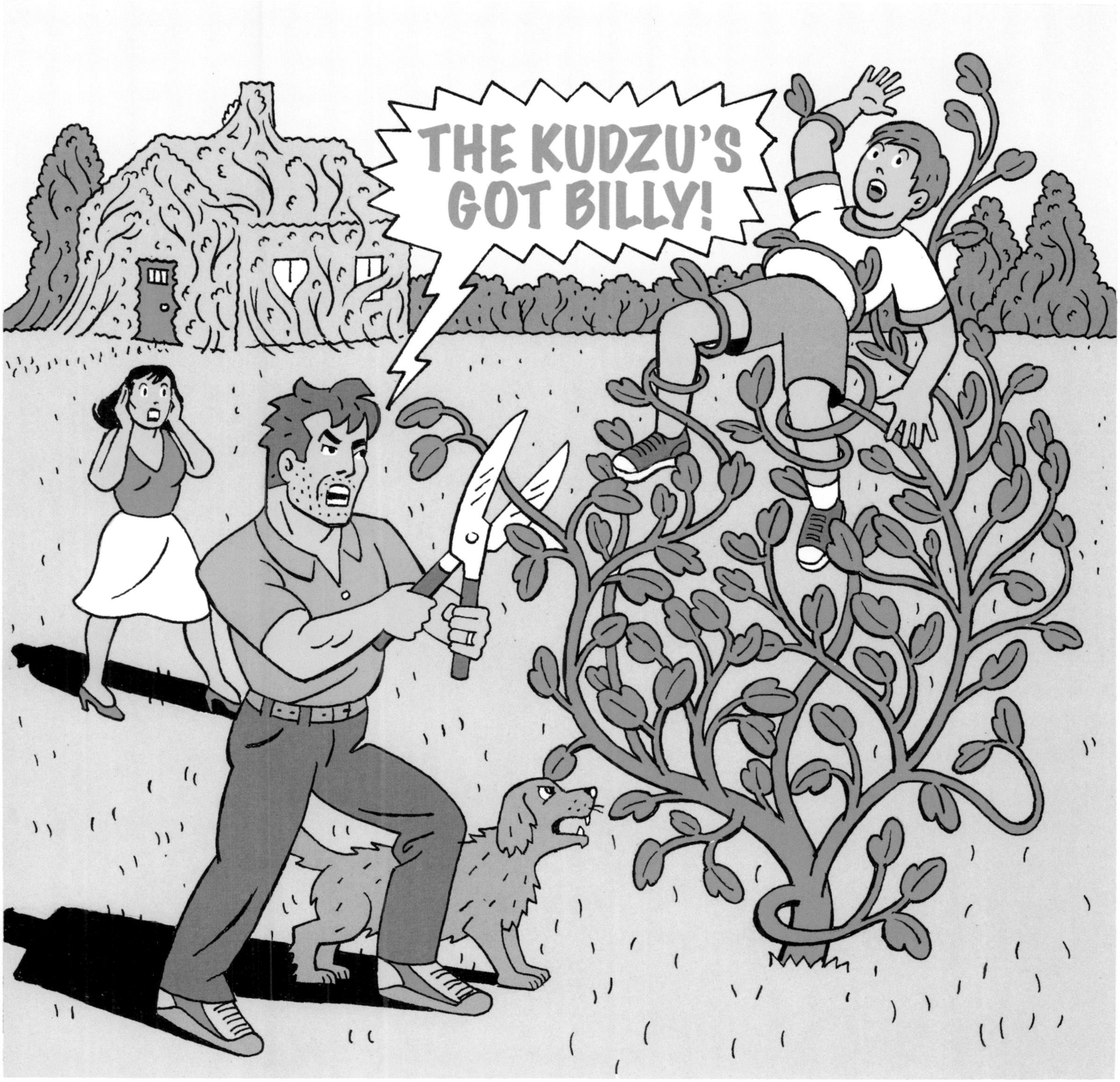
THE KUDZU'S GOT BILLY!

THE TOP 10 AVALANCHES MOSTLY CAUSED BY GLOBAL WARMING

Warmer air holds more moisture, which creates more winter snowfall, putting more snow on top of a glacier or a slope. If there has been more summer rain, the water saturates the ground below and acts as a lubricant. With more weight on top and less friction on the bottom to hold the glacier or the slope in place . . . avalanche!

The first three avalanches are ranked by size and speed.
The remaining seven are listed roughly chronologically.

1. **Aru Glacier, western Tibet, July 21, 2016**
   247 million cubic feet of snow and ice collapsed off the glacier, spreading more than five miles in three minutes at top speeds of nearly 200 mph, killing nine people.

2. **Another glacier in the Aru Range, western Tibet, September 24, 2016**
   Similar to the collapse off Aru Glacier—as big and fast and as stunning to glaciologists, but this one caused no fatalities.

3. **Kolka Glacier on Mount Kazbek, North Ossetia, Russia, September 21, 2002**
   A 20-million ton avalanche rampaged eight miles down Karmadon Gorge at 179 mph, burying several villages and a Russian film crew, leaving 125 dead.

4. **Siachen Glacier region, Ghanche, Pakistan, April 7, 2012**
   An avalanche hit the Gayari military base, killing 129 soldiers and 11 civilians.

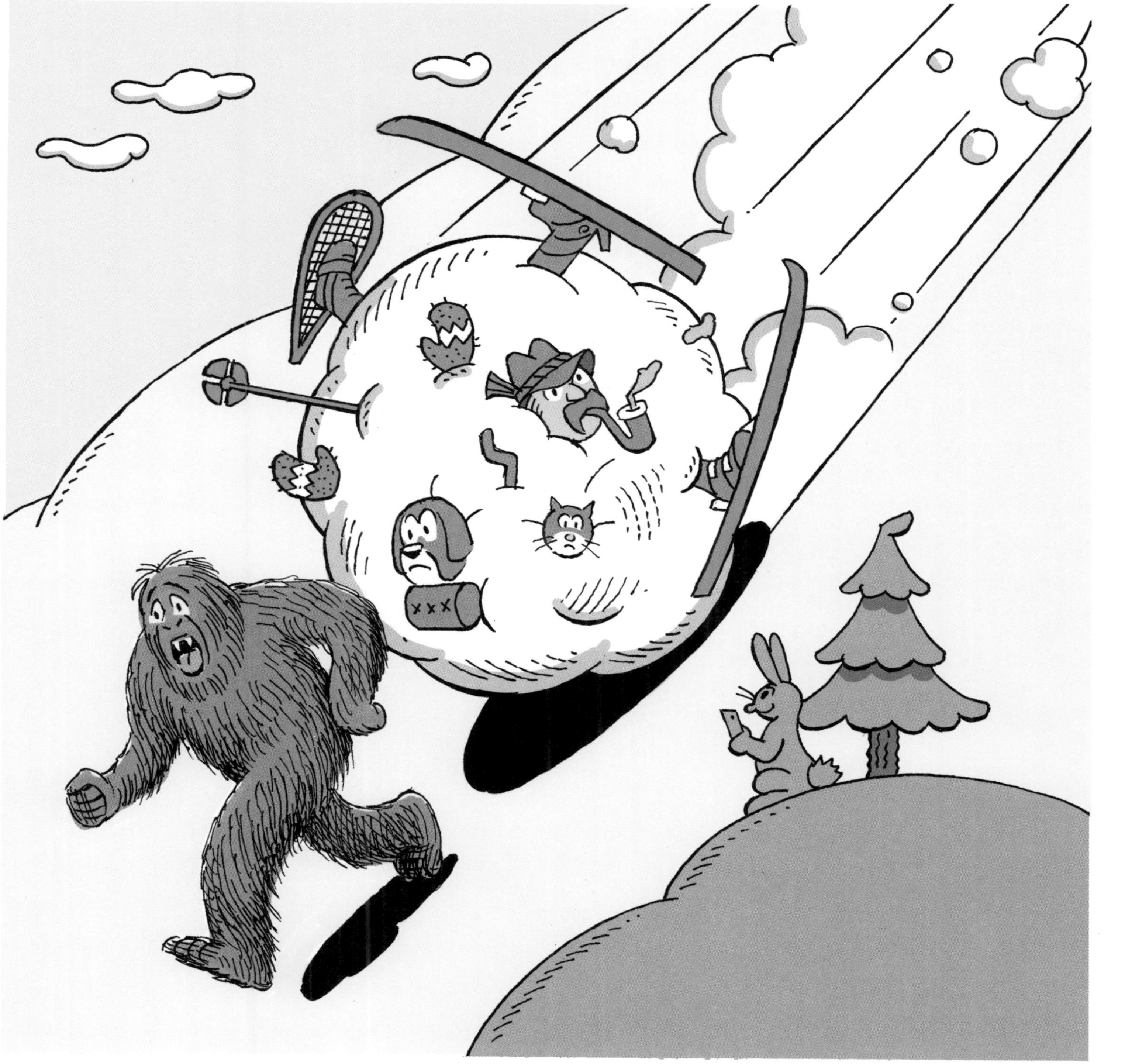

5. **Mount Annapurna region, western Nepal, May 5, 2012**
   More than 60 people, including three Ukrainian tourists, were killed as flash floods, triggered by an avalanche, washed away Nepali homes.

6. **Avalanche on Mount Manaslu, central Nepal, September 23, 2012**
   This killed ten people, including nine European climbers.

7. **Avalanche on Mount Everest, April 18, 2014**
   This, which killed 16 Sherpas, was until then the deadliest disaster in Mount Everest's history.

8. **Afghanistan avalanches, February 24-28, 2015**
   40 avalanches in Panjshir Province partly caused by rising temperatures killed at least 310 people.

9. **The Alps, 2015**
   Since January, more than 100 skiers had died, most of them buried in avalanches.

10. **Afghanistan-Pakistan border, February 4-6, 2016**
    More than 100 people were killed.

THE TOP 10 COSTLIEST CLIMATE CHANGE-RELATED DISASTERS WORLDWIDE IN 2018

Consider just the United States. In 2018, the U.S. was hit by 14 separate billion-dollar climate-related disasters: two hurricanes, three tornadoes, three hailstorms, two winter storms, two severe thunderstorms, one drought and one series of wildfires. And the three years of 2016, 2017 and 2018 were historic: the average number of billion-dollar disasters was more than twice the long-term average. For example, in 1980, when records began to be kept, there were only three, adjusted for inflation.

1. U.S. – Hurricanes Florence and Michael	$32 billion
2. California, U.S. – Camp and Woolsey fires	$9-$13 billion
3. Japan – floods	$9.3-$12.5 billion
4. China – floods	$9.3 billion
5. Australia – drought	$5.8-$9 billion
6. Europe – drought	$7.5 billion
7. Argentina – drought	$6 billion
8. Kerala, India – floods	$3.7 billion
9. Cape Town, South Africa – drought	$1.2 billion
10. Philippines and China – Typhoon Mangkhut	$1-$2 billion

Why is a tornado like a redneck divorce? Somebody's going to lose a trailer.

If your home is hit by a dolphin, do not go out to see if the dolphin is okay. That's how hurricanes trick you into going outside.

THE TOP 12 CITIES LIKELY TO RUN SHORT OF DRINKING WATER PARTLY BECAUSE OF CLIMATE CHANGE

Climate change means more droughts *and* more heavy rainfall—rainfall that land, rivers, reservoirs, water and sewer systems, etc. can have difficulty handling. This spells trouble for cities that already have drinking water problems.

1. **Cape Town**
   In 2017, the city experienced its worst drought in a century. On January 1, 2018, the city government imposed restrictions of 87 liters of water per person per day. In February it tightened this to 50 liters—and prepared for a "Day Zero" when municipal water supplies would be largely shut off and residents would have to go to collection points for a daily ration of 25 liters. This was avoided, and the winter of 2018 brought good rains. But Cape Town remains the world's most likely large city to some day run out of water.

2. **Sao Paulo**
   In a 2015 crisis, partly caused by a 2014-2017 drought, the city had less than 20 days supply of water. To stop looting, police had to escort water trucks. The crisis is over . . . for now.

3. **Bangalore**
   The city's boom as a tech hub is running up against an antiquated water and sewage system. Half of the city's drinking water is lost to waste. And not a single one of its lakes has water suitable for drinking or bathing.

4. **Beijing**
   A human being needs 1,000 cubic meters of water per year. Beijing's 20-plus million residents average only 145 cubic meters. China has almost 20% of the world's population but only 7% of the world's fresh water.

5. **Cairo**
   The source of 97% of Egypt's water, the Nile is increasingly filling with untreated agricultural and residential waste. Among lower-middle-income countries, Egypt ranks high for the number of deaths due to water pollution. The UN predicts critical shortages by 2025.

6. Jakarta

Because fewer than half of its residents have access to piped water, people are digging wells—which drain the aquifers. And newly-laid concrete and asphalt stops Jakarta's once-open land from absorbing rain and replenishing the aquifers. The land is sinking; 40% of this capital city is now below sea level . . . and the sea is rising. Because of this, in August 2019, Indonesia announced it would move its capital to Borneo.

7. Moscow

One legacy of Soviet-era industrialization is pollution. Officials admit that 35%-60% of Russia's reserves of drinking water fail sanitary standards. And Moscow's water supply is 70% dependent on surface water—very vulnerable to pollution.

8. Istanbul

In drier months, the city is now experiencing water shortages. At the start of 2014 its reservoirs were at less than 30% of capacity.

9. Mexico City

Its pipes lose 40% of the water that goes through them. Partly as a result, 20% of the city's residents get running water for just part of the day; another 20% get running water only a few hours a week.

10. London

Running close to capacity, it is likely to have supply problems by 2025 and "serious shortages" by 2040.

11. Tokyo

As it relies heavily on surface water, it is particularly vulnerable to drought—which has hit every decade or so. A 2014 report evaluated Tokyo as the largest water-stressed city in the world.

12. Miami

As sea levels rise, more seawater leaks into the Biscayne Aquifer, the city's main source of water. Neighboring cities are also being hit. Saltwater intrusion forced Hallandale Beach, just a few miles north, to close six of its eight wells.

"Have you heard that you can drink from the Dnieper River?"
"You think that's amazing? You can eat from the Moscow River."

"According to environmentalists' estimates,
the water from the Moscow River will soon be worth $105 per barrel."

THE TOP 10 FASTEST-WARMING U.S. CITIES

Degrees increase per decade

	°F	
1. Reno	1.39	
2. Phoenix	1.12	(tied with Ft. Myers, FL as the third hottest U.S. city: 75.1)
3. Las Vegas	1.04	(tied with Tucson and Austin, TX, as the 17th hottest at 69.4)
4. Riverside, CA	.95	
5. Prescott, AZ	.89	
6. Chattanooga	.82	
7. Tucson	.80	(tied with Las Vegas and Austin, TX, as the 17th hottest at 69.4)
8. Minneapolis	.76	
9. El Paso	.75	
10. St. Louis	.72	

Miami is the hottest at 77.2, McAllen, TX, is second at 75.6

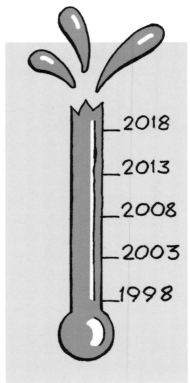

THE TOP 11 U.S. CITIES WHOSE RAT POPULATION IS GROWING FAST

As the climate warms, rats proliferate. And some cities' rat populations increase at faster rates than others. Every year, Orkin rates America's rattiest cities. In 2018 as in 2017, Chicago topped the list. The next six cities barely moved up or down. Los Angeles was +1, New York was -1, Washington was +1, San Francisco was -1, Detroit was +1 and Philadelphia was -1. But most other cities rose or fell more dramatically.

Here are the eleven that, from 2017 to 2018, moved up the most:

1. Portland, Maine   from 53th to 34th: +19

2. Charleston, West Virginia   from 64th to 47th: +17

3. Burlington, Vermont   from 54th to 43rd: +11

4. San Diego, California   from 35th to 26th: +9

5. Dayton, Ohio   from 55th to 48th: + 7

6. Charlotte, North Carolina   from 28th to 22nd: +6

6. Columbus, Ohio   from 31st to 25th: +6

6. Raleigh-Durham, North Carolina   from 33rd to 27th: +6

6. Orlando, Florida   from 47th to 41st: + 6

10. Cleveland, Ohio   from 13th to 8th: +5

10. Nashville, Tennessee   from 40th to 35th: +5

THE TOP 10 YEARS AND U.S. STATES EXPERIENCING FOREST FIRES

Warmer weather means lots more mountain pine beetles, which kill trees. That may turn forest into tinderboxes.

The top 10 years for forest fires in the U.S. by acreage burned, 1960-2017.

The top 10 states in terms of increased acreage burned by wildfires. Change in annual burned acreage between 1984-1999 and 2000-2014.

	Acres burned		Acres per sq. mi.
1. 2015	10,125,149	1. Idaho	3.58
2. 2006	9,873,745	2. Oregon	2.56
3. 2017	about 9,800,000	3. Washington	1.90
4. 2007	9,328,045	4. Arizona	1.75
5. 2012	9,326,238	5. Alaska	1.59
6. 2011	8,711,367	6. New Mexico	1.43
7. 2005	8,689,389	7. Montana	1.37
8. 2004	8,097,880	8. Oklahoma	1.28
9. 2000	7,393,493	9. Nevada	1.17
10. 2002	7,184,712	10. Texas	1.14

During the last 30 years, human-caused climate change has nearly doubled the number of acres burned in the western United States by wildfires. Since the 1970s, temperatures in the southwest have increased by more than one degree Celsius. According to the National Academy of Sciences, for each additional degree of Celsius, the area burned by western wildfires will double, triple or even quadruple.

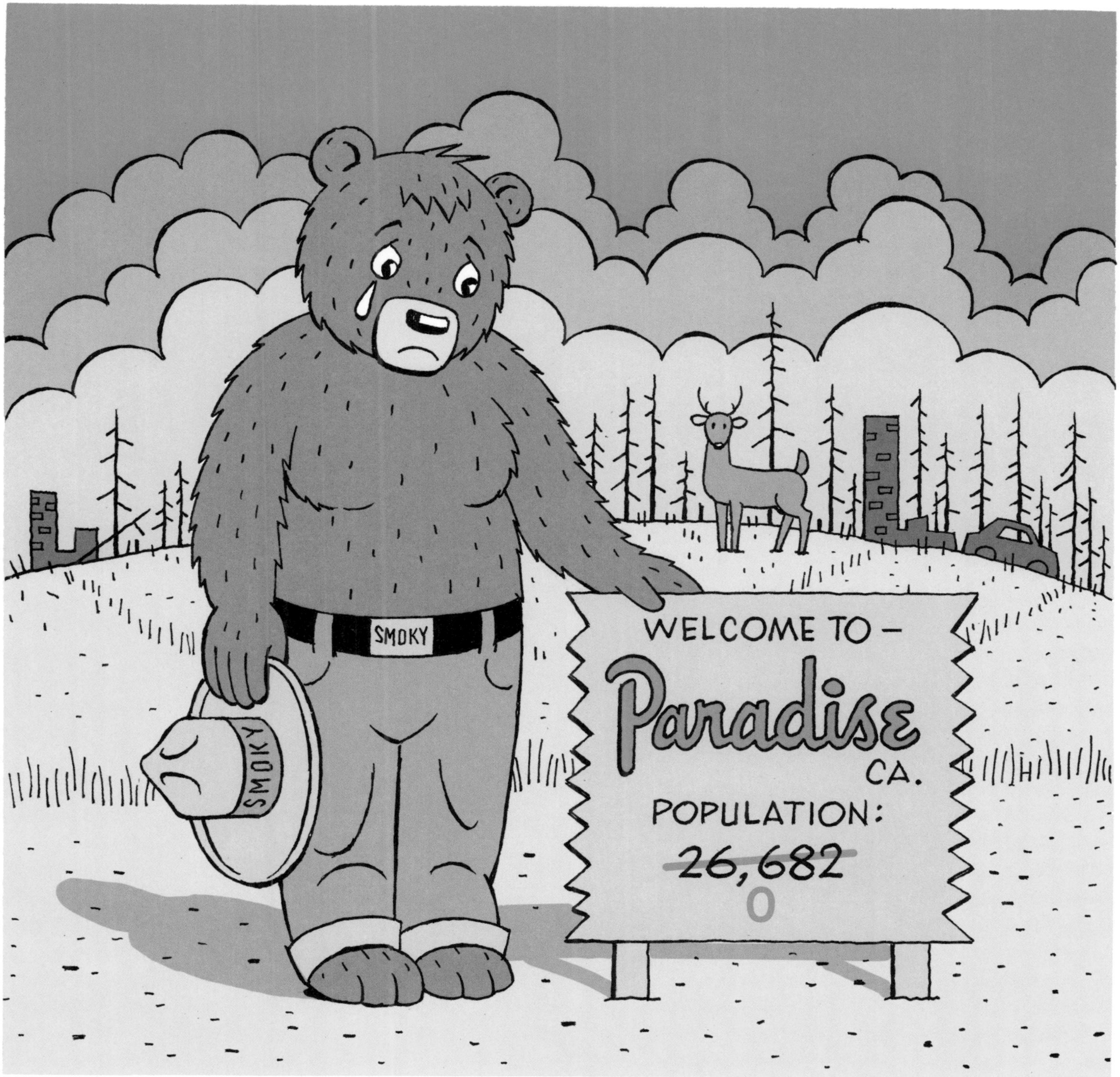
SMOKY
SMOKY
WELCOME TO –
Paradise
CA.
POPULATION:
26,682
0

GLOBAL WARMING: THE BAD THINGS IT'S PROBABLY GOING TO DO TO US.

THE TOP 10 ECONOMIC STRESSES ON THE UNITED STATES DUE TO CLIMATE CHANGE

1. Increased heat-related mortality in the Gulf states and the Southwest. (This is certainly more than just an economic loss, isn't it?)

2. Increased infrastructure damage along the Gulf and Atlantic coasts.

3. Decreased agricultural yields in the Midwest, the Great Plains and the Southwest.

4. Decreased water supply in the West.

5. Increased energy demand in the Southwest.

6. Increased wildfires in the Southwest and the Rockies.

7. Increased damage to urban drainage systems in the central Great Plains.

8. Decreased shellfish harvests in the Pacific Northwest.

9. Increased road damage in the northern Rockies and northern Great Plains.

10. Increased human migration out of the South and Southwest.

If warming continues at present rates, it could shave three to six percent off U.S. GDP by 2100. And that's an optimistic forecast.

THE TOP 12 DISEASES COMING WITH CLIMATE CHANGE

Not the top 10 . . . instead, the top 12. And not in order of importance . . . instead, more or less in alphabetical order. This is how *Scientific American* reports them, and why mess with *Scientific American*?

1. **Bird flu**
   H5N1 infections, now common in farmed poultry, are spreading to wild birds. As for people? Only 240 have died . . . so far.

2. **Babesiosis**
   Once confined to the tropics, this malaria-like disease has cropped up in Italy and Long Island, NY. It's rare in humans . . . so far.

3. **Cholera**
   Thriving in warm waters, it kills 100,000 people a year. And waters are getting warmer.

4. **Ebola**
   It kills people and, as of this writing, has no cure. Outbreaks usually follow heavy rainfall or droughts—and climate change will bring more of these.

5. **Parasites**
   Higher temperatures and more rainfall will help many parasites thrive in the wild and find hosts, including humans.

6. **Lyme disease**
   In the U.S., cases have more than doubled since the 1990s. Due in part to climate change, the Lyme tick's range is growing.

7. **Plague**
   Same as with parasites: there's more territory for the rodents and the infected fleas they carry.

8. **"Red tides"**
   As coastal waters get warmer, they will probably experience more blooms of poisonous algae.

9. **Rift Valley fever**
Climate change is helping mosquitos spread this fever through Africa and the Middle East, killing livestock and people.

10. **Sleeping sickness**
Global warming will help spread the tsetse fly, putting an additional 45 to 77 million people at risk by 2090.

11. **Tuberculosis**
As droughts bring livestock and wildlife closer together at watering holes, TB will spread.

12. **Yellow fever**
Same as with Rift Valley fever (see above): more territory for the mosquitos that carry this disease.

What's more: In the early 20th century, more than a million reindeer died of anthrax in Siberia. There are 7,000 burial grounds with infected carcasses. In the summer of 2016, thawing permafrost in the Yamal Peninsula released some of this anthrax. Dozens of people were hospitalized and one child died. As more permafrost melts . . .

Mad coward disease (noun): *a brain-eating disease spread by global warming; affecting some politicians, it is characterized by a fear of being "primaried" by people even crazier than themselves, thus causing the politicians to deny global warming.*

THE TOP 10 WAYS A WARMER ARCTIC WILL AFFECT THE WORLD

Arctic temperatures continue to rise faster than anywhere else in the world. So there are fewer polar bears, more buckling roads from melting permafrost, etc.—that's local. But the Arctic's influence also goes global.

1. **Albedo effect**
   As Arctic Ocean ice melts, the top of the world turns from white to blue. Since dark surfaces absorb far more heat, global temperatures rise even more.

2. **Methane release from the seabed**
   Vast quantities of methane rest in frozen form on the continental shelf, less than 200 meters under the Arctic Ocean. As that ocean warms, the methane is released.

3. **Methane release from permafrost**
   In 2006, Siberian permafrost released 3.8 million tons of methane. In 2013, the last year for which there is a number, it released 17 million tons. At this rate . . . ?

4. **Sea level rise from melting Alaskan glaciers**
   The rapid retreat of these glaciers represents about half the loss of mass by glaciers worldwide and the largest contribution of glacial melt to rising sea level.

5. **Melting the Greenland ice sheet**
   Rising Arctic air temperatures are accelerating the surface melting of this ice sheet. Each year, the melt adds about 72 cubic miles of water to the ocean, raising sea levels.

6. **Increase in water vapor**
   Since warmer air holds more moisture, the polar atmosphere holds more and more water vapor. Water vapor is a greenhouse gas, trapping radiation, leading to more heating.

7. **Slowdown of the global ocean conveyor belt**
   The belt's "engine" is near the North Pole. But as Arctic waters get warmer, they can jam the belt. Since 2004, the Atlantic current has weakened 30%. If this continues, climate is affected worldwide. For example, the Indian and Asian monsoon areas dry up (see page 56).

8. **Major shifts in the northern hemisphere's jet stream**
   Warmer Arctic air slows the jet stream, making weather more "stuck." In summer, this can create drought and more heat. In winter, it can bring longer-lasting snowstorms.

9. **Stress on migrating birds**
   Several hundred million birds migrate to Alaska each summer. As the treeline advances northward, major breeding areas will disappear. There will be many fewer such birds.

10. **More fossil fuel extraction**
    There are major oil and gas reserves not just in the Alaskan Arctic but also in the Canadian, Norwegian, Greenlandic and Russian Arctic. As these become more accessible to drilling, the world's transition to renewables gets pushed farther away.

Baked Alaska (noun): *the soon-to-be condition of Alaska*

THE TOP 7 CONSEQUENCES AS THE "NORTH ATLANTIC CONVEYOR BELT" IS DIMINISHED AND POSSIBLY DIVERTED

The Atlantic Meridional Overturning Circulation (AMOC), also called the North Atlantic conveyor belt, is the system in which warm water flows north in the upper layers of the Atlantic and colder water flows south in the deep Atlantic. Part of the AMOC, the Gulf Stream flows north past the British Isles and Norway.

Since 1957, the net flow of the Gulf Stream has dropped 30%—and, as the Earth has become warmer, more fresh water flows into the North Atlantic. As this warming and freshening continues, the Gulf Stream could be diverted toward the equator. This downturning would:

1. Seriously cool northwestern Europe.

2. Heat the high latitudes of the Southern Hemisphere.

3. Dry the tropics.

4. Change—and probably diminish—the Atlantic fisheries.

5. Change oceanic CO_2 and oxygen levels.

6. Change terrestrial vegetation.

7. Accelerate regional sea level rise.

Scientists say there is a 90% probability that the AMOC will continue to decrease in strength during this century and a 10% probability that it will collapse in this century, with potentially severe consequences.

THE TOP 10 NATIONS AT RISK IN SEA LEVEL RISE

2010 population below median locked-in sea level* if temperatures rise 4°C.

Millions of people		Percent of population	
1. China	145	1. Vietnam	52%
2. India	55	2. Bangladesh	32%
3. Bangladesh	48	3. Japan	27%
4. Viet Nam	46	4. Egypt	25%
5. Indonesia	44	5. Malaysia	24%
6. Japan	34	6. Thailand	23%
7. United States	25	6. Myanmar	23%
8. Philippines	20	8. Philippines	22%
9. Egypt	19	9. Indonesia	18%
10. Brazil	16	10. China	11%

—Climate Central

* The sea level rise we don't see now, but which carbon emissions and warming have locked in for later years

THE TOP 10 WORLD CITIES AT RISK IN SEA LEVEL RISE

2010 population below median locked-in sea level rise* if temperatures rise 4°C.

Millions of people		Percent of population	
1. Shanghai, China	22.4	1. Shanghai, China	76%
2. Tianjin, China	12.4	2. Hanoi, Vietnam	60%
3. Dhaka, Bangladesh	12.3	2. Haora, India	60%
4. Calcutta, India	12.0	4. Khulna, Bangladesh	58%
5. Mumbai, India	10.8	5. Shantou, China	54%
6. Hong Kong, China	10.1	6. Calcutta, India	51%
7. Jakarta, Indonesia	9.5	7. Mumbai, India	50%
8. Taizhou, China	8.9	8. Hong Kong, China	46%
9. Khulna, Bangladesh	7.6	9. Dhaka, Bangladesh	38%
9. Hanoi, Vietnam	7.6	9. Osaka, Japan	38%

—*Climate Central*

* The sea level rise we don't see now, but which carbon emissions and warming have locked in for later years

THE TOP 10 ISLAND NATIONS THREATENED BY RISING SEA LEVELS

Ranked by percent of area that will be below sea level:

1. **Maldives, in the Indian Ocean**
   With 80% of its 1,200 islands no more than three feet above sea level, the Maldives will be completely submerged in 30 years. To dramatize this fate, top government officials donned scuba gear and held the world's first underwater cabinet meeting.

2. **Kiribati, in the South Pacific, halfway between Hawaii and Australia**
   Spread across an area the size of Alaska, many of its 33 coral atolls and reef islands, with a population of 100,000, is no more than 6.6 feet above sea level. By 2050, Kiribati may be unlivable; by 2100, Kiribati may be gone.

3. **Bahamas, in the Atlantic, north of Cuba and southeast of Florida**
   Like the Maldives, 80% of the Bahamas is no more than 3 feet above sea level. It's the third richest country in the Americas, behind only the U.S. and Canada, with an economy based on tourism and finance. Can it switch to an economy based on scuba diving?

4. **Marshall Islands, in the Pacific, near the equator**
   Much of the Marshalls—1,156 islands and islets—is less than six feet above sea level. Rising seas are already washing away many graves. Its 70,000 living people have a free pass to emigrate to the U.S.—which may become very enticing.

5. **Tuvalu, in the South Pacific, south of Kiribati**
   The average height of the nation—three reef islands and six atolls—is 6.6 feet above sea level. Its highest elevation is 15 feet, the lowest maximum elevation of any nation except the Maldives. Its 10,000 people may have to relocate to Australia, New Zealand or Fiji.

6. **Bahrain, in the Arabian Gulf**
   The financial center of the Middle East, Bahrain has the region's freest and fastest growing economy. The average annual salary is $107,000; its 1.4 million people are well off. But by 2100, up to 22% of its more than 30 islands could be under water.

7. **Seychelles, in the Indian Ocean, 900 miles east of Kenya**
   A nation of 115 islands, Seychelles is so beautiful it's been compared to the Garden of Eden. Now its beaches, its number one tourist attraction, are being eaten away. A wall protects its resort hotels from the rising seas . . . but for how long?

8. **Antigua and Barbuda, where the Atlantic and the Caribbean meet**
   Tourism employs nearly 90% of the nation's population. For every .04 inch of sea level rise, Barbuda will lose about 3.3 feet of land. By 2100, that's about 130 feet of shoreline. As the nation's beaches go, so will its tourism.

9. **Singapore, just off the southern tip of the Malay peninsula**
   Most of its important centers of population (5.4 million), industries, commerce, ports and airports are less than two meters (6.6 feet) above sea level. 70% of its coastline is protected by seawalls and rock slopes—how effective for how long?

10. **Cook Islands, in the South Pacific, northeast of New Zealand**
    Here the sea level rise since 1993 is 4 millimeters per year, about 20% greater than the global average. The islands are known for protecting foreigners' assets from legal claims in their home countries—how long can Cook protect itself from the sea?

On October 17, 2009, Maldives' President Mohammed Nasheed, his vice president, the cabinet secretary and 11 cabinet ministers sat around a table 20 feet down, on the sea floor, and signed a document calling on all countries to cut their carbon dioxide emissions.

THE TOP 10 U.S. STATES AT RISK IN SEA LEVEL RISE

An effectively inundated community (EIC) is a community having 10% or more of its livable land area flooded at least 26 times per year.

Number of EICs in each state in the year 2100 based on three scenarios of flooding: intermediate-low (IL), intermediate-high (IH) and highest (H).

	IL	IH	H
1. Louisiana	112	131	146
2. New Jersey	50	103	131
3. Florida	19	58	90
4. North Carolina	26	49	63
5. Maryland	30	39	51
6. Virginia	8	24	38
7. Massachusetts	5	18	28
8. Texas	10	17	26
9. South Carolina	12	19	22
10. Georgia	6	10	18

—*Elementa: Science of the Anthropocene*

Number of people living less than one meter above sea level.

1. Florida	1,600,000
2. Louisiana	880,000
3. California	325,000
4. New York	300,000
5. New Jersey	154,000
6. Virginia	75,000
7. South Carolina	60,000
8. North Carolina	58,000
9. Massachusetts	52,400
10. Georgia	28,000

— *Environmental Research Letters*

THE TOP 10 WAYS THAT GLOBAL WARMING HITS THE BIG EASY HARD

1. New Orleans: Sea level expected to rise 4.3 feet by 2065.

2. Louisiana by 2050: "100-year" flood levels, 9.4 feet today, expected to be 11 feet . . . "100-year" coastal floodplain, 5,000 square miles today, expected to be more than 6,900 square miles . . . and 260,000 more people will be at risk of coastal flooding.

3. Coastal Louisiana: Losses from hurricane winds, land subsidence and sea level rise will rise $500 million per year, half of which is related to climate change.

4. New Orleans: Surge and flooding from Katrina was 15%-60% higher than it would have been under the climate and sea level conditions around 1900.

5. New Orleans: Number of days per year with at least 4 inches of rainfall up 79% in the last 30 years.

6. New Orleans: Temperature up 2.76°F in last 30 years.

7. New Orleans: Since 1970, 8.8 more days per year above 95°F. Number of days above 95°F expected to rise from 16 today to 80 by 2065.

8. New Orleans: Number of "danger days" (heat index above 105°F) expected to rise from 35 today to 120 in 2050. More heat will mean more heat strokes and kidney problems—and more ozone, which increases the risk of death from heart and lung disease.

9. New Orleans: Mosquito season up 15 days since 2006. More mosquitos will mean more risk of West Nile virus, dengue fever, yellow fever, Chagas and malaria. More ticks will mean more risk of Lyme disease. There will be more shellfish toxins.

10. Louisiana: By 2050, summer drought threat level will more than double and wildfire threat level will nearly double.

THE TOP 10 U.S. COUNTIES MOST VULNERABLE TO SEA LEVEL RISE IN 2100

Assuming a rise of 1.8 meters (5.9 feet).

Ranked by number of people at risk

	Number of People	Percent of Population
1. Miami-Dade, Florida	1,967,018	35.9
2. Broward, Florida	1,543,944	36.8
3. Pinellas, Florida	391,872	18.4
4. Lee, Florida	299,514	22.0
5. Jefferson, Louisiana	289,706	27.8
6. Nassau, New York	257,560	10.2
7. San Mateo, California	249,020	16.2
8. Orange, California	225,720	3.2
9. Charleston, South Carolina	195,698	26.9
10. Ocean, New Jersey	176,360	13.4

The surface rock of nearly all of Miami-Dade and much of Broward is very porous limestone. By 2100 it will probably be filled with seawater.

South Beach Diet (noun): a weight-loss program whose success will come from a human being's inability to eat while underwater

THE TOP 10 PLACES PRONE TO DROUGHT, WHICH CLIMATE CHANGE MAY EXACERBATE

In 2008, Goldman Sachs called water "the petroleum of the next century"—and, as climate change triggers more droughts, those droughts have helped trigger conflicts in Syria, Somalia, Afghanistan, etc. More conflicts loom. The India-Pakistan dispute over Kashmir is largely about control over the headwaters of the River Indus—which, due to shrinking glaciers, could be reduced by 8% by 2050. Climate-change droughts are a threat in . . .

The top 10 countries

1. Ethiopia

2. Somalia

3. Eritrea

4. Uganda

5. Sudan

6. Afghanistan

7. India

8. China

9. Iran

10. Morocco

The top 10 megacities

1. Calcutta, India

2. Karachi, Pakistan

3. Los Angeles, U.S.

4. Chenna, India

5. Lahore, Pakistan

6. Ahmadabad, India

7. Santiago, Chile

8. Belo Horizonte, Brazil

9. Luanda, Angola

10. Yanyon, Myanmar

Water (noun): the basis of all life, increasingly present as either too little (fresh water, needed by cities) or too much (sea water, rising upon cities)

THE TOP 10 POPULAR SONGS REWRITTEN IN LIGHT OF THE DISCOVERY THAT GLOBAL WARMING COULD DAMAGE MALE FERTILITY

In a study published in November 2018, researchers at the University of East Anglia, working with beetles, have shown that "Heat waves reduce male fertility and sperm competitiveness, and successive heat waves almost sterilize males." What's more, the offspring of the males who endured the heat lived shorter lives. Yes, the researchers worked with beetles, but the study's lead author pointed out that previous research has shown that heat shock can damage reproduction in the males of warm-blooded animals and can lead to infertility in mammals.

For human males, the temperature of the testicles must be cooler than the inside of the body. In a warming world, this will be increasingly problematic.

Hence, the rewritten pop songs:

1. We've having a heatwave, a tropical heatwave,
   The temperature's rising, it isn't surprising: you're sterile
                     Ella Fitzgerald

2. Well, I'm hot blooded, check it and see
   I feel a fever burning inside me
   Roasting my sperm
                  Foreigner

3. We didn't start the fire
   It was always burning
   Since the world's been turning
   But we've cranked it higher
   So now if you're yearning
   To give her a baby, forget it

                         Billy Joel

4. Happiness is a warm gun
   Much too warm, it's shooting blanks

                         The Beatles

5. I'm just a hunk, a hunk of burning love
   And believe me, I'm reliable
   My burning sperm's not viable

                         Elvis Presley

6. Hot child in the city
   Hot child in the city
   Runnin' wild and lookin' pretty
   Hot child in the city
   But no hot boy can make her pregnant—so hold your pity

                         Nick Gilder

7. Come on, baby, light my fire—but not too much

                         The Doors

8. The heat is on, on the street
   Inside your head, on very beat
   And inside your testes, got your semen
   Burning like a demon

                         Glenn Frey

9. Some like it hot, so let's turn up the heat 'til we fry
   And if we can't conceive a baby, we'll know why

   The Power Station

10. Goodness gracious great damaged balls of fire

   Jerry Lee Lewis

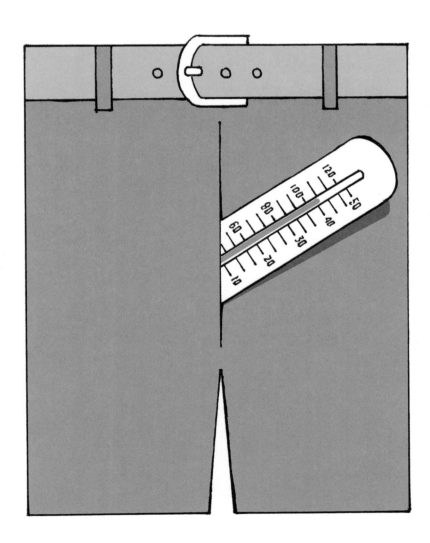

GLOBAL WARMING: HEROES, VILLAINS, PROFITEERS AND FOOLS.

THE TOP 10 COUNTRIES DEALING WITH CLIMATE CHANGE

The Climate Change Performance Index is published annually by Germanwatch, the NewClimate Institute and the Climate Action Network. While the 2019 CCPI ranks no country as among the three best, we have tweaked this list to do so.

While Americans compose slightly less than 5% of the world's population, we consume 25% of its energy resources. By comparison, Japan, also highly industrialized, uses 6% of the world's energy while having 2% of its population. And Japan isn't even among the top 10 best countries dealing with climate change.

The top 10 best
(the higher the number, the better)

1. Sweden	76.28 (best!)	
2. Morocco	70.48	
3. Lithuania	70.47	
4. Latvia	68.31	
5. U.K.	65.92	
6. Switzerland	65.42	
7. Malta	65.06	
8. India	62.93	
9. Norway	62.80	
10. Finland	62.61	

The top 10 worst
(the lower the number, the worse)

1. Saudi Arabia	8.82 (worst!)	
2. United States	18.82 (2nd worst)	
3. Iran	23.94	
4. South Korea	28.53	
5. Taiwan	28.80	
6. Australia	31.27	
7. Canada	34.26	
8. Kazakhstan	36.47	
9. Russia	37.59	
10. Malaysia	38.08	

THE TOP 10 MILESTONES IN THE DISCOVERY OF HUMAN-DRIVEN GLOBAL WARMING

A timeline (not ranked not by importance):

1. **1859 John Tyndall**
   This Irish scientist proves that some gases (such as CO_2 and methane) absorb more energy than others (such as oxygen and nitrogen), thus laying the basis for what will be called "the greenhouse effect."

2. **1896 Svante Arrhenius**
   This Swedish scientist suggests that burning fossil fuels will add CO_2 to the atmosphere, which will raise Earth's average temperature.

3. **1938 Guy Stewart Callendar**
   Arguing that Arrhenius's forecast is coming true, this British engineer presents evidence that temperature and CO_2 have been rising over the past half century.

4. **1957 Roger Revelle**
   This American scientist finds that the oceans will not absorb the CO_2 produced by humans.

5. **1960 Charles David Keeling**
   From recordings he makes at the Mauna Loa Observatory, this American scientist demonstrates that CO_2 in the atmosphere is rising. "The Keeling Curve" now measures its build-up.

6. **1966 Cesare Emilani and Wallace Broecker**
   From analysis of deep-sea cores and ancient corals, they conclude that small changes can flip the world's climate system from a stable state to an unstable one.

7. **1967 Syukuro Manabe and Richard Wetherald**
   Making the first detailed calculation of the greenhouse effect, they find that doubling the current level of CO_2 would increase global temperature about 2°C.

8. **1971 SMIC Conference**
   Experts from 14 nations gather in Stockholm for the first international conference specifically on climate change. Their "Study of Man's Impact on Climate" says the change may be rapid and dangerous.

9. **1972 John Sawyer**
   This British meteorologist makes this prediction for the year 2000: "The increase of 25% CO_2 expected by the end of the century therefore corresponds to an increase of 0.6°C in the world temperature." Sawyer, who will die in 2000, is spot on.

10. **1979 U.S. National Academy of Sciences report**
    At the direction of the Carter White House, Jules Charney, the "father of modern meteorology," brings together top scientists to assess the CO_2 issue. With input from climatologist James Hansen, the Charney report predicts a global warming of three degrees Celsius if no action is taken.

The Charney Report would become accepted fact within the U.S. government, the scientific community and the oil-and-gas industry . . . at least for a few years.

The report finds it highly credible that doubling CO_2 will bring a global warming of 1.5-4.5°C.

In the 1980s, a scientific consensus begins to form. Testifying to Congress in June 1988, James Hansen states that human-caused warming has already measurably affected global climate. The summer of 1988, the hottest on record until then, prompts the first wide public attention to man-made global warming—and prompts corporations and wealthy individuals to start spending millions of dollars to convince the public that there's no problem.

"Some circumstantial evidence is very strong, as when you find a trout in the milk."
—Henry David Thoreau

"People will generally accept facts as truth only if the facts agree with what they already believe."
—Andy Rooney

THE TOP 10 STEPS BY WHICH THE BIGGEST OPPORTUNITY TO COMBAT GLOBAL WARMING WAS LOST, 1979-1989

In June 1979, in Tokyo, leaders of the world's seven wealthiest nations signed a statement resolving to reduce carbon emissions. In November 1989, in the Netherlands, delegates from 60 nations met to approve a framework for a binding treaty—and the United States would need to lead.

In 1979, someone looking ahead ten years would have thought the U.S. *would* lead—partly because the Charney Report (see previous list) was becoming accepted fact within the U.S. government, the scientific community and the oil-and-gas industry.

Then things changed:

1. **October 1980.** The National Commission on Air Quality wants proposals for legislation for a stable energy climate. Two dozen policy gurus and scientists—experts who agree on major points and have made a commitment to Congress—meet near St. Petersburg, Florida to figure this out. After two days, they fail to draft a single paragraph. Four days later, Reagan is elected president.

2. **1981-1982.** Reagan is determined to undo the environmental achievements of presidents Carter, Nixon, Johnson, Kennedy and even Theodore Roosevelt. James Hansen, now director of the NASA Goddard Institute for Space Studies, leads six other NASA scientists in publishing a paper urging humankind to develop alternate sources of energy. Soon after, the U.S. Energy Department tells Hansen his climate-modeling research will not be funded. When his funding lapses, Hansen has to lay off half his staff.

3. **1982.** Learning of the White House's plans to end the Energy Department's carbon dioxide program, Congressman Al Gore decides to hold a hearing to shame the White House before it can put them into action. On March 25, 1982, Hansen testifies before Gore's subcommittee and makes big news. Dan Rather devotes three minute of CBS Evening News to the greenhouse effect. The head of Exxon's research division says Exxon will invent a future of renewable energy. The Energy Department's carbon-dioxide program is largely preserved, but otherwise the U.S. government is not doing anything.

4. **1983-1984.** On October 19, 1983, a commission of The U.S. National Academy of Sciences issues a 500-page report, "Changing Climate." In the report, the commission's chairman argues that action must taken immediately or else it will be too late. But in his press interviews he argues the opposite: There is

no urgent need for action. "Caution, not panic." Playing off this, Reagan's science adviser recommends only "continued research." Exxon publicly walks away from developing renewable energy. The American Petroleum Institute, which has had its own carbon-dioxide research program, cancels it.

5. **1985.** In May, an article in *Nature* by British scientists gives rise to the perception of the "hole in the ozone layer" crisis. World leaders, including Reagan, quickly endorse a solution. This makes American and other scientists wonder if recommendations for solving a *real* crisis—global warming—might now be heeded. Their resulting report contains the most forceful warnings yet issued by a scientific body.

6. **1986-1987.** In June 1986, the U.S. Senate holds a hearing on ozone and carbon dioxide. In September 1987, Reagan's EPA administrator says that just as there is now an international agreement on ozone, there will likely be one on global warming.

7. **November 1987.** The Reagan Administration is talking about addressing global warming. So is Congress: there are eight days of hearings, and three committees have introduced legislation to establish a national climate-change policy. James Hanson, about to testify before Congress, sends his formal statement to NASA which sends it to the White House . . .which writes falsehoods into it. Refusing to put his name on the final statement, Hanson appears before Congress as a private citizen.

8. **1988-1989.** On June 23, 1988, in the middle of the hottest year in human history (see next list), Hansen testifies before Congress in his official capacity. *The New York Times* headlines, "Global Warming Has Begun, Expert Tells Senate. Sharp Cut in Burning of Fossil Fuels Is Urged to Battle Shift in Climate." Hansen's testimony spurs action. On April 14, 1989, a bipartisan group of 24 senators urges the new president, George Bush, to cut CO_2 emissions. And Bush has proclaimed himself an environmentalist.

9. **1989.** John Sununu, Bush's Chief of Staff, decides that Hansen's scientific arguments are "technical garbage." Sununu gets Allen Bromely, a nuclear physicist from Yale, named Bush's science adviser, and Bromley labels Hansen's findings "technical poppycock." The American Petroleum Institute establishes the Global Climate Coalition, which approaches scientists skeptical of global warming and pays them $2000 to write op-eds. In October, these scientists begin to be quoted in national publications whose articles about global warming now say things like, "Many respected scientists say the available evidence doesn't warrant doomsday warnings."

10. **November 1989.** In the Netherlands—where delegates from 60 nations have met to approve a framework for a binding treaty on CO_2 emissions—the U.S. is represented by Allen Bromley. At John Sununu's urging, Bromely forces the conference to abandon its commitment to freeze these emissions.

—Based on *Losing Earth: The Decade We Almost Stopped Climate Change*
by Nathaniel Rich, *New York Times Magazine*, August 1, 2018

THE TOP 10 WARNING SIGNALS IN AMERICA IN THE SUMMER OF 1988

It was the hottest and driest summer in history.
It should have told us something.

1. Fires in Yellowstone National Park consumed 800,000 acres, and the smoke could be seen 1,600 miles away, in Chicago.

2. In Wisconsin, the Fox and Wisconsin Rivers completely evaporated. The governor banned cigarette smoking outdoors in parts of the state.

3. For the first time, Harvard University closed because of the heat.

4. One day in Philadelphia, in Veterans Stadium where the Phillies were hosting the Cubs, the on-field thermometer read 130 degrees. During a pitching change, every player (except the catcher and the entering reliever), coach and umpire fled to the dugouts.

5. New York City's mosquito population quadrupled and its murder rate hit a record high.

6. Spontaneous combustion caused the 28th floor of Los Angeles's second-tallest building to burst into flames.

7. Fleeing the continental United States for wetlands, ducks swelled Alaska's pintail duck population to 1.5 million, up from 100,000.

8. In Texas, farmers fed their cattle on cactus.

9. Stretches of the Mississippi flowed at less than one fifth of normal capacity. Thousands of barges beached at Greenville, Mississippi, St. Louis and Memphis.

10. In Clyde, Ohio, a Sioux medicine man from South Dakota, who claimed to have performed 127 successful rain dances, danced for three days . . .and it rained less than a quarter of an inch.

Indeed, these warning signs, the record-breaking heat and Congressional hearings this summer (see previous list) prompt the first wide public attention to global warming—and prompt corporations and wealthy individuals to start spending millions of dollars to convince the public that there's no problem. As a result, much of the public will be convinced.

THE TOP 10 CLIMATE-CHANGE DENIERS

1. Senator James Inhofe (R-OK)
He has compared the EPA to the Gestapo and has said "man-made global warming is the greatest hoax ever perpetrated on the American people." To prove his point about climate change, he once brought a snowball onto the floor of the Senate. Tossing the snowball, he said, "It's very, very cold out."

2. Marc Morano
He began his career with Rush Limbaugh and went on to work for Inhofe. Now he is executive director of ClimateDepot.com and communications director for the Committee for a Constructive Tomorrow, an anti-science "think" tank. He has said, "I'm not a scientist, although I do play one on TV occasionally. Okay, hell, maybe more than occasionally."

3. Chris Horner
He is a senior fellow for the Energy and Environment Legal Institute. Funded by coal companies, he harasses climate scientists. On Fox News he said that John Holdren, Obama's senior science advisor, is "if not borderline Communist—Communist."

4. Myron Ebell
Trump chose Ebell to head his EPA transition team. Opposing the Endangered Species Act, Ebell mocked "soft feelings for cuddly little critters." He has advocated the elimination of federal conservation regulations and has campaigned against federal policies which restricted property owners in U.S. national parks and forests. He worked to make regulating the tobacco industry "politically unpalatable."

5. Steve Milloy

He worked at the Advancement of Sound Science Coalition, established by the tobacco industry. There he ran junkscience.com which was dedicated to "debunking" claims regarding passive smoking, global warming and DDT.

6. Patrick Michaels

He contends that global warming will be minor and may even be beneficial. He has argued that "Congress should pass no legislation restricting emissions of carbon dioxide." His work is largely made possible by fossil-fuel companies; in August 2010, he admitted that 40% of his funding came from the oil industry.

7. Bjorn Lomborg

Former director of the Danish government's Environmental Assessment Institute, he has argued that predicted temperature rises could save more than 1.3 million lives a year. The Danish Committee on Scientific Dishonesty once declared him guilty of exactly that (a government review later cleared him). Rajendra Pachauri, chairman of the UN's climate change panel, has compared him to Adolph Hitler.

8. Matt Ridley

Okay, so he's not a denier. In fact, he says, "I think recent global warming is real, mostly man-made and will continue." He's on this list because, as a man made wealthy by coal mining on his family's land and as a hereditary peer in the British House of Lords, Viscount Matthew White Ridley lobbies for coal and opposes renewable energy and any actions against man-made climate change—which he thinks is unlikely to be dangerous.

9. Christopher Monckton

Viscount Monckton says, "Global warming will not affect us for the next 2,000 years and if it does, it won't have been caused by us." He once led a Tea Party crowd in a call-and-response: "Global warming is . . . ?" "Bullshit!" In 2014, he claimed, "There has been no global warming for 14 full years." (Note: 2014, 2013 and 2012—each warmer than the year before—were all all among the seven warmest years ever.)

10. Fred Singer

Singer says, "Since 1979 . . . the climate has been cooling just slightly." (Note: Since 1979, global temperature has risen about 0.5°C.) He says if global warming does occur, it will reduce sea-level rise. And besides, "People like warmer climates. There's a good reason why much of the U.S. population is moving into the Sun Belt."

THE TOP 10 DUMBEST THINGS SAID BY CLIMATE-CHANGE DENIERS

1. Carbon dioxide "literally cannot cause global warming."

> —Joe Bastardi, meteorologist appearing on Fox News

Bastardi said CO_2 can't cause warming because it doesn't "mix well in the atmosphere" (false). He also said warming would violate the First Law of Thermodynamics (also false).

2. "Snow skiing would be hurt—but water skiing will benefit."

> —William Nordhaus, Yale economist

Nordhaus also said, "Cities are increasingly climate-proofed by technological changes like air-conditioning and shopping malls."

3. "We must demand that more coal be burned to save the Earth from global cooling."

> —Don Blankenship, CEO of Massey Energy, a coal company

After the deaths of 29 miners in his Upper Big Branch Mine in 2010, Blankenship served one year (May 2016 - May 2017) in federal prison for having conspired to willfully violate mine safety and health standards.

4. Climate change is impossible because "God's still up there."

> —U.S. Senator James Inhofe (R-Oklahoma)

And, God help us, Inhofe is still in the U.S. Senate.

5. God buried fossil fuels "because he loves to see us find them."

> —Bryan Fischer, a former director at the American Family Association

Fischer also claims the Holocaust was caused by homosexuals. He has supported kidnapping children from same-sex households and smuggling them into "normal" homes.

6. "The President was wearing a trench coat, it was so cold, but he's talking about global warming."

       —U.S. Congressman Steve Scalise (R-Louisiana)

He said this in reference to Obama's 2013 inauguration speech. Memo to Steve: Weather is not the same as climate, weather is not the same as climate, weather is not the same as climate. . . .

7. "I thought it must be true until I found out what it cost."

       —U.S. Senator James Inhofe (R-Oklahoma)

Yes, the senator gets two entries. Memo to Jim: The International Energy Agency estimates that for every year the world delays doing anything significant to curb climate change, we'll pay $500 billion later on.

8. Safeguarding the climate is "a worldview that elevates the Earth above man."

       —Rick Santorum, former U.S. Senator (R-Pennsylvania)

Santorum also said that we were put on Earth to use it "for our benefit, not for the Earth's benefit."

9. "100 years is a long time. . . .There is an extremely high chance that the very nature of human society itself will have changed by that time in ways that render this entire issue moot."

       —Karl W. Smith, economist and writer for *Forbes*

Sure, maybe in 100 years human beings will have shed their bodies and be living as consciousnesses uploaded into the cloud. Or maybe not.

10. It feels hotter than it did 30 or 40 years ago because of "all this air conditioning, and it's a huge difference when you go outside."

       —Rush Limbaugh

(No comment.)

THE TOP 10 CLIMATE-DISINFORMATION ORGANIZATIONS SUPPORTED BY THE KOCH BROTHERS

Ranked by amount given to them by Koch foundations up through 2011 (last year for which data is available).

1. Cato Institute: more than $5 million since 1997

2. Heritage Foundation: more than $4.5 million since 1997

3. Americans for Prosperity: $3,609,281 since 2007

4. Heartland Institute: millions (no other data available)

5. Manhattan Institute for Policy Research: nearly $2 million since 1997

6. American Enterprise Institute: more than $1 million since 2004

7. American Legislative Exchange Council: more than $850,000 since 1997

8. Beacon Hill Institute at Suffolk University: some part of $725,000 since 2008

9. Competitive Enterprise Institute: funding since the 1980s

10. Institute for Energy Research: (no data available)

In all, since 1997, the Koch brothers have given at least $100,343,292 directly to 84 groups denying climate change science. Most of the Koch fortune comes from Koch Industries, historically rooted in fossil fuel operations.

THE TOP 10 THINGS DONALD TRUMP HAS SAID ABOUT CLIMATE CHANGE

1. "The concept of global warming was created by and for the Chinese in order to make U.S. manufacturing non-competitive." Trump, 2012

2. "We should be focused on magnificently clean and healthy air and not distracted by the expensive hoax that is global warming." Trump, 2013

3. "Obama's speech on climate change was scary. It will lower our standard of living and raise costs of fuel & food for everyone." Trump, 2013

4. "Secretary of State John Kerry just stated that the most dangerous weapon of all today is climate change. Laughable." Trump, 2014

5. "When will our country stop wasting money on global warming and so many other truly stupid things and begin to focus on lower taxes?" Trump, 2014

6. "Just out—the polar ice caps are at an all-time high, the polar bear population has never been stronger. Where the hell is global warming?" Trump, 2014

7. "Windmills are the greatest threat in the U.S. to both bald and golden eagles. Media claims fictional 'global warming' is worse." Trump, 2014

8. "As ISIS and Ebola spread like wildfire, the Obama administration just submitted a paper on how to stop climate change (aka global warming)." Trump, 2014

9. "Wow, 25 degrees below zero, record cold and snow spell. Global warming, anyone?" Trump, 2015

10. "I know much about climate change. It'd be—received environmental awards." Trump, 2016

Donald Trump (noun): A windbag who, if turned from evil to peaceful purposes, could by himself power the world's wind farms.

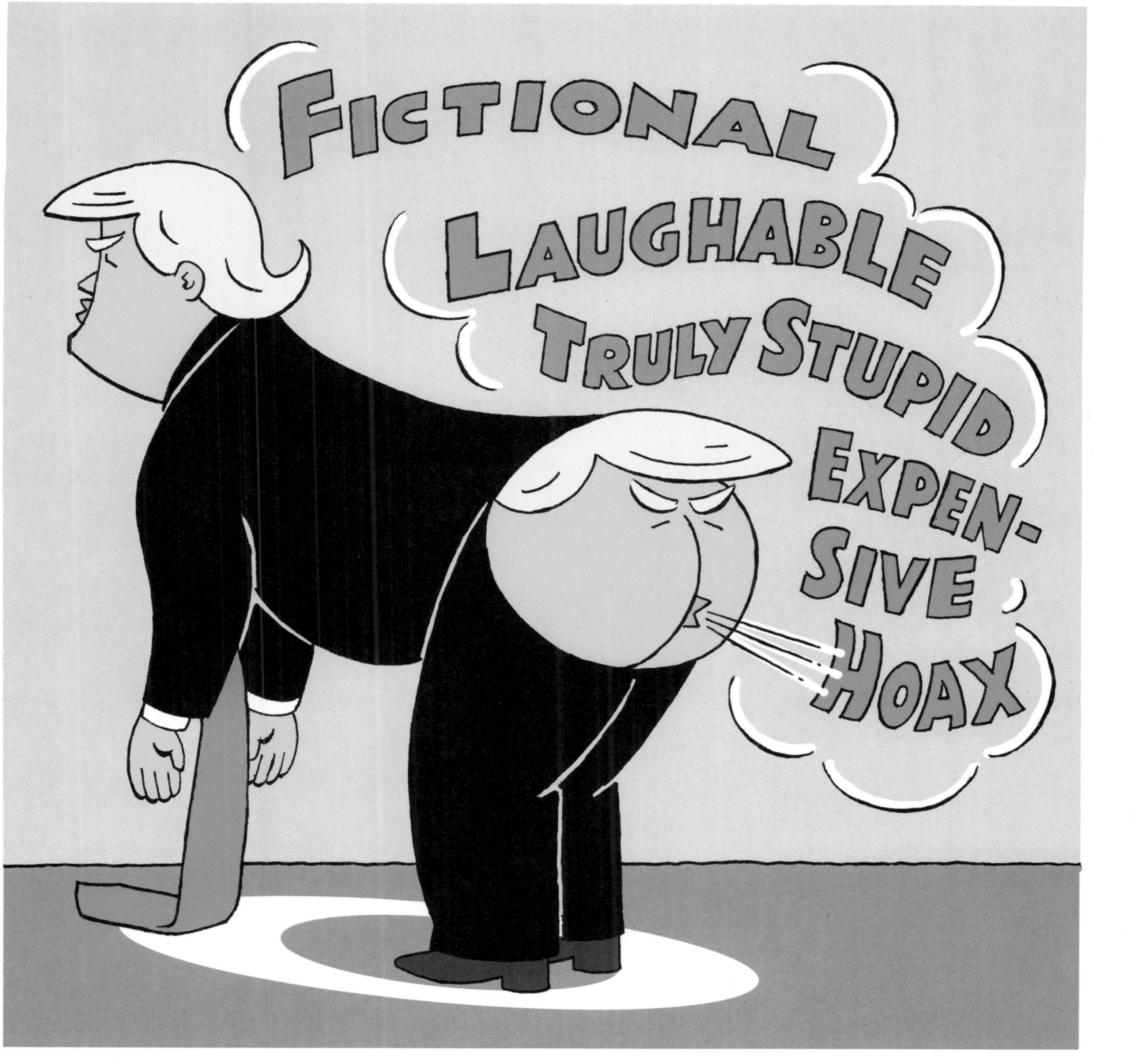
FICTIONAL
LAUGHABLE
TRULY STUPID
EXPEN-
SIVE
HOAX

THE TOP 10 INDUSTRIES THAT WILL PROFIT FROM GLOBAL WARMING

1. Private equity firms making profitable bets on what commodities will soon be scarce. Ex: KKR's investment in a Bermuda hedge fund that trades weather derivatives.

2. Financial services firms helping their wealthy clients buy farmland and water rights.

3. Energy companies planning to drill in the Arctic. Ex: Royal Dutch Shell, Exxon Mobil.

4. Insurance companies selling protection and raising rates.

5. Companies making genetically-modified seeds able to withstand harsher climates. Ex: Monsanto. And companies making fungicides and seed coatings to make plants more resilient. Ex: BASF SE.

6. Arctic shipping companies. Ex: Nordic Bulk Carriers.

7. Manufacturers of air-conditioning equipment.

8. Manufacturers of flood walls systems. Ex: The Massachusetts firm, Flood Control America.

9. Renewable energy companies.

10. Manufacturers of consumer products to protect against sun exposure: new types of clothing, eyewear, umbrellas and (natch!) sunscreen.

Private enterprise (noun): *the ability to make a buck off the very last drowned and/or baked human*

THE TOP 10 ORGANIZATIONS FIGHTING THE LOSING BATTLE AGAINST CLIMATE CHANGE

Before the Industrial Revolution, the Earth's atmosphere contained 280 parts per million (ppm) of carbon dioxide. In 2008, it was 392 ppm. That year, with the goal of getting it back down to 350 ppm, some activists founded 350.org. In 2013, the level hit 400 ppm; as of June 2019, it was 413.92. At the current rate, within 50 years it will be 500 ppm. But these organizations keep fighting the good fight.

1. 350.org

2. Environmental Defense Fund

3. Sierra Club Foundation

4. Union of Concerned Scientists

5. Greenpeace

6. EarthJustice

7. Center for Climate and Energy Solutions

8. The Solutions Project

9. Nature Conservancy

10. National Resources Defense Council

THE TOP 10 PEOPLE FIGHTING THE LOSING BATTLE AGAINST CLIMATE CHANGE

In 2013, CO_2 in the Earth's atmosphere hit 400 parts per million (ppm); as of June 2019, it was 413.92. At the current rate, within 50 years it will be 500 ppm.

1. **James Hansen**
   From 1981 to 2013, he was head of NASA's Goddard Institute for Space Science. His testimony to Congress in 1988 sparked public awareness of the dangers of global warming.

2. **Bill McKibben**
   "The world's best green journalist," he has educated millions of readers about climate change. A co-founder of 350.org, he has been arrested many times for civil disobedience protesting attacks on the environment.

3. **He Jianjun**
   As deputy director of China's Expert Committee on Climate Change which provides the scientific basis for China's climate-change planning, he is enormously influential.

4. **Jenna Nicholas**
   She is the project manager of Divest-Invest Philanthropy, a coalition of wealthy individuals and major institutions committed to divest $6 trillion in assets from fossil fuels over five years.

5. **Hela Cheikhrouhou**
   Directing the UN Green Climate Fund, this Tunisian technocrat disburses billions of dollars to help developing nations mitigate and adapt to climate change.

6. **Akon**
   His Akon Lighting Africa has installed more than 100,000 solar street lamps, 1,000 solar microgenerators and 200,000 household solar electric systems—while creating thousands of jobs in 15 African countries.

7. **Felipe Calderon**

As president of Mexico, he was key to Mexico becoming the first developing nation to set binding emissions-reductions targets. He now chairs a global commission which promotes sustainable growth while mitigating climate change.

8. **Gavin Schmidt**

Succeeding James Hansen as director of NASA's Goddard Institute for Space Studies, he is also a leading climate blogger. He won the first Climate Communications Prize from the American Geophysical Union.

9. **Sheldon Whitehouse**

A Democratic U.S. Senator from Rhode Island, he gives a "Time to Wake Up" speech about climate change in the Senate every single week.

10. **Steve Howard**

Formerly the CEO of The Climate Group, working with governments and companies to shrink their carbon footprints, he is now chief sustainability officer of IKEA. IKEA has pledged $1 billion for renewable energy and climate adaptation projects.

Honorable mention goes to three celebrities: Robert Redford, Leonardo DiCaprio and Arnold Schwarzenegger who, as governor of California, championed the landmark law that is the basis of the state's cap-and-trade program.

And then of course, there's Al Gore and Greta Thunberg.

THE TOP 10 MOVIES AND NOVELS WHICH GET CLIMATE CHANGE WRONG

Because movies usually have far more influence than books, they get the first five slots, in descending order of ridiculousness.

1. *The Day After Tomorrow* (2004), starring Dennis Quaid and Jake Gyllenhaal, directed by Roland Emmerich. A scientifically impossible superstorm creates rapid worldwide climate change, mainly flash freezing. Inspired by the novel *The Coming Global Superstorm*.

2. *Geostorm* (2017), starring Ed Harris, Andy Garcia and a lot of other people who should have known better. What causes the climate to go apocalyptically haywire? Of course: satellites.

3. *Hell* (2011), produced by (among other people) Roland Emmerich. The Earth's temperatures have risen 10 degrees Celsius. Why? Solar flares have destroyed our atmosphere. Hey, global warming isn't *our* fault.

4. *Snowpiercer* (2013), starring Chris Evans, Tilda Swinton, John Hurt and Ed Harris (again!). A geoengineering attempt to stop global warming has created a new ice age.

5. *The Arrival* (1996), starring Charlie Sheen and Lindsay Crouse. Aliens have secretly landed. To kill all humans and make Earth habitable for themselves, they've built underground bases now pumping greenhouse gases into the atmosphere. Here, too, global warming isn't our fault. It's those sneaky aliens.

Now, the novels. Some thriller writers hate environmentalists and either deny global warming or believe it's a good thing. And for some (like some movie-makers), global freezing is either more believable or more dramatic.

6. *State of Fear* (2004) by Michael Crichton. Eco-terrorists plot mass murder to publicize the danger of global warming which, says Crichton, won't happen. In 2005, climate-change denier Senator James Inhofe had Crichton deliver his expertise-free views to Inhofe's Senate committee.

7. *Fallen Angels* (1991) by Larry Nevin, Jerry Pournelle and Michael Flynn.
   Wikipedia: "A radical technophobic green movement dramatically cuts greenhouse gas emissions, only to find that man-made global warming was staving off a new ice age."

8. *The Coming Global Superstorm* (1999) by Art Bell and Whitley Strieber.
   Global warming suddenly causes freezing. This novel was basis of the movie *The Day After Tomorrow*.

9. A tie: *Ice!* (1978) by Arnold Federbush and *The Sixth Winter* (1979) by John Gribbin.
   In the 1970s, some scientists feared global cooling and warned of a coming ice age, and this was taken seriously by serious media. So Federbush could be forgiven—except he has an ice age come in mere months. Gribbin outdoes him; he has it come in mere weeks.

10. *Fifty Degrees Below* (2005) by Kim Stanley Robinson.
    Human-caused climate change has made the Gulf Stream stall, plunging the East Coast into the words of the book's title. Yes, the North Atlantic Conveyor Belt could collapse (see page 56) and cool the surrounding land—but "*fifty degrees below*" represents a loss of at least fifty scientific I.Q. points.

An Inconvenient Truth (2006), Al Gore's Oscar-winning documentary, told movie-goers the equivalent of "Eat your spinach" when what most movie-goers want to do is gorge on fake-buttered popcorn.

GLOBAL WARMING:
WHAT CAN BE DONE.

THE TOP 10 WAYS A CITY CAN TRY TO PROTECT ITSELF AGAINST RISING SEAS

1. **Build sea gates, a.k.a. storm-surge barriers.**
   The Netherlands, St. Petersburg (Russia), Venice and Shanghai have them—they're open to ships and tides; they close during storms.

2. **Build barrier islands and artificial reefs.**
   Build reefs from stone, rope and wood pilings. In a harbor like New York City, seed them with oysters and other shellfish (25% of New York Harbor used to be oyster beds). As sea levels rise, the reefs of shells will grow.

3. **Build water storage facilities.**
   In a flood or a rainstorm, water can be channeled into these. In Rotterdam, a single underground parking garage can hold 2.5 million gallons.

4. **Build floating communities.**
   By 2040, Rotterdam plans to have as many as 1,200 homes floating on its harbor. French Polynesia will host a "city of floating islands" with renewable power and sustainable aquaculture.

5. **Employ "sand engines."**
   In one province of the Netherlands, the government dredged up enough sand to make a peninsula the size of 250 football fields. Over the next 20 years, wind, waves and tides (the "zandmotor") will spread its sand 15 miles up and down the coast.

6. **Build levees, install pumps.**
   As in New Orleans.

7. **Restore freshwater wetlands and mangrove swamps.**
   Try this in places like Florida.

8. **Require new buildings to be set further inland and higher off the ground.**
   As required by New York City.

9. **Encourage homeowners to build with resilient materials like fiber cement sheets, stone, steel, hardwood and glass blocks.**
   As in Queensland, Australia.

10. **Pray.**

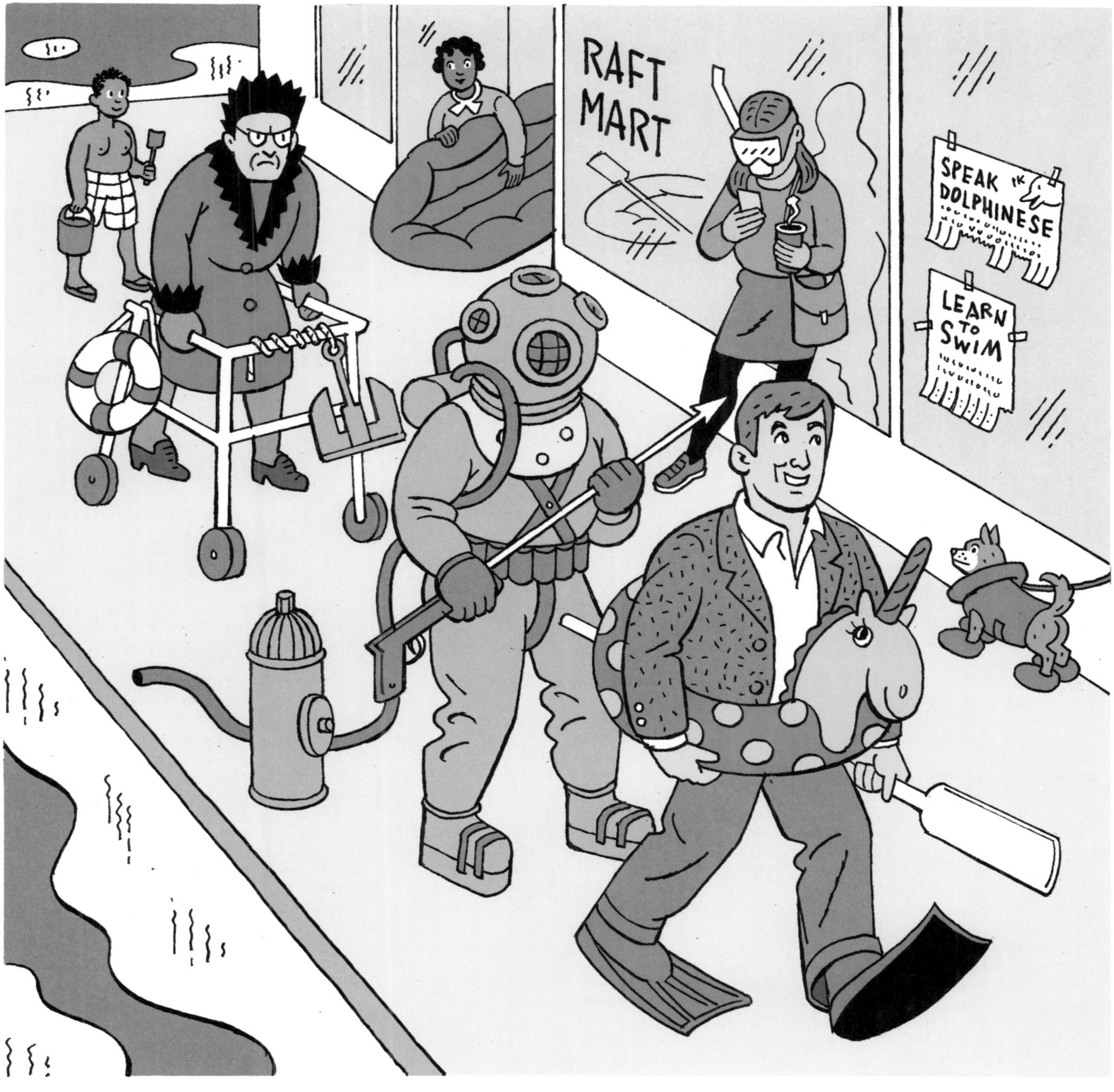
RAFT MART
SPEAK DOLPHINESE
LEARN TO SWIM

THE TOP 10 GEOENGINEERING SOLUTIONS TO GLOBAL WARMING: SOLUTIONS 1, 2, 3 AND 4. OVER OUR HEADS.

Ranked in descending order of the seriousness with which these technofixes are being considered.

1. **Pump light-reflecting sulfate aerosols into the upper atmosphere or stratosphere.**
   There is already a natural proof of concept: The 1991 eruption of Mount Pinatubo spewed 10 million tons of sulfur into the atmosphere and cooled the Earth roughly 1 degree Fahrenheit for about a year. So run tubes up to dirigibles at 65,000 feet and pump out sulfate aerosols. The risk: sulfate aerosols produce sulfuric acid, which damages ozone; depletion of the ozone layer could lead to more skin cancer. And the sulfuric acid could come down as acid rain, decimating plant and fish life.

2. **Put something into orbit to filter, block or reflect sunlight.**
   Physicist Lowell Wood proposes a mesh of aluminum threads a millionth of an inch in diameter and a thousandth of an inch apart. He says it "would be like a window screen" that "wouldn't actually block the light but would simply filter it." The screen would cost almost nothing to operate and would look like a tiny black dot on the sun. Other suggested ways to deal with too much sunlight: clouds of moon dust or a planet-girdling ring of trillions of tiny reflective disks. Or one giant umbrella.

3. **Make clouds brighter.**
   Seeding clouds with tiny salt particles would make clouds whiter, boosting their reflectivity ("albedo"). It's argued that doing this to just three percent of the clouds over the world's oceans would reflect enough sunlight to curb global warming. Between 5,000 and 30,000 unmanned ships—wind-powered and GPS-steered—would sail the oceans, spraying a fine saltwater mist into the air. The risk: this might make it harder for rainclouds to form, so don't do this upwind of any place where there's a drought.

4. Move the Earth farther away from the sun.

Pick out an asteroid or comet about 60-65 miles in diameter. Strap a chemical rocket to it. Then fire the rocket at just the right time to direct the asteroid or comet so it sweeps close to Earth and transfers some of its gravitational energy to Earth and nudges Earth out into a slightly further orbit. The risk: if this works, the Moon probably gets stripped away from Earth, radically upsetting our climate. And if instead of "sweeping close to Earth," the comet or asteroid hits us? Probably it sterilizes Earth.

THE TOP 10 GEOENGINEERING SOLUTIONS TO GLOBAL WARMING: SOLUTIONS 5, 6, 7, 8, 9 AND 10. HERE ON EARTH.

Ranked in descending order of the seriousness with which these technofixes are being considered.

5. Make the ocean absorb more CO_2—by dumping iron or antacids.
   The Southern Ocean around Antarctica is devoid of life. So fertilize it with iron. For each pound of iron, enough plankton would hatch to devour 100,000 pounds of CO_2. The risk: these waters are rich in nutrients—which are carried northward to where fish need them. Huge plankton blooms in the Southern Ocean could devour these nutrients and turn all oceans sterile. Another way to make the ocean absorb more CO_2: reduce its acidity by dumping in huge amounts of limestone or other alkalines.

6. Filter CO_2 from the air with giant "wind scrubbers."
   Build scrubbers, 200 feet high and 165 feet wide. Equip them with porous filters. A binding chemical gets pumped through filters to trap CO_2 particles as they drift past. Then the CO_2 is stripped off. A single scrubber would snag 90,000 tons of CO_2 a year. The downside: separating CO_2 from the binding chemical would require a lot of energy. And to capture all the CO_2 that humans add to the atmosphere, you'd need scrubber towers covering an area at least the size of Arizona.

7. Make cropland brighter, make deserts brighter, make oceans brighter.
   Planting crops with bright leaves or using genetic modification to get even brighter leaves could, over the next 100 years, reflect sunlight equal to removing 195 billion tons of CO_2 from the atmosphere. Desert reflectivity could be increased by covering deserts with white plastic film. And ocean reflectivity could be increased with micron-sized bubbles. The risk: brighter crops could warm the land and decrease precipitation; brighter deserts could disrupt weather patterns; those ocean bubbles could choke marine life.

8. Pump deep, cold nutrient-rich waters to the surface of oceans.
   This would boost algae growth; algae eat carbon dioxide. Scientist James Lovelock suggests starting with 10,000 pipes in the Gulf of Mexico.

9. Irrigate vast swaths of desert to grow trees. Trees take carbon dioxide out of the air and release oxygen into it. Mangroves are especially good at this.

10. Grow slime on buildings.
    Cover buildings with strips of carbon-eating algae. Before the algae decomposes and gets really slimy, collect it and reprocess it as fuel.

Geoengineering (noun)*: A solution comparable to resorting to bariatric surgery after a lifetime of overeating*

THE TOP 10 PEOPLE PUSHING RESEARCH IN GEOENGINEERING— AND MAYBE EVEN IMPLEMENTATION

In July 2012, "climate entrepreneur" Russ George dumped 120 tons of iron sulfate onto 15,000 square miles of the Pacific, spawning a massive plankton bloom. Assuming the plankton would absorb CO_2 and create "carbon credits," George said this could be a $100-billion business. His rogue experiment caused an uproar. Since then, geoengineering has been pushed mostly by establishment types. They are led by . . .

1. **Bill Gates**

   While he holds patents on methods to prevent hurricanes, he's more interested in controlling the climate. His personal money helps fund Intellectual Ventures and the Fund for Innovative Climate and Energy Research (FICER), both of which promote geoengineering research. He also has a major stake in Carbon Engineering, a Canadian geoengineering company.

2. **Nathan Myhrvold**

   This former head of technology at Microsoft is part-owner of Intellectual Ventures. He has proposed a project called Stratoshield in which giant hoses would be lifted by balloon to spray aerosols.

3. **Murray Edwards**

   A tar-sands billionaire in Alberta, Canada, he has a major stake in Carbon Engineering.

4. **David Keith**

   One of Bill Gates's two chief climate advisers, this Harvard professor helps run FICER and is the founder, president and majority owner of Carbon Engineering. As head of the Keith Group, he has advocated using sea salt to brighten ocean clouds, to reflect sunlight back into space.

5. **Ken Calderia**

   Gates's other chief climate adviser, this Stanford professor helps run FICER and works for Intellectual Ventures. The holder of a carbon capture patent, he says, "If any patent I am on is ever used for the purpose of altering climate, then any proceeds that accrue to me for this use will be donated to nonprofit NGOs and charities."

6. Lowell Wood

A Ph.D. in astrophysics and an advocate of geoengineering, he works for Intellectual Ventures. He has surpassed Thomas Edison as the most prolific inventor in terms of patents held. Says Ken Calderia, "Lowell enjoys playing the role of Dr. Evil. He's a planetary engineer."

7. Dan Whaley

Founder and CEO of Climos, a San Francisco geoengineering company. Climos has said, "We are in active collaboration on the scientific, technical and regulatory steps necessary to bring a next-generation ocean iron fertilization (OIF) project to realization."

8. Margaret Leinen

Former head of geosciences at the National Science Foundation and head of the Climate Response Fund (CRF), which promotes geoengineering. She is also the former chief scientific officer of Climos.

9. Sir Richard Branson and Niklas Zennstrom

Through his Carbon War Room, Branson has helped fund research by the Royal Society into solar radiation management. Zennstrom, co-founder of Skype, has also funded research into geoengineering.

10. Phil Rasch and Jay Apt

Rasch is chief climate scientist for the Pacific Northwest national laboratory, a research institution funded by the U.S. Department of Energy. He and Jerome "Jay" Apt, a professor at Carnegie Mellon, have received FICER money.

Not pushing for geoengineering research but providing U.S. government guidance on research restrictions: the National Committee on Energy Policy, Sasha Mackler, research director.

THE TOP 10 THINGS YOU CAN DO TO REDUCE GLOBAL WARMING (THEY WON'T MAKE ANY REAL DIFFERENCE BUT THEY MAY MAKE YOU FEEL GOOD)

The real point is to increase your self-esteem.

1. Reduce, reuse, recycle.

2. Use less heat and air conditioning.

3. Change a light bulb.

4. Drive less and drive smart.

5. Buy energy-efficient products.

6. Use less hot water.

7. Use the "off" switch and then unplug.

8. Plant a tree.

9. Get a report card from your utility company.

10. Encourage others to conserve.

Do all this and you'll feel warm all over . . .and you'll reduce global warming by exactly one-zillion-zillionth of one percent. As Leonardo DiCaprio said in his address at the UN on September 23, 2014, "To be clear, this is not about telling people to change their light bulbs or buy a hybrid car. The disaster has grown beyond the choices that individuals make."

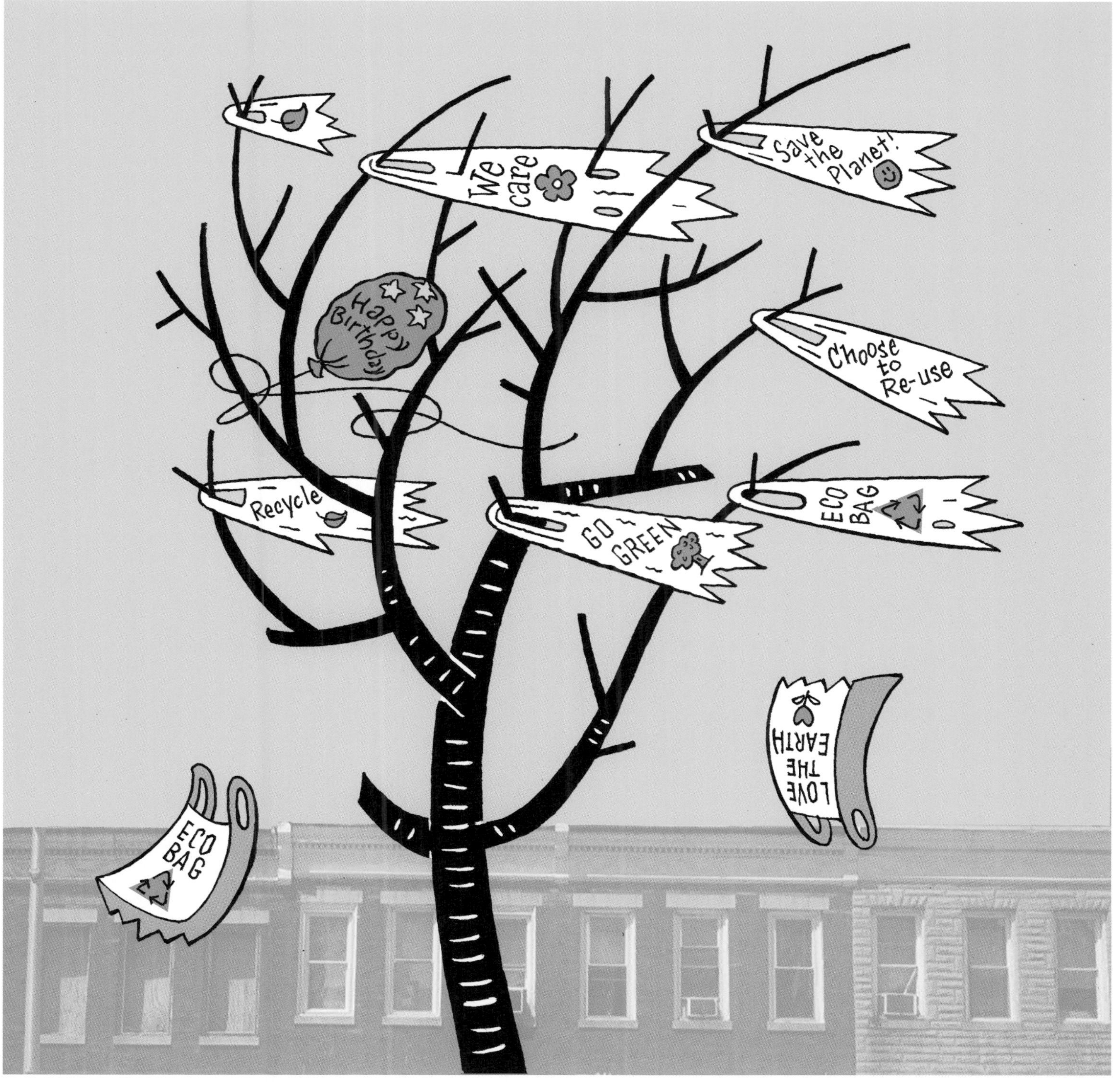
We care
Save the Planet!
Happy Birthday
Choose to Re-use
Recycle
GO GREEN
ECO BAG
LOVE THE EARTH
ECO BAG

GLOBAL WARMING: TEARS AND LAUGHTER.

THE TOP 10 MOST DISCOURAGING NON-FICTION BOOKS ABOUT CLIMATE CHANGE

Maybe Amazon should offer a two-for-one deal: buy one of these and get a free copy of *Final Exit*, that bestseller on how to commit suicide.

1. *The Uninhabitable Earth: Life After Warming* by David Wallace-Wells

2. *Losing Earth: A Climate History* by Nathaniel Rich

3. *Learning to Die in the Anthropocene: Reflections on the End of a Civilization* by Roy Scranton

4. *Requiem for a Species: Why We Resist the Truth About Climate Change* by Clive Hamilton

5. *The Collapse of Western Civilization: A View from the Future* by Naomi Oreskes and Erik Conway

6. *The Great Derangement: Climate Change and the Unthinkable* by Amitav Ghosh

7. *The Water Will Come: Rising Seas, Sinking Cities and the Remaking of the Civilized World* by Jeff Goodell

8. *Field Notes from a Catastrophe: Man, Nature and Climate Change* by Elizabeth Kolbert

9. *Dire Predictions: Understanding Climate Change* by Michael E. Mann and Lee R. Kump

10. *Reason in a Dark Time: Why the Struggle Against Climate Change Failed* by Dale Jamieson

Anthropocene (noun): *the current geological age; the period, from the Industrial Revolution onward, during which human activity has been the dominant influence on climate and the environment; as this activity is tending toward human extinction, perhaps the shortest geological age ever*

THE TOP 10 BUMPERSTICKERS AND T-SHIRTS ABOUT GLOBAL WARMING

1. The environment says, "F__k me? No, f__k you."

2. How do I know there's no global warming? Because Trump tells the truth and scientists lie.

3. What if climate change is a hoax and we create a better world for nothing?

4. When the seas rose, the dinosaurs moved inland. Try moving 100 American cities.

5. When you finally realize climate change is real, try not to blame feminists and gays.

6. Save the Earth for future generations? What have they ever done for us?

7. Well, at least the war on the environment is going well.

8. There's a warm place reserved for people who deny global warming.

9. There is no Planet B.

10. Unfortunately, the climate is changing faster than we are.

THE TOP 10 PHRASES THAT GLOBAL WARMING WILL MAKE OBSOLETE

1. "a blizzard of facts"—will become "a sandstorm of facts"

2. "a snowball's chance in hell"—a snowball won't have a chance anywhere

3. "on thin ice"—will be meaningless, because all ice will be thin

4. "move at a glacial pace"—in other words, very fast

5. "he got out over his skis"—will have to mean waterskis

6. "tough sledding"—will be meaningless, because all sledding will be tough

7. "cold shoulder" and "out in the cold"—will be meaningless, along with "you're getting warm," because everyone will always be warm

8. "they froze her out"—along with "chill out," will be impossible

9. "my eyes glaze over"—will be impossible

10. "a day at the beach"—will mean "brutal" because any remaining beaches will be boiling hot and bordered by poisonous jellyfish

And say goodbye to any pirate saying "Shiver me timbers"
and the joke, "I went to a fight and a hockey game broke out."

THE TOP 10 SNARK

1. "We estimate that there are perhaps 20,000 prehistoric hunter-gatherers frozen up in those glaciers. Now, if they simply thaw and wander around, it's not a problem, but if they find a leader—a Captain Caveman, if you will—we'll be facing an even more serious problem. "
—John Hodgman
Daily Show correspondent

2. "According to a new U.N. report, the global warming outlook is much worse than originally predicted. Which is pretty bad when they originally predicted it would destroy the planet."
—Jay Leno

3. "Experts say this global warming is serious, and they are predicting now that by the year 2050, we will be out of party ice."
—David Letterman

4. "Global warming. It's the kids I feel sorry for, because if sea levels do rise, they'll drown first."
—(source unknown)

5. "President Bush has a plan. He says that if we need to, we can lower the temperature dramatically just by switching from Fahrenheit to Celsius."
—Jimmy Kimmel

6. "The U.S. leads the world in people who think climate science is fake but pro wrestling is real."
—John Fugelsang

7. "Global warming isn't real because I was cold today! Also great news: World hunger is over because I just ate!"
—Stephen Colbert

8. "If only the people who worry about 'traditional marriage' cared about 'traditional climate.'"
—@LOLGOP

9. "On Groundhog Day, we hope Punxsutawney Phil will not see his shadow—meaning spring will arrive early. Yes, only in America do we accept weather predictions from a rodent but deny climate change evidence from scientists."
— (source unknown)

10. "One of the ten best things about global warming: Furnaces convert easily to tornado shelters."
—John E. Brandenberg and Monica Rix Paxson

EVERYTH

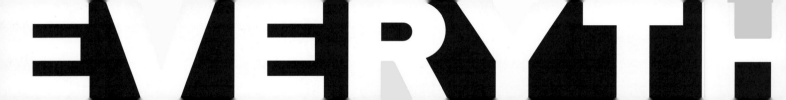

ING ELSE

NUCLEAR WAR

THE TOP 12 TIMES WHEN THE CUBAN MISSILE CRISIS COULD HAVE BECOME NUCLEAR WAR

The crisis began on October 15, 1962 when objects photographed by U.S. U-2 spy planes flying over Cuba were identified as Soviet missiles. As the crisis intensified, more and more incidents were seen by U.S. or Soviet officials as the other side preparing for war or actually going to war—and possibly requiring that "our side" move closer to, or even initiate, a nuclear response. And some incidents risked taking—and even took—that decision out of the hands of top officials and put it the hands of people far down the chain of command.

These 12 incidents are listed chronologically.

1. **October 22, 1962: Some NATO bases mistakenly go to DEFCON 3**
   While almost all U.S. armed forces went to DEFCON 3, to avoid provoking the USSR, the U.S. Army in Europe did not. For the same reason, the Supreme Commander of NATO decided not to have NATO go to DEFCON 3. But, due to miscommunication, several NATO commanders in Germany, Italy, Turkey and the U.K. put individual bases on DEFCON 3. The Soviets could have interpreted this as signaling an imminent attack.

2. **October 24, 1962: An exploding Soviet satellite is misinterpreted as an ICBM attack**
   Intended to make a flyby of Mars, Sputnik 22 was launched and was in a parking orbit around Earth. When its engines were reignited to head it toward Mars, it exploded. Some U.S. officials misinterpreted this as an ICBM attack.

3. **October 25, 1962: A Minnesota bear gets reported as a Soviet nuclear strike**
   Around midnight, a sentry at an Air Force base in Duluth, Minnesota spotted a shadowy figure trying to climb over the security fence. He shot at it and raised the "sabotage" alarm—which went to airfields throughout the region. But Volk Field, a National Guard base in La Crosse, Wisconsin, got the "air raid" alarm. Believing the U.S. was under attack, Volk crews rushed their nuclear-armed F106-A fighter jets onto the tarmac. Calling his Duluth counterpart for confirmation, the Volk commander was told about the mistake. Volk's F106-As were stopped before takeoff. The "saboteur" trying to climb the fence had been a bear.

4. **October 26, 1962. Rushed online, some U.S. radar stations rush to judgment**
   U.S. radar stations under construction were brought online as quickly as possible, leading to repeated false alarms. An unannounced test firing of a Titan II ICBM off the coast of Florida was momentarily misinterpreted by one new station—which nearly sounded the alarm for nuclear attack.

5. **October 26, 1962. One man in a missile silo could start World War III**

   As the crisis escalated, Minuteman ICBMs at Malmstrom Air Force Base in Montana were rushed into full deployment. And, by mistake, all the launch-enabling equipment and codes were placed in a silo alongside the corresponding missile. A single person could have launched a nuclear-armed missile.

October 27, 1962, "Black Saturday," the most dangerous day of the crisis, has been called the most dangerous day in human history. The U.S. had moved to DEFCON 2—one step short of nuclear war. Unknown to the U.S., the Soviets already had nuclear warheads at two missile sites in Cuba ready to destroy American cities and had nuclear-tipped cruise missiles in a "firing position" 15 miles from the U.S. naval base at Guantanamo Bay. And Castro was urging Khrushchev to use nuclear weapons to "liquidate" the imperialist enemy.

6. **October 27, 1962. The Soviets go to wartime frequencies**

   As the Soviets fueled nuclear-armed ICBMs, wireless communications between divisions of the Soviet military and its Strategic Rocket Forces were transferred to wartime frequencies. This told U.S. officials that the U.S. could be attacked at any moment.

7. **October 27, 1962: F-102s with nuclear missiles scramble to protect a U-2 that has strayed over Russia**

   A U.S. U-2 spy plane was flying near the North Pole, sampling the air for radiation that would point to Soviet nuclear tests. Thrown off-course by the aurora borealis, the pilot strayed over the USSR—and MiGs flew up with orders to shoot it down. Two U.S. F-102 fighters scrambled to provide protection to the unarmed U-2.

Because the U.S. was on heightened alert, the F-102s' conventional weapons had been replaced with missiles with nuclear warheads. In theory, only the president could authorize their use. In practice, they were under the control of the pilot. And if a MiG were about to fire on the U-2 or on a F-102, how could a U.S. pilot not respond?

Although no shots were fired, this U-2 intrusion—on the tensest day of the Cuban Missile Crisis—could be seen by the Soviets as a harbinger of an all-out U.S. nuclear attack. The U-2 made it back to Alaska. And somebody got word to the U.S. command to suspend U-2 flights near the USSR.

8. **October 27, 1962: An unarmed U.S. U-2 spy plane is shot down over Cuba**
American leaders had agreed that if any U.S. plane were shot down over Cuba, the U.S. would attack. After the crisis, it came to light that Khrushchev, fearing such retaliation, had ordered Soviet troops in Cuba not to shoot any U.S. planes. What happened here? Acting on his own, a Soviet lieutenant general ordered, "Destroy Target Number 33." In response, U.S. military leaders overwhelmingly urged Kennedy to attack Cuba's air defenses the next morning. Correctly suspecting Khrushchev had not authorized downing unarmed reconnaissance planes, Kennedy said no. The pilot of this U-2, Major Rudolph Anderson, was the only person to die in the Cuban Missile Crisis.

9. **October 27, 1962: Captain Arkhipov saves the world**
U.S. warships enforcing the blockade of Cuba detected four Soviet submarines approaching Cuba. Unbeknownst to the U.S., each had a nuclear-tipped torpedo that could deliver a blast two-thirds the strength of the bomb dropped on Hiroshima. Moscow had given all four permission to launch this torpedo independently if attacked by depth charges. One submarine, codenamed B-59, having lost contact with Moscow for several days, did not know the blockade was in effect. When U.S. warships dropped depth charges on either side of B-59 to force it to surface, the crew thought that perhaps war had been declared. Should it launch its nuclear torpedo?

On most Soviet submarines this required the consent of only two people: the captain and the political officer. But onboard B-59 was also Vasili Arkhipov. While Arkhipov was only B-59's "second captain," he held same rank as its captain. Crucially, because he commanded the entire submarine flotilla, his consent was also required. B-59's Captain Valentin Savitsky argued for launch. An intelligence officer on B-59 recalled Savitsky shouting, "We're going to blast them now! We will die, but we will sink them all!" Political Officer Ivan Maslennikov agreed. Arkhipov dissented. He argued that B-59 should surface and get orders from Moscow. He prevailed. Most experts agree that had B-59 launched its nuclear torpedo, an all-out nuclear war would have been triggered.

10. **October 28, 1962: A test tape of a Soviet attack is mistaken for the real thing**
Just before 9:00 am, radar operators at Moorestown, New Jersey reported to NORAD headquarters that a nuclear attack from Cuba was underway, with impact expected near Tampa, Florida at 9:02 am. All NORAD was alerted. What had happened? The radar operators didn't know that a test tape simulating a missile launch from Cuba was being run on their own machinery. Simultaneously, a satellite had come over the horizon and they mistook it for an incoming missile. There was a radar post that normally would have notified Moorestown about the satellite but, because of the Cuban Missile Crisis, it had been assigned to other work. 9:02 am came and went with Tampa untouched.

11. **October 28, 1962: An orbiting satellite is mistaken for two incoming missiles**
Having just become operational, the Laredo, Texas radar site mistook an orbiting satellite for two

missiles incoming over Georgia—and warned NORAD. Believing the warning had come from the more reliable (!) Moorestown post, NORAD prepared to intercept the missiles. And Moorestown failed to contradict the false warning.

12. November 2, 1962: Colonel Penkovsky tries to blow up the world

Oleg Penkovsky, a colonel in Soviet military intelligence, had become disillusioned with the Soviet regime and felt Nikita Khrushchev's actions could lead to nuclear war. So, starting in April 1961, he gave valuable information to the U.S. and Great Britain. Perhaps most importantly, his information had, on October 15, 1962, helped the U.S. identify the U-2 photographs of Cuba as Soviet missiles.

Now, what if Penkovsky learned the USSR was about to launch a nuclear attack but he had had no time to pass on any corroborating information? Penkosvky, the CIA, and Britain's MI6 had agreed to this signal: He was to call the CIA, and/or MI6, blow three times into his phone's mouthpiece and then hang up. On November 2, 1962, two such calls came. While, on October 28 the Cuban Missile Crisis seemed to have ended, on November 2 Soviet missiles were still in Cuba and U.S. forces remained at DEFCON 3—so Penkovsky could have been warning about the real thing.

What had happened? Unbeknownst to the CIA and MI6, on October 22 the KGB had arrested Penkovsky. While he had probably told the KGB about the signal he could send to the CIA and MI6, he had probably not revealed what it really meant, only that it meant "unexpected danger." So the KGB let him send the signal. Why did he send it? Since Penkovsky knew he would be executed for treason, he was probably trying to take the USSR down with him by pushing the West to launch a nuclear strike.

Why didn't he succeed? Sensing the signal was a false alarm, the MI6 officer who received it did nothing. The CIA officer who received it alerted Langley, and Langley sent another officer to the Moscow "dead drop" to see if Penkovsky had provided anything else. This officer was arrested by the KGB—so the CIA also concluded the signal was a false alarm.

On May 16, 1963, in Moscow's Lubyanka Prison, Oleg Penkovsky was executed.

Khrushchev remembers:

"I remember President Kennedy once stated . . .that the United States had the nuclear missile capacity to wipe out the Soviet Union two times over, while the Soviet Union had enough atomic weapons to wipe out the United States only once . . .When journalists asked me to comment . . .I said jokingly, "Yes, I know what Kennedy claims, and he's quite right. But I'm not complaining . . .We're satisfied to be able to finish off the United States first time 'round. Once is quite enough. What good does it do to annihilate a country twice? We're not a bloodthirsty people."

THE TOP 14 TIMES NOT INCLUDING THE CUBAN MISSILE CRISIS WHEN A LOT OF PEOPLE COULD HAVE BEEN NUKED

Ten of these were false alarms. But numbers 7, 10 and 12 were false alarms that very nearly became nuclear war. In number 3, one or more nuclear bombs nearly detonated on U.S. soil. In number 13, six nuclear warheads were vulnerable to theft. In number 14, 50 ICBMs were vulnerable to unauthorized launch. Thus, 3, 7, 10, 12, 13 and 14 carried the most risk. Aside from that, it's hard to assign any "order of importance." So all 14 incidents are listed chronologically.

1. **November 5, 1956: A flight of swans is seen as Soviet warplanes**
   During the Suez Crisis, the U.S. feared the USSR might take unilateral action against the British and French forces attacking Egypt. With tensions high, NORAD (North American Air Defense Command) simultaneously received these reports: unidentified aircraft over Turkey, Soviet MiG-15 fighters over Syria, a downed British Canberra medium bomber and unexpected maneuvers by the Soviet Black Sea Fleet through the Dardanelles into the Mediterranean. These possible signs of a Soviet attack could have triggered a NATO response.

   But these turned out to be: scheduled exercises by the Soviet Fleet, a British bomber brought down by mechanical reasons, a fighter escort for the Syrian president returning from Moscow . . . and a wedge of swans over Turkey.

2. **October 5, 1960: The rising moon is seen as dozens of Soviet nuclear missiles**
   On this date, NORAD's early warning radar in Thule, Greenland, reported with 99.9% certainty that a massive Soviet nuclear attack was underway: dozens of missiles would hit the U.S. in 20 minutes. According to some accounts, amid tension and confusion and even panic, NORAD went to its maximum alert.

   What argued against this being an attack: Soviet leader Nikita Khrushchev was in New York City. What this attack really was: the moon rising over Norway reflecting radar waves back to the Thule radar and fooling its computers.

3. **January 24, 1961: A nuclear bomb nearly spreads fallout from North Carolina to New York City**
Three and a half days after JFK's inauguration, around midnight on January 23-24, over North Carolina, a U.S. B-52 Stratofortress carrying two 3.8 megaton thermonuclear bombs developed a fuel leak in its right wing. Attempting an emergency landing, the pilots were unable to keep the plane stable. Losing control, they ordered the crew to bail out. At 1,000 to 2,000 feet, as the gyrating aircraft broke up, the two bombs—each 12 feet long and weighing 6,200 pounds, each with 250 times the destructive power of the Hiroshima bomb, each partially armed—separated from the plane. Aircraft wreckage and the bombs plunged toward farmland 12 miles north of Goldsboro.

One bomb safely parachuted to the ground and snagged on a tree. But the parachute on the second bomb failed. Slamming at 700 miles per hour into swampy, muddy ground, this bomb broke into pieces. When the tree-snagged bomb was disarmed, it was discovered that three of its four arming mechanisms had engaged. And when the pieces of the other bomb were unearthed, it was discovered that all four mechanisms had engaged. The fourth mechanism—a simple, low-voltage switch—was actually in the "armed" position and should have triggered the bomb.

Robert McNamara, secretary of defense at the time, said that only "by the slightest of margins, literally the failure of two wires to cross, a nuclear explosion was averted." The explosion would have spread lethal fallout north to Washington, Baltimore, Philadelphia and New York City.

4. **November 24, 1961: The failure of a single switch has U.S. bombers ready to take off**
SAC (Strategic Air Command) headquarters in Omaha lost contact with the early warning radar in Thule, Greenland. When SAC tried to call NORAD headquarters in Colorado to find out what the problem was, the line was dead. Fearing this simultaneous breakdown meant the U.S. was under attack, SAC's entire alert force was ordered to prepare for takeoff. Fortunately, a U.S. bomber over Thule made contact with the facility and the alert was called off. The cause: the failure of a single AT&T switch in Colorado.

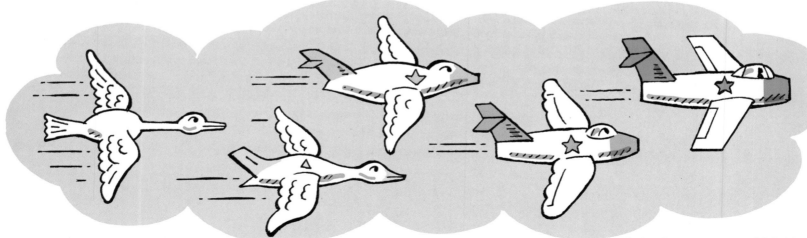

A flight of swans is seen as MiG-15s.

5. **November 9, 1965: A blackout sets off alarms of a nuclear attack**
   Alarms are spread across the U.S. so that, in case of a nuclear explosion, the location of the strike can be quickly transmitted to the Command Center of the Office of Emergency Planning before the resulting failure of some of the power grid. At 5:27 pm on November 9, 1965, when much of the northeast was hit by a power failure, the alarms in this area should have gone from green to yellow—meaning a failure not caused by a nuclear explosion. But two alarms in different cities went red—meaning a nuclear attack. The Command Center went on full alert.

6. **May 23, 1967: A solar storm is interpreted as the Soviets jamming U.S. radars**
   In Alaska, Greenland and the United Kingdom, all three of the Northern Hemisphere radar sites of the U.S. Air Force BMEWS went offline. Believing the Soviet Union was jamming them in preparation for war, U.S. commanders quickly began preparing to launch more nuclear-equipped aircraft. In truth, a solar storm that had begun on May 18 was hitting the Earth with solar flares and coronal mass ejections.

7. **November 9, 1979: A simulated Soviet nuclear attack is displayed as the real thing**
   At 2:35 am, President Carter's national security adviser Zbigniew Brzezinski was awakened by a phone call from his military assistant William Odom telling him that 250 Soviet missiles had been launched at the United States. Knowing the president had only seven minutes to decide to order retaliation, Brzezinski told Odom he would stand by for a further call to confirm the Soviet attack. And he told Odom to confirm that SAC was launching its planes. Odom called back to report that 2,200 missiles had been launched—it was an all-out attack. One minute before Brzezinski intended to call the president, Odom called a third time to say that other warning systems were not reporting Soviet launches.

   What had happened? Software simulating a Soviet missile attack then being tested on NORAD computers had somehow been mistakenly transferred into the regular warning displays at the headquarters of NORAD, SAC and NMCC (National Military Command Center).

   "Sitting alone in the middle of the night, Brzezinski had not awakened his wife, reckoning that everyone would be dead in half an hour."—Robert M. Gates, former U.S. Secretary of Defense

8. **March 15, 1980: A Soviet missile appears to be heading toward the U.S.**
   As part of a training exercise, a Soviet submarine near the Kuril Islands (a Soviet possession near Japan) launched four SLRMs. American early warning sensors determined that one missile would impact the United States. The situation naturally resolved itself.

9. **June 3 and June 6, 1980: A 46-cent chip turns 000 missiles into 200 missiles**
   Routinely, NORAD computers sent SAC messages that said 000 ICBMs or SLBMs (short-range ballistic missiles) had been launched at the United States. But on these two days, some messages said 002 and then 200. In response, SAC ordered its bombers and tankers to start their engines. When early warning systems such as BMEWS reported no missiles, SAC took no further action. What had happened? A 46-cent computer chip had made "typographical errors."

10. **September 26, 1983: Colonel Petrov saves the world**

Starting in May 1981, thinking the U.S. was preparing for a first strike, the Soviets were on hair-trigger alert. This made risky incidents . . . riskier.

On September 26, Lt. Colonel Stanislav Petrov, age 44, was the officer on duty in the command center of the Soviet early warning system. If the system detected inbound missiles, Soviet doctrine required an immediate and massive nuclear counter-attack. Shortly after midnight, with a howling siren, the system reported first one ICBM heading from the U.S. toward the Soviet Union and then four more. Believing these were false alarms, Petrov disobeyed protocol and did not tell his superiors.

Later it was determined that these "missiles" were sunlight glinting on high altitude clouds under the orbits of Soviet satellites. At first praised by his superiors, Petrov was later reassigned to a less sensitive post, took early retirement and suffered a nervous breakdown. He died in May 2017.

11. **November 7-11, 1983: The Soviets believe a NATO exercise is a prelude to a nuclear attack**

Able Archer was an annual NATO command post exercise culminating in a simulated DEFCON 1 and nuclear attack. Because the 1983 version was much more realistic than those of previous years, Soviet leaders believed it might be a cover for preparations for a real nuclear attack. In response, they put nuclear-capable aircraft in East Germany and Poland on high alert and may have prepared ICBMs for launch. Only when Able Archer 83 ended did the Soviets stop fearing an immediate attack.

12. **January 25, 1995: A study of the Northern Lights nearly leads to "lights-out"**

Scientists were about to launch a large, four-stage Black Brant rocket off the coast of Norway to fly 930 miles above the Earth near Russia to study the aurora borealis. Before launch, they notified the Russian military. But the word never got to the right officials, and the Norwegians didn't realize that the Brant's radar signature looks just like that of a Trident missile (and U.S. Trident submarines often patrol the Norwegian Sea). So as the Brant streaked up into the night near Russian airspace, radar operatives at Russia's Olengorsk early warning station reported an "incoming missile." As the Brandt separated, dropped one of its engines and fired another, it looked like a multiple-reentry missile carrying eight to ten nuclear warheads. And now, in the next five minutes, it could be not be tracked by Russian radar. In these five minutes, Russian leadership had to decide whether to launch a nuclear counterattack on the U.S.

Russian submarine commanders were ordered to full battle alert; Russian president Boris Yelstin was awakened and given the Cheget, the "nuclear briefcase." (This is the only time when a nuclear briefcase has actually been broken out and opened up, ready for use.) Doubting this was a U.S. attack, Yeltsin did nothing. Reacquiring the "missile," Russian radar confirmed it was heading harmlessly out to sea.

13. **August 29-30, 2007: Six U.S. nuclear weapons, possibly fully operational, go missing**

Six advanced cruise missiles were loaded in a pylon on the wing of a B-52 bomber at Minot Air Force Base in North Dakota. While they were supposed carry dummy warheads, the missiles actually had nuclear warheads. For fifteen hours the bomber sat overnight on the tarmac without the special guard required for nuclear weapons. It then flew for more than three hours to Barksdale Air Force Base in Louisiana where it sat for another nine hours similarly unguarded. Finally a maintenance crew discovered what the warheads really were.

For 36 hours, these warheads were not reported missing, were not protected by mandatory security measures for nuclear weapons and, for all anyone knows, may have been fully operational. Was this a mistake? Said a former assistant secretary of defense, "This wasn't just a mistake. I've counted, and least 20 things had to have gone wrong for this to have occurred."

14. October 23, 2010: The U.S. loses command and control of 50 ICBMs
For nearly an hour, a launch control center at Warren Air Force Base, Wyoming lost command and control of its 50 ICBMs, about one-ninth of America's ICBM arsenal. Had there been any unauthorized launch attempt, the center could neither have detected nor canceled it. What had happened? During routine maintenance of one of the computers, a circuit card had been installed improperly.

"Death wears bunny slippers."—The unofficial motto of U.S. missileers because, 60 feet underground, in the control room of a missile silo, while one missileer monitors control panels, his partner sleeps in a bed opposite.

THE TOP 9 NUCLEAR ARSENALS
(AS FAR AS IS KNOWN, THERE IS NO 10TH)

	Total warheads	Deployed warheads	Retired Warheads
Russia	6,850	1,600	2,700
United States	6,450	1,750	2,800
Israel	60-400	?	
France	300	280	
China	280	?	
United Kingdom	215	120	
Pakistan	140-150	0	
India	130-140	12	
North Korea	10-20	0	

THE TOP 2 TIMES THAT A COUNTRY OTHER THAN THE U.S. AND THE USSR CAME CLOSE TO USING ITS NUCLEAR WEAPONS

1. October 8, 1973: Losing the Yom Kippur War, Israel prepares to go nuclear

Two days into the war, with Egyptian and Syrian forces overwhelming Israeli defenders, Israeli Defense Minister Moshe Dayan ordered his country's 13 nuclear bombs loaded onto jets and ordered his country's 20 Jericho nuclear missiles into readiness. But Israel's conventional forces soon drove back the Egyptians and Syrians. If they hadn't . . . ?

2. June-July 1999: In the Kargil War, Pakistan prepares to go nuclear

In early May, a Pakistan-India war broke out in Kargil in the states of Jammu and Kashmir. On June 24, Pakistan's Prime Minister Nawaz Sharif and Army Chief of Staff Pervez Musharraf were at or near a military base when an Indian fighter pilot—thinking the base was his assigned target—nearly bombed it. If this had happened, the surviving Pakistani leadership might have moved toward "going nuclear" against India. Even so, Pakistan was soon preparing to deploy and possibly use nuclear weapons, and India could have retaliated with its own nuclear weapons. Learning of Pakistan's nuclear moves on July 4, President Clinton told Sharif that Pakistan had to withdraw its troops. Sharif complied. By July 14, both sides had ceased their military operations.

THE TOP 2 COMMENTS BY SOMEONE WHO WAS LOOKING FORWARD TO HAVING A NUCLEAR ARSENAL

1. "I'm not afraid of nuclear war. There are 2.7 billion people in the world; it doesn't matter if some are killed. China has a population of 600 million; even if half of them are killed, there are still 300 million people left. I'm not afraid of anyone."

   —Mao Zedong, November 1957 (about to initiate the "Great Leap Forward," which, between 1958 and 1962, killed at least 45 million Chinese)

2. "If the worst came to worst and half of mankind died, the other half would remain while imperialism would be razed to the ground and the whole world would become socialist; in a number of years there would be 2,700 million people again and definitely more."

   —Mao Zedong, October 1954

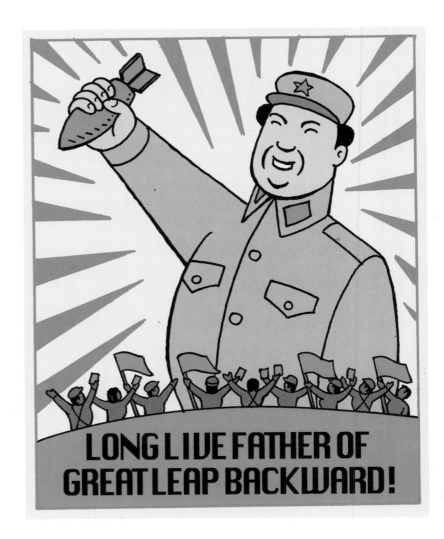

LONG LIVE FATHER OF GREAT LEAP BACKWARD!

THE TOP 10 QUOTES ON THE NATURE, VALUE AND CONSEQUENCES OF NUCLEAR WAR

1. "The living will envy the dead."

   —Nikita Khrushchev

2. "Nuclear war would really set back cable."

   —Ted Turner

3. ". . . one forty-five caliber automatic, two boxes of ammunition . . .one hundred dollars in gold, nine packs of chewing gum, one issue of prophylactics, three lipsticks, three pair of nylon stockings. Shoot, a fella' could have a pretty good weekend in Vegas with all that stuff."

   —Major T.J. "King" Kong in *Dr. Strangelove*,
   reciting some of the contents of a survival kit
   in a SAC B-52 carrying nuclear bombs over Russia

4. "In nuclear war all men are cremated equal."

   —Dexter Gordon

5. "I know not with what weapons World War III will be fought, but World War IV will be fought with sticks and stones."

   —Albert Einstein

6. "There is a further advantage (to hydrogen bombs): . . .now that the practically unlimited supply of hydrogen can be utilized, there is considerable reason to hope that homo sapiens can put an end to himself, to the great advantage of such less ferocious animals as may survive."

   —Bertrand Russell

7. "Mr. President, I'm not saying we wouldn't get our hair mussed."

   —General Buck Turgidson in *Dr. Strangelove*,
   responding to the president saying a nuclear war would be mass murder

8. "Some programs have been theatrical masterpieces, but all we're seeing is the negative side of nuclear war."

—Senator Barry Goldwater

9. "If there are enough shovels to go around, everybody's going to make it . . ..It's the dirt that does it."

—T.K. Jones, Deputy Under Secretary of Defense under Reagan, meaning, with a shovel, anyone can dig a fallout shelter

10. "Mr. President, we must not allow a mineshaft gap."

—General Buck Turgidson, embracing Dr. Strangelove's idea that after a nuclear war there would be "the chance to preserve a nucleus of human specimens . . . at the bottom of some of our deeper mineshafts." Turgidson has pointed out that one hundred years from now the Soviets will still be expansionists and therefore, today, "We must prevent them from taking over other mineshaft space, in order to breed more prodigiously than we do."

THE TOP 10 REMOTE ISLANDS ON WHICH YOU MIGHT BE ABLE TO SURVIVE AN ALL-OUT NUCLEAR WAR AND ITS AFTERMATH

Working from the theory that the Northern Hemisphere will get the worst of nuclear winter, we've listed only islands in the Southern Hemisphere. Working from the theory that you don't know how to survive on your own, we've listed only islands that already have some people there, who might be willing to let you in and help you live.

1. **Tristan da Cunha**

   A group of British Overseas Territories islands in the middle of the South Atlantic (more than 2,000 miles from South America, 1,700 miles from Africa). It includes St. Helena, where Napoleon was exiled, which is the most remote inhabited island in the world, with fewer than 300 people.

2. **Pitcairn Island**

   The only British Overseas Territory in the South Pacific, it is best known as the haven of the mutineers of the British ship *HMS Bounty* who settled there in 1790. Current population is about 50.

3. **Easter Island**

   Chilean island in the southeastern Pacific, 1,300 miles from Pitcairn and 2,182 miles from mainland Chile, population about 7,750. Famous for its giant carved heads of a people who managed to perish without nuclear war.

4. **Floreana Island**

   Part of the Galapagos Islands, 563 miles west of Ecuador. It is home to about 100 people.

5. **Niue**

   An island country in the South Pacific, 1,500 miles northeast of New Zealand. It is home to about 1600 people.

6. **Kerguelen Islands**

   Also known as the Desolation Islands, a raw and chilly French territory in the Southern Ocean north of Antarctica and 2,050 miles south of Madagascar. France maintains a permanent presence of 45 to 100 soldiers, scientists, engineers and researchers.

7. **Amsterdam Island**

   In the southern Indian Ocean, equidistant (about 2,000 miles) from Madagascar, Australia and Antarctica. Administered by France, it is the seasonal home of about 30 researchers.

8. **Macquarie Island**

   About halfway between New Zealand and Antarctica, administered by Australia, it has a research station whose staff varies from 20 to 40 people during the year. Its permanent residents include four million penguins.

9. **Raoul Island**

   680 miles north-northeast of New Zealand's North Island, it has a permanently manned weather station.

10. **Falkland Islands**

    Three hundred miles east of South America's southern Patagonian coast, this British Overseas Territory is home to about 3,400 people. In 1982, the British defeated Argentina's attempt to seize the Falklands. If they aren't remote enough, go 80 miles southeast to . . .

11. **South Georgia and the South Sandwich Islands**

    This British Territory is "home" to some British officials and researchers, 35 in the summer, 16 in the winter. Wikipedia tells us that "Toothfish are vital to the island's economy; as a result Toothfish Day is celebrated on 4 September as a bank holiday."

A caveat:

In the late 1930s, foreseeing a world war, an American minister and his wife decided to move to a remote place where they would be safe. They moved to the South Pacific island of Guadalcanal. In the Battle of Guadalcanal, August 1942 to February 1943, the island became the killing ground for more 25,000 American and Japanese soldiers, sailors and airmen.

"Make the rubble bounce." Early in the Cold War there were enough nuclear weapons to destroy the human race. Why add more, asked Winston Churchill? "Why make the rubble bounce?"

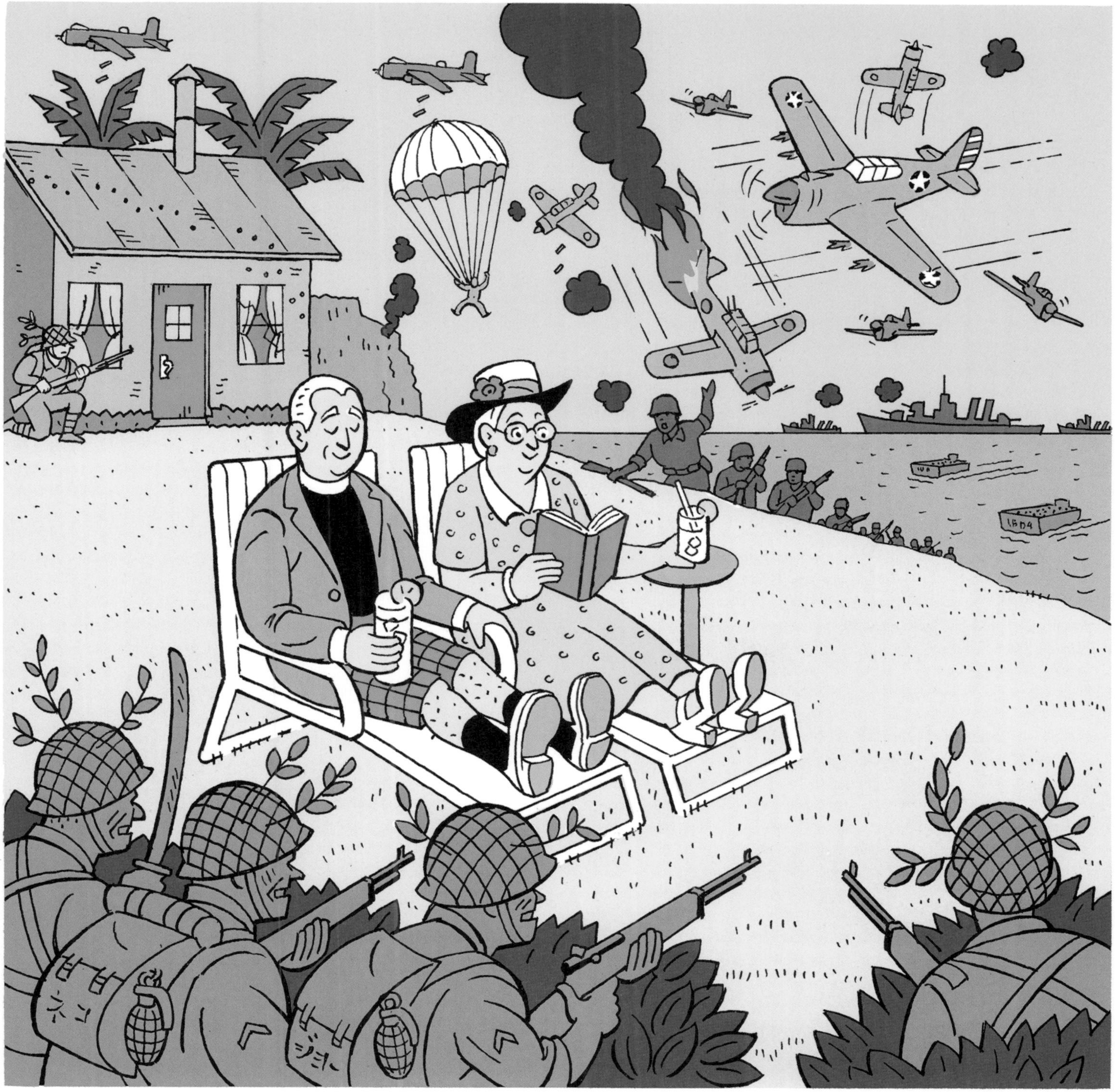

THE TOP 10 VIDEO GAMES WITH NUCLEAR WEAPONS

On the assumption that nuclear weapons can't be used without triggering a global nuclear war, the three best video games either immerse you in such a war or put you in a position to start one. Since this assumption was powerful during the Cold War, the two best games emerged from the 1980s, when nuclear tensions were high. *DEFON* (2006) is a throwback to that time. Post–Cold War, with the threat of global nuclear war less on people's minds (until now?), video games show nuclear weapons being used without triggering such a war.

And while some recent video games are set after a global nuclear apocalypse, the "nuclear" seems incidental—the apocalypse could just as easily have been the result of something else. Hence, two good examples of this genre, *Fallout* and *Metro: Last Light*, are not included in this Top 10.

1. **Balance of Power (1985)**
   As the President of the United States or the Secretary General of the Soviet Union, you try to outdo the other superpower without provoking it too much. If you provoke it too much? This can lead to brinksmanship which can lead to global nuclear war—in which case the game ends and this message appears: "There is no animated display of a mushroom cloud with parts of bodies flying through the air. We do not reward failure."

2. **Missile Command (1980)**
   Your six cities are being attacked by ballistic missiles and, in later (and increasingly difficult) levels of the game, by missiles from planes and satellites. Commanding counter-missiles, you try to destroy the incoming nukes. At the conclusion of each level, you're awarded points depending on how many cities and missiles you have left. But unless you're really, really good, eventually all your cities will be destroyed. The game is a contest to see how long you can last before The End.

3. **DEFCON (2006)**
   Players are given a screen that recalls the "big boards" that represented nuclear war in movies such as *Dr. Strangelove*, *Fail Safe* and, especially, *WarGames*. Commanding one of six parts of the world and armed with nuclear and conventional weapons, you try to kill as much of the enemy's population as possible while limiting the deaths of your people. Gameplay begins at DEFCON 5 and counts down 30 minutes in real time to DEFCON 1 when you can use your nukes. Then pure-white nuclear explosions bloom in "cold near-silence" and the death toll for each city flickers up, "evoking icy dread."

4. Call of Duty 4: Modern Warfare (2007)

It's 2011. A civil war breaks out in Russia and an anti-Western group led by Khaled Al-Asad seizes power in a small but oil-rich Middle Eastern country. Al-Asad gets a Russian nuclear device. As U.S. Marines assault his forces, the device goes off; the aftermath is a grim, "fiery hellscape." In Russia, the leader of the ultranationalists, Imran Zakhaev, takes control of a nuclear launch facility. When British and U.S. forces try to reclaim it, Zakhav launches ICBMs at the U.S. Eastern Seaboard, but the good guys destroy the missiles. Then. . . .

5. Nuclear War (1989)

In this satirical nuclear battle among five world powers, each player (one human, one computer-controlled) is represented by a caricature of a national leader. Available are: Ronnie Raygun (Ronald Reagan), P.M. Satcher (Margaret Thatcher), Infidel Castro (Fidel Castro), Col. Malomar Khadaffy (Muammar al-Gaddafi), Ayatollah Kooksmamie (Ruhollah Khomeini), Mao the Pun (Mao Zedong), Jimi Farmer (Jimmy Carter), Tricky Dick (Richard Nixon), Mikhail Gorabachef (Mikhail Gorbachev) and Ghanji (Mahatma Gandhi). The winner is anyone who, at the end, has some population while everyone else on earth is dead. With its silly, juvenile names, why list this game as high as 5? Because if the winner is computer-controlled, that leader jumps for joy in a blasted wasteland, crowing, "I won! I won!" . . . an ending that brilliantly conveys the idiocy of nuclear war.

6. World in Conflict (2007)

The game is set in an alternate 1989 in which the Soviet Union invades Western Europe, triggering World War III. Then Soviet forces attack and occupy Seattle, Washington. You have access to tactical nukes and, indeed, the U.S. uses one on Soviet forces in a town outside Seattle. You see the terrible consequences of fallout. But you also see the grandeur of the explosion: a pillar of smoke shot through with realistic "god rays." Then, in case the U.S. can't recapture Seattle, the U.S. president approves a back-up plan: nuke it.

7. **Civilization (series of six games, from 1991 to 2018)**
You're charge of a civilization: Roman, Aztec, American, etc. Starting at the dawn of civilization, moving up through present times and beyond, you try outdo your opponents. You "eXplore, eXpand, eXploit, and eXterminate." Eventually you have access to nukes. In *Civilization II*, a nuclear attack is followed by skull icons on the map. Then . . .? "Somehow, moving tanks into the target city afterwards didn't feel like much of a victory, which was probably the point."

8. **Trinity (1986)**
Combining history, mythology and fantasy, this strange game has been called a "prose poem." As you're flying back from London, a Russian ICBM heads for your plane. Going through mysterious doors, you narrowly escape, watching nuclear bombs explode at London (near future) . . . low earth orbit (near future) . . . underground in Nevada (1970) . . . Eniwetok Atoll (1952) . . . Siberia (1949) . . . and Nagasaki (August 1945). Last is the Trinity test site in New Mexico (July 1945) where, unless you do something, things will go horribly wrong. *Computer Gaming World* called this game "a tense, ethical tightrope walk through the Cold War."

9. **Supreme Commander (2007)**
It's the 37th century and the Infinite War has raged for more than a millennium throughout the Milky Way galaxy among the United Earth Federation, the Cybran Nation and the Aeon Illuminate. While the chief weapon is a planet killer named Black Sun, players have lesser weapons such as nuclear missiles. But a nuke-counter-nuke escalation is economically draining. And "when you destroy a commander they almost always go nuclear and destroy their own nearby units in the process." Does this imply that a nuclear war is a mutual suicide pact?

10. **Command and Conquer: Red Alert 2 (2000)**
Like all games in this series, it's set in an alternate 1972 in which the Soviet Union invades the United States. *PC Gamer U.S.* named it the best real-time strategy game and the best multiplayer game of 2000. What role do nuclear weapons play? With time travel, mind control, "prism technology that creates massive energy beams" and a "Chronosphere" that can teleport troops, nukes are almost incidental. So why is this game is on this list? Because its nuclear explosions yield a very nice radioactive green glow. The game's original cover art had a plane heading toward a burning World Trade Center; after 9/11 it was quickly changed.

All quotes are from *How PC Games Depict the Bomb* by
Tom Senior and Samuel Roberts, *PC Gamer*, May 21, 2018

THE 10 MOST POWERFUL NUCLEAR WEAPONS EVER BUILT

1. **Tsar Bomba: 50 megatons, the equivalent of 3,800 Hiroshima bombs**
   Exploded by the Soviet Union on October 30, 1961 over Novaya Zemlya Island in the Russian Arctic Sea. To limit radioactive dust, its actual yield of 100 megatons was reduced by 50 percent. If dropped on New York City, it could kill at least 7.6 million people.

2. **Mk-41: 25 megatons**
   The most powerful thermonuclear weapon ever fielded by the United States. About 500 were produced between 1960 and 1962 and remained in service until July 1976.

3. **TX-21 "Shrimp": 14.8 megatons**
   Exploded by the United States during its biggest-ever nuclear weapon test, on March 1, 1954, at Bikini Atoll in the Marshall Islands.

4. **Mk-17: 10-15 megatons**
   The first operational hydrogen bomb of the U.S. Air Force, it had a loaded weight of slightly more than 20 tons. About 200 were produced by 1955, retired from service in 1957.

5. **Mk-24: 10-15 megatons**
   Between 1954 and 1955, the U.S. produced 105 of these, retired from USAF service in 1956.

6. **Ivy Mike: 10.4 megatons**
   A U.S. hydrogen bomb based on the device exploded in a test on May 9, 1951. Not a deliverable weapon, it was used only to validate certain concepts.

7. **Mk-36: 10 megatons**
   Between 1956 and 1958, the U.S. produced 940 of these, retired from USAF service by 1962.

8. **B53: 9 megatons**
   The oldest nuclear bomb in the U.S. inventory, it was retired from USAF service in 1997.

9. **Mk-16: 7 megatons**
   Based on the Ivy Mike bomb, it was the only liquid fuel nuclear weapon ever built by the U.S. Retired from service by April 1954, replaced by solid-fuel thermonuclear weapons such as Mk-17 (see number 4) and TX-14 (see number 10).

10. TX-14: 6.9 megatons

The first fielded solid-fuel thermonuclear weapon of the U.S., exploded in test in April 1954. Retired in October 1954. Some of these were recycled into the Mk-17 weapons.

The most powerful nuclear free-fall weapon in the U.S. arsenal today is the B83 bomb, with a maximum yield of 1.2 megatons.

THE TOP 10 THINGS TO DO TO SURVIVE A NUCLEAR ATTACK AS ACTUALLY TOLD TO AMERICANS IN THE 1950S

1. Get in a bomb shelter. If you can't do that . . .

2. Get in a basement. If you can't do that . . .

3. Get under a table. If you can't do that but you're inside . . .

4. Put your hands over your head. If you're in a car . . .

5. Get under the dashboard. If you're out in the open and you have the time . . .

6. Dig a hole, cover it with a loose board and newspaper or fabric.* If you can't dig a hole . . .

7. Duck into the nearest doorway or under a tree. If no doorway or tree is available . . .

8. Drop flat against the curb. Unless you're in a bomb shelter or a covered hole . . .

9. Keep your eyes shut. And at all times . . .

10. Wear protective clothing. If you're wearing coat, pull it over your head. No coat? Women: A full dress will protect more of your body. Men: A hat with a wide brim will protect your face.

* Advice from atomic physicist Ralph E. Lapp (1917-2004) who worked on the Manhattan Project

Maxi-skirt (noun): *in the 1950s, a woman's maximum protection against fallout*

THE TOP 10 LIFE FORMS THAT WOULD SURVIVE A NUCLEAR WAR

Listed in descending order:

1. **Deinococcus radioduran**
Nicknamed "Conan the bacterium" by scientists and once listed by the Guinness Book of World Records as the "most radiation resistant life form," it's a "polyextremophile," meaning it's better at everything than even an "extremophile" such as . . .

2. **The tardigrade**
Called a "little water bear," this eight-legged micro-animal is an "extremophile," meaning it can be boiled, frozen, sent to space, deprived of water and, after being clinically dead for almost a decade, brought back to life.

3. **The mummichog**
Able to turn its genes on and off and redesign body parts to cope with new environments, this fish can survive in any temperature, any salinity and any mixture of chemicals, even in severe chemical spills. Taken to the Skylab space station in 1973, they did just fine, swimming in zero gravity, and so did their offspring.

4. **The fruit fly**
With less surface area to absorb radiation, fewer cells to be affected by radiation and slow cell division, Drosophilla can survive radiation up to around 64,000 rads. 1,000 rads kills humans.

5. **The lingulata**
In the history of the earth there have been five mass extinctions and this brachiopod (an animal with a hinged shell, like a clam) has survived all of them . . . survived 99% of all species that have ever lived.

6. **The braconid wasp**
These parasitoid wasps (they lay eggs inside other animals) can withstand up to 180,000 rads of radiation. The only question: after a nuclear war would they find any prey species to lay their eggs in?

7. **The amoeba**
They're fairly resistant to radiation and, as a single-celled organism, when they multiply they don't mutate. Plus they can go into a dormant cyst state—curl up in a protective layer and stay that way indefinitely.

8. The scorpion

Relatively unchanged since their appearance 430 million years ago, scorpions are survivors. Unharmed by ultraviolet radiation, they could likely also survive nuclear radiation. Since they can be frozen and brought back to life, they may be able to survive a nuclear winter.

9. The cockroach

Yes, popular culture says cockroaches should be number 1 on this list. And, yes, they're thought to have survived the Hiroshima bomb detonation from about 1,000 feet away. And, yes, they can live a month without eating. But in a test, only 10 percent of cockroaches survived 10,000 rads. So they're down here at number 9.

10. Escherichia coli (E. Coli)

Able to survive 6,000 rads, they make up 80 percent of our intestinal flora. So if all of us die in a nuclear war, maybe some of these can live on in some of our guts?

CYBERWAR

THE TOP 10 CYBER POWERS

1. U.S.

2. U.K.

3. Russia

4. China

5. Israel

6. Iran

7. North Korea

8. "Could be somebody sitting on their bed that weighs 400 pounds."
   —Donald Trump, September 27, 2016

9. "Could be some guy in his home in New Jersey."
   —Donald Trump, December 7, 2016

10. "We believe it was the DNC that did the 'hacking' to distract from the many issues facing their deeply flawed candidate and failed party leader."
    —Donald Trump, June 15, 2016

THE TOP 10 POLITICAL CYBERATTACKS TO DATE

The ones we know about, listed chronologically:

1. Moonlight Maze, 1998-1999

In the world's first known cyberattack, Russians hackers penetrated the Pentagon, NASA, the Department of Energy, the U.S. Army, and research institutions such as Los Alamos and Sandia National Laboratories. They apparently stole maps of U.S. military installations around the world, troop configurations and doctrine, and blueprints of military hardware. Among the many clues that pointed to Russia: the attackers' working hours aligned with a typical working day in Moscow and the attackers didn't work during Russian Orthodox holidays.

2. Titan Rain, 2003-05

In the first cyberattack by China that was made public, hackers penetrated the U.S. Departments of State, Homeland Security, and Energy; NASA; Sandia National Laboratories; the Redstone Arsenal; other parts of the U.S. military; and many U.S. defense contractors, including Lockheed Martin.

3. 2008 attack on the U.S. Department of Defense

In the worst breach of U.S. military computers in history, a USB flash drive went into a laptop computer attached to the U.S. Central Command. From there, a Russian worm spread undetected to other systems. The Pentagon spent nearly 14 months cleaning the worm and, to stop this from happening again, banned USB drives.

4. Stuxnet and Operation Olympic Games, June 2010

Called the world's first digital weapon, Stuxnet—developed jointly by the U.S. and Israel—is a malicious computer worm, typically inserted on a USB flash drive. In what the Pentagon called Operation Olympic Games, it manipulated the computer controllers of Iran's nuclear facility in Natanz, forcing its centrifuges to gyrate wildly out of control and destroy themselves. Stuxnet set Tehran's atomic program back at least two years.

In autumn 2012, in retaliation, an Iranian cyberattack breached or paralyzed 46 of American's largest financial institutions. And in 2013 Iranian hackers tried to take control of a very small dam 15 miles north of New York City, possibly as a dry run for an attack on a much larger part of America's power grid.

5. Great Britain (!) hacks Belgium, 2010-2013

In "Operation Socialist," the British government successfully breached the Belgian telecommunications company Belacom to gain roaming data for mobile devices, allowing it to execute "man-in-the-middle" attacks. Edward Snowden called this the first documented case of one EU nation cyberattacking another.

6. Russian attacks on Ukraine, 2010-onward

2010: Russian hackers created havoc in the Ukrainian government computer systems.
2014: Tried to disrupt the May 2014 presidential election.
2014-2016: Attacked, and may have destroyed, a huge number of artillery pieces in the Ukrainian Army.
December 23, 2015: Staged the first known successful attack on a power grid, leaving about 230,000 people without electricity.
2015: Also attacked a mining company and a large railway operator.
Today: Attacks continue.

7. Operation Newscaster, 2011-2014

Probably the work of Iran, this operation targeted at least 2,000 senior U.S. military and diplomatic personnel, congresspeople, journalists, lobbyists, think tankers and defense contractors in the U.S. and six countries either allied with the U.S. or where the U.S. has major strategic interests. After creating fake personas on many social media sites, it tried to "befriend" target victims to steal their email passwords and then their data. Newscaster was called "the most elaborate cyber espionage campaign using social engineering that has been uncovered to date from any nation."

8. North Korean attack on Sony Pictures, November 2014

After releasing confidential data about Sony Pictures, including emails, executives' salaries and copies of then-unreleased Sony films, the hackers demanded Sony withdraw its film *The Interview*, a comedy about a plot to assassinate North Korean leader Kim Jong-Un. The hackers threatened terrorist attacks on any theaters showing the movie. This cyberattack was the first by a nation to inflict commerical damage on a single company and a warning to the U.S. as a whole: look what we can do.

9. Office of Personnel Management data breach, 2014-2015

A Chinese theft of about 21.5 million records—the personnel records of every* federal employee, every federal retiree and up to one million former federal employees—this is among the largest breaches of U.S. government data ever. In its aftermath, the director and the CIO of the OPM resigned. (* Perhaps only the CIA, which does not use the OPM system, was unscathed.)

10. **Russian attack on the Clinton campaign, 2016**

Early in 2016, Russian hackers stole emails from the Democratic National Committee (DNC). In June and July 2016, working with Russia, WikiLeaks released 19,252 of these emails and 8,034 attachments. On November 6, 2016, two days before the election, it released 8,263 more DNC emails. And in the month before the election WikiLeaks, working with Russia, published more than 20,000 pages of emails from John Podesta, chair of the Clinton campaign, that the Russians had also stolen.Clinton's poll numbers declined after the emails were released. It is highly likely that without the Russian cyberattacks, she would have won the presidency.

And a huge attack waiting in the wings:

Nitro Zeus

Developed early in the Obama administration, this cyberattack plan was for use in case diplomatic efforts to limit Iran's nuclear program failed and military conflict ensued. With electronic implants in Iranian computer networks, it could have disabled Iran's air defenses, communications systems and crucial parts of its power grid. A more narrowly focused cyberplan was developed to, if need be, disable Iran's Fordo nuclear enrichment site.

Stuxnet (noun): *a stone thrown by people who live in a glass house*

THE TOP 10 CYBERATTACKS THAT COULD HIT YOU

Ranked in ascending order from annoying (1, 2, and 3) to disturbing (4) to painful (5, 6 and 7) to potentially or definitely lethal (8, 9 and 10)

1. Your medical records
In the last year more than 75 percent of the health care industry was infected with malware.

2. Your appliances
As your washing machine, dishwasher, refrigerator, etc. get connected to the Internet of Things, they can be attacked—and used to extort ransom from you or simply cause mayhem for you.

3. Your home security
Think it's smart to live in a "smart home?" Hackers can access your locks, door and fire alarms, security lighting and temperature controls.

4. Your vote
The U.S. election infrastructure is dangerously vulnerable. Says a leading voter security expert, "Forty states are using computer technology that is a decade old or more and often they are not receiving software updates or security patches."

5. Your computer
You've heard about hackers getting control of people's computers, right? Here's a new reason: since cryptocurrency coin mining requires a lot of computing power, miners might try to "cryptojack" your computer and add it to their arsenal.

6. Your identity
Nearly 60 million Americans have been affected by identity theft. Every year about one in twenty is hit . . . and this number is rising.

7. Your money
Think it's smart to have digital money? Cryptocurrency hacking and stealing is on the rise: more than $1 billion in 2018. And what about "regular" money? Each year identity theft costs Americans about $17 billion.

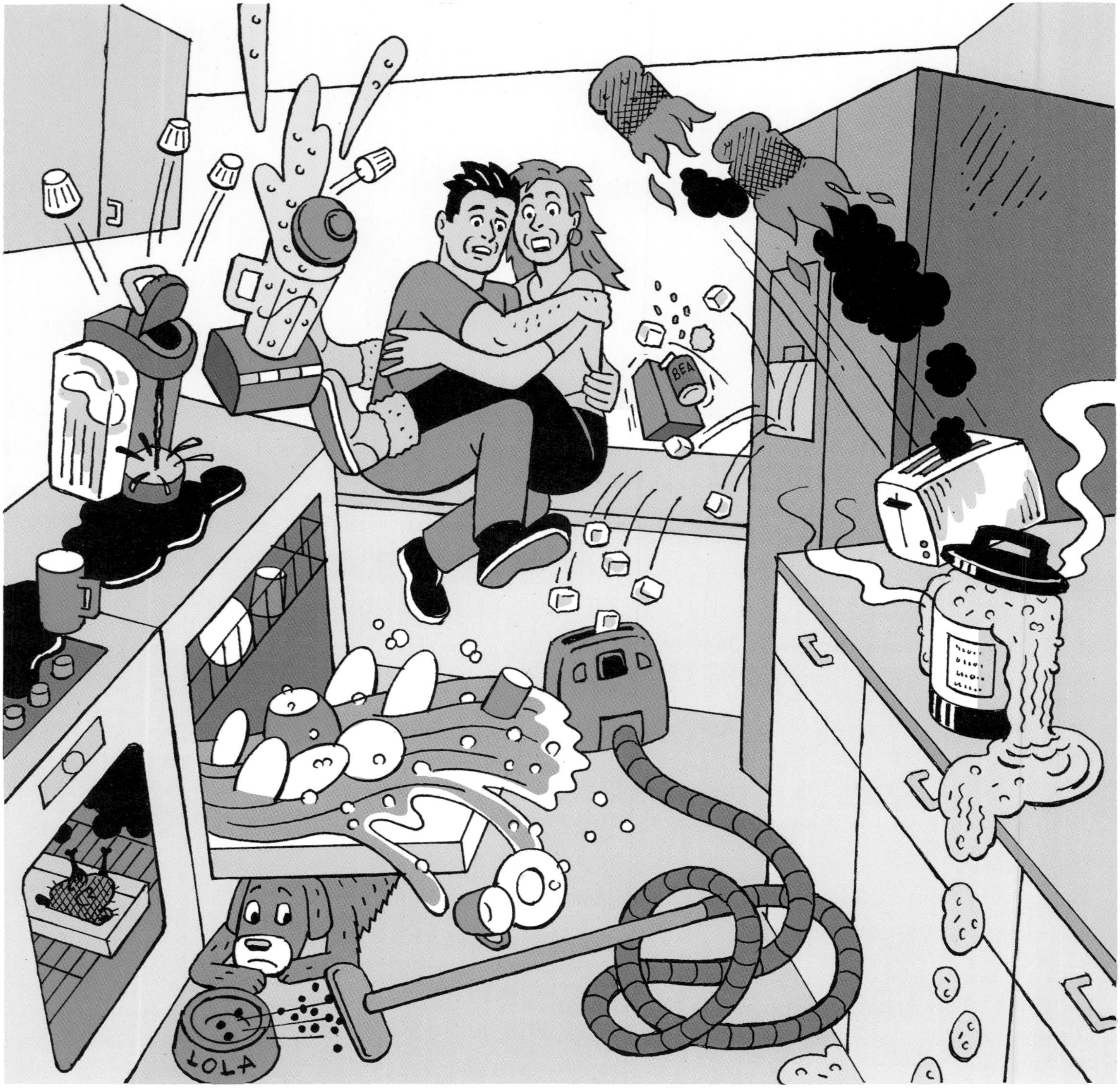
BEA
LOLA

8. Your car

As one security expert puts it, "Today's cars are basically computers on wheels and as such they're becoming a bigger target for hackers." Hackers can change you car's direction, disable the brakes. . . .

9. Your electricity—and therefore your food, water, etc.

48 percent of CEOs of power and utility companies say a cyberattack on their infrastructure is inevitable. And a recent U.S. government report says the U.S. would not be able to thwart "a catastrophic power outage of a magnitude beyond human experience"—affecting food, water, transportation and healthcare.

10. Your life

They probably can't do it yet, but hackers may soon enough be able to blow up a nuclear plant or a plane . . . smash a train . . . let loose a deadly virus. . . .

ransomware (noun): *an intruder that lets someone tell you, "Nice little dishwasher you've got there, be a shame if anything happened to it."*

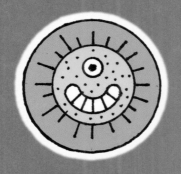

BIOWAR AND PANDEMICS

THE TOP 10 PANDEMICS IN HISTORY

1. Tuberculosis: one billion dead in the 19th and 20th centuries
Tuberculosis in humans can be traced back 9,000 years. Throughout the 17th, 18th and 19th centuries, it caused 25 percent of all deaths in Europe. In the 19th century (when, because its victims lost such weight, it was called "consumption") it killed one out of every seven Americans and Europeans. Today, 1.8 billion people, one-fourth of the world's population, are infected with tuberculosis; in the U.S., 5–10 percent are infected. In 2017, it killed 1.6 million people, mostly in developing countries.

2. Smallpox: 300-500 million dead in the 20th century
Smallpox has probably been in human populations since 10,000 BC and has been found in Egyptian mummies 3,000 years old. It's caused huge numbers of deaths in Eurasia in the last 2,500 years, and in Africa and the Pacific in the last 1,500 years. Introduced into the Americas in the early 16th century, it probably killed nearly all the native inhabitants. In the 18th century, it killed an estimated 400,000 Europeans per year. As recently as 1967, it was killing two million people per year.

3. Measles: 200 million dead between 1855 and 2005
Measles has been a human disease for the last 1,500 years. In populations not previously exposed to it, it can be devastating. In 1529 in Cuba, it killed two-thirds of the natives who had survived smallpox. In the 1850s it killed 20 percent of all Hawaiians. In 1875 it killed one-third of all Fijians. The first successful vaccine became available in 1963.

4. Black Death: 75-200 million dead in the 14th century
Probably originating in Central Asia, bubonic plague spread west along caravan routes. Then, in 1346, besieging the Crimean city of Kaffa, Mongols—as a form of biowarfare—threw their infected dead over the walls. From there, the plague spread by fleas on black rats on merchant ships. In Europe, it was called the Pestilence or Great Mortality; it peaked in 1347-1351, killing 30 to 60 percent of the population and was responsible for religious, social and economic upheavals. Overall, in Eurasia, it may have killed as many as 200 million people. Two hundred years was required for world population to recover.

5. Spanish flu: 20-100 million dead (best estimate: 75 million) in 1918
In 1918 the flu infected 500 million people, about one-third of the planet's population and killed anywhere from one in 25 to one in five. It killed 675,000 Americans. During World War I, more U.S. soldiers died from the flu than were killed in battle. Since 1918 there have been several other flu pandemics; in 1957-58 flu killed two million people worldwide, in 1968-69 flu killed one million worldwide.

6. **Cholera: 40 million dead since 1817**

Likely originating on the Indian subcontinent, cholera became widespread with the first pandemic in 1817. Since then there have been six more cholera pandemics, reaching more and more parts of the world, from Europe to the Americas. The most recent such pandemic originated in Indonesia in 1961. Every year cholera kills about 120,000 people.

7. **Plague of Justinian: 25-50 million dead from the 6th century into the 8th century**

Now known to be the first bubonic plague epidemic, it is named after Justinian I, emperor of the Eastern Roman Empire at the time of its initial outbreak in 541 AD. At its peak it may have killed up to 5,000 people a day in Constantinople when, as there was no room to bury all the dead, the city smelled of the dead. Altogether, it killed perhaps 40 percent of the city's inhabitants and up to 25 percent of all people in the eastern Mediterranean. It may have contributed to the military successes of the Goths and the Arabs against a weakened empire. It hit last in 750 AD.

8. **HIV: 35 million dead from the early 1980s to 2017**

AIDS (acquired immune deficiency syndrome) is believed to have originated in non-human primates in Africa, then transferred to humans in the early 20th century. Spread primarily by unprotected sex, HIV (human immunodeficiency virus) currently has no cure nor any effective vaccine. In 2016, about 36.7 million people were living with HIV (sub-Saharan Africa is the most affected) and it caused one million deaths. Antiretroviral therapy may lead to a near-normal life expectancy. Without treatment, death comes, on average, in 11 years, from cancer or an opportunistic infection.

9. **Cocoliztli Epidemic: 5-15 million from 1545 to 1548**

Probably originating in the southern and central Mexican highlands, cocoliztli (the Aztec word for "pestilence") hit with high fever and blistering, followed by internal bleeding, damage to the gastrointestinal, respiratory and other systems and then death, often within a week. Perhaps 80 percent of Mexico's native population died, and during the 16th century there were five more such outbreaks. The exact cause of cocoliztli is unknown. It may have been an Old World bacterium brought by Spaniards who were themselves healthy.

10. **Third Plague epidemic: 12 million from 1882 to 1912**

The first bubonic plague epidemic was the Plague of Justinian; the second was the Black Death. While this one began in Yunnan province in China in 1855, it did not become an epidemic until it hit Hong Kong in 1894. From there it spread to all parts of China, to India (where it killed 10 million) and then, with a much lower death toll, around the world.

And here are the first two known pandemics (see next page).

WHILE THESE KILLED FEWER PEOPLE THAN THE TOP 10, THEY WERE DEVASTATING TO THEIR POPULATIONS.

1. **The Antonine Plague: up to 5 million from 165 to 180 AD**
   Possibly smallpox or measles, and named after the Roman emperor Marcus Aurelius Antonius, this pandemic was brought to the Roman Empire by troops returning from the Near East. It killed as much as one-third of the population in some areas (2,000 a day in Rome) and in 169 AD may have killed Marcus Aurelius's co-regent, the emperor Lucius Verus.

2. **The Plague of Athens: 75,000-100,000 from 430 to 426 BC**
   Possibly typhus, this hit in the second year of the Peloponnesian War, killing 25 percent of the city-state's population. While it hit on the verge of a possible Athenian victory (and killed the Athenian leader, Pericles), the Spartans—fearing contact with a diseased enemy—withdrew their troops. The plague destroyed Athens' social order and made Athenians feel the gods had abandoned them.

catapult (verb)*: how an army besieging a city can have fun with its bubonic-plague-infected dead (see also "having a fling")*

THE TOP 10 INSTANCES OF BIOLOGICAL WARFARE IN THE LAST 100 YEARS

Biological warfare began in 1500-1200 BC when the Hittites drove victims of tularemia (an infectious disease with a 60% death rate) into enemy lands, causing an epidemic. In the last 100 years, biowar has become more sophisticated. The top 10 instances during that time:

1. **1931 and 1937-1945 : The Japanese use plague, cholera, etc.**
   In 1931, when a five-member delegation of the League of Nations came to China to investigate Japan's invasion of that country, the Japanese served the delegation fruit laced with cholera. Apparently it didn't work. Starting in 1937, using plague-inflected fleas and cholera-covered flies, the Japanese killed 400,000 Chinese civilians. They also used bioweapons on Chinese troops.

   Then, in its war against the U.S: In 1944, a Japanese submarine with unspecified bioweapons was sent to defend Saipan from American invasion—but was sunk. In 1944, the Japanese hoped to attack the U.S. mainland with balloon bombs filled with plague, anthrax, rinderpest and smut fungus. In 1945, in "Operation Cherry Blossoms at Night," kamikaze planes were to drop plague-infected fleas onto San Diego. According to some sources, fearing retaliation by the U.S., Tojo rejected this plan. Other sources say the attack, set for September 22, 1945, was prevented only by Japan's surrender on August 15.

2. **1942: The Soviets use tularemia**
   A naturally occurring bacterial illness, tularemia is usually transmitted by ticks and rodents. But in 1942, during the siege of Stalingrad, huge numbers of surrounding Germans became ill (fever, chills and lack of energy) with the rare pulmonary form, which points to the use of a aerosol weapon. In any event, the German offensive was temporarily halted.

3. **May 1945: Having considered using infected rats, the Nazis use sewage**
   In the closing days of the war, German troops deliberately polluted a reservoir in northwestern Bohemia with sewage. Earlier, the Germans considered having submarines launch infected rats on the English coast—but it was determined the rats would drown before reaching land. And Germany researched how to weaponize bubonic plague and how mosquitos could infect Allied troops with malaria.*

4. September 7, 1978: The Soviets use Ricin

Georgi Markov, a well-known Bulgarian novelist and playwright, had escaped to England, where he spoke on the BBC and other radio networks against the Bulgarian communist regime. Fired from a specially modified umbrella, the poison ricin, derived from castor beans, was injected into Markov's thigh. He died a few days later.

5. 1979-80: Rhodesia uses cholera and anthrax

The Rhodesian government of white settlers used both against against black nationalist guerillas. Cholera was put into water pumps and drinking water. Anthrax, used to kill cattle and thus deprive the enemy of food, also killed at least 182 people.

6. 1981: Somebody may have used dengue-2 fever in Cuba

From May to October, in three widely separated parts of Cuba, there were more than 300,000 reported cases, with 158 fatalities. Cuba said this was an attack by the United States. Some U.S. officials believe it was caused by Cuban troops returning from parts of Africa where the dengue-2 strain is found.

7. 1980s: Iraq uses anthrax

Some Iranian prisoners, tied to stakes in the open, were exposed to an anthrax bomb. Others, confined to beds in an underground chamber, were sprayed with anthrax—as medical researchers watched. Thus dozens of "human guinea pigs" died from internal hemorrhaging.

8. 1984: American followers of an Indian guru use typhoid fever

Attempting to stop people from voting in a local election so their own candidates could win, Oregon followers of the Indian guru Bhagwan Shree put typhoid fever bacteria into salad bars and salad dressing in eight restaurants. This bioterrorist attack, the first and largest in U.S. history, sickened 751 people and hospitalized 45 of them.

9. 1989: South Africa uses cholera and yellow fever

During its fight against black nationalists, the South African apartheid government ordered an operative to contaminate the water supply of refugee camp in Namibia—an attempt foiled by the high chlorine count in the treated water.

10. 2001: An American biowarfare researcher uses anthrax

Beginning on September 18, letters containing anthrax spores were sent to several U.S. media offices and to two U.S. senators. Five people died and scores more were injured, some permanently. In 2005, the FBI began focusing on Bruce Edwards Ivins who had worked with bioweapons at Ft. Detrick. In July 2008, Ivins committed suicide. The (disputed) consensus: Ivins, mentally unbalanced, was the sole perpetrator. His motives remain unclear.

*As for the Allies: During World War II, the British weaponized tularemia, anthrax, brucellosis and botulism toxin. And the U.S. had 5,000 bombs filled with anthrax spores.

THE TOP 10 U.S. GOVERNMENT FIELD TESTS OF (MORE OR LESS) SIMULATED BIOWEAPONS

1. **September 26 and 27, 1950. Operation Sea-Spray, San Francisco Bay**
   Onto San Francisco, a Navy ship sprayed two types of bacteria—Bacillus globigii* and Serratia marcescens. These were chosen for their similarities to Bacillus anthracis, which causes anthrax. On September 29, patients in Stanford University Hospital came down with S. marcescens infections. One died.

2. **1951. Near Newport News, Virginia**
   For some reason, the U.S. Army theorized that an enemy might target blacks at military bases. Since African-Americans are more susceptible than whites to a fungal disease called Valley Fever, the Army simulated this by releasing the fungus Aspergillus from briefcases at the Norfolk Naval Supply Center where most workers were black. Aspergillus was known to cause lethal infections.

3. **1954-1973. Operation Whitecoat, Fort Detrick, Maryland**
   More than 2,300 conscientious objectors (many of them trained U.S. Army medics, many of them Seventh-Day Adventists) allowed themselves to be infected with bacteria—tularemia or Q fever—and then given antibiotics to cure the infections. No one died but some claim to have lingering health affects: asthma and headaches. The government says Operation Whitecoat contributed to developing vaccines and drugs for various diseases.

4. **Mid-1950s-1973. Project SHAD, on U.S. Navy ships throughout the world**
   In Project SHAD—Shipboard Hazard and Defense—about 6,000 military personnel took part in 46 tests of chemical and biological weapons. Many did so unknowingly. They were exposed to Bacillus globigii, Serratia marcescens and Escherichia coli.

5. **September 1954. Operation Big Itch, Dugway Proving Ground, Utah****
   The U.S. military dropped bombs full of the tropical rat flea (Xenopsylla cheopis). The fleas survived the fall and soon attached themselves to hosts—proving that fleas could be used a carrier of a bioweapon.

6. **May 1955. Operation Big Buzz, Savannah, Georgia . . . And April-November 1956. Operation May Day, Savannah, Georgia**
   In each operation, the U.S. military dispersed more than 300,000 uninfected mosquitos in predominantly black neighborhoods to see how many would get indoors and bite people. Many did. These were tests of how well mosquitos would work as carriers of yellow fever.

7. 1956. Operation Drop Kick, Avon Park, Florida

With the same goals as Operations Big Buzz and May Day, the U.S. military dispersed about 600,000 uninfected mosquitos in a predominately black neighborhood. After this operation and the Savannah operations, Army personnel posing as public health officials photographed and tested the people who were bitten.

8. 1961. Operation Bellwether, Dugway Proving Ground, Utah

According to an official report, "releases of uninfected, starved, virgin female mosquitos were used to evaluate the effects of varying the vector and host ratio," as well as "determining the effect of the presence or absence of overt movement of the human samplers upon the outdoor biting rate."

9. June 6, 1966. New York City

In the subway stations at 23rd Street and 7th Avenue and at 23rd Street and 8th Avenue, U.S. Army scientists dropped onto ventilation grates light bulbs packed with Bacillus globigii, with about 87 trillion organisms in each light bulb. As intended, the light bulbs shattered. The scientists concluded that by June 10 one million people had been exposed.

10. 1969. The White House

It is said that by placing "germs" in the White House air conditioning system, the U.S. Army "assassinated" President Nixon.

* According to the National Academy of Sciences, Bacillus globii is now recognized as a pathogen which can cause food poisoning and, in rare cases, death.

** On September 28, 1994, the U.S. General Accounting Office reported, "From 1951 through 1969, hundreds, perhaps thousands of open-air tests using bacteria and viruses that cause disease in humans, animals and plants were conducted at Dugway. . . . It is unknown how many people in the surrounding vicinity were also exposed to potentially harmful agents used in open-air tests at Dugway."

Light bulb (noun): *when lit, the symbol for a bright idea, such as smashing light bulbs in the New York City subway to release more than 87 trillion Bacillus globigii*

THE TOP 10 BIOAGENTS KNOWN TO HAVE BEEN WEAPONIZED AND STOCKPILED BY THE SOVIETS

After signing an international convention in 1972 to stop producing bioweapons, the USSR set up a program to do exactly that. Called Biopreparat and employing 25,000 people, it included 19 research institutes, six production plants and many storage facilities. By 1989, it dwarfed any U.S. effort. Says one U.S. official, "If we produced a pound of anything, they produced a hundred to five hundred."

Much information about Biopreparat comes from its First Deputy Director, Kanatjan Alibekov—now Ken Alibeck—who defected to the U.S. in 1992. While Biopreparat was officially canceled by President Gorbachev in 1909 and again by President Yeltsin in 1992, Alibeck said Russia kept developing new biological agents, ostensibly for defense.

Listed in descending order of lethality, what the Soviets weaponized and stockpiled:

1. **Plague (Yersinia pestis)**
   The death rate for untreated pneumonic plague is 100 percent and it kills within 24 hours. In the 1980s, the Soviets produced large quantities of plague organisms that were resistant to antibiotics.

2. **Glanders (Burkholderia mallei)**
   Glanders is an infectious disease, primarily of horses, mules and donkeys. In humans, in its septicemic form, it has a high mortality rate: 50 percent when treated, 95 percent when untreated. Allegedly, the Soviets used weaponized glanders in Afghanistan from 1982 to 1984.

3. **Anthrax (Bacillus anthracis)**
   Inhalation anthrax has a death rate of more than 80 percent. In 1979, in a military facility near Sverdlovsk, a weaponized form was accidentally released and killed at least 105 people. Alibeck says the KGB destroyed all hospital records and other evidence.

4. **Marburg virus**
   Alibeck says research in turning Marburg (usual death rate: 24–88 percent) into a weapon was conducted outside the Siberian city of Novosibirsk in the Vector Institute under the leadership of Dr. Nikolai Ustinov. While injecting guinea pigs with Marburg, Ustinov accidentally injected himself. From his corpse, his colleagues isolated an especially deadly form which, in Ustinov's honor, they

named Marburg Variant U. In the early 1980s, it could have been mounted in ICBM warheads on several days notice. As of 1991, the Soviets were ready to manufacture large quantities of Variant U.

5. Ebola

Ebola has death rate of 50 percent. In 1996, in a bioweapons lab in the Moscow suburb of Sergiev Posad a technician named Nadezhda Makovetskaya was drawing blood from Ebola-infected horses. Despite wearing two layers of gloves, she pierced herself with the needle. She died quickly and was buried, according to one account, in a "sack filled with calcium hypochlorite." In 2004, the same thing happened here to another technician, Antonina Presnyakva; she also died.

6. Botulism (Botulinum toxin)

Untreated, botulism has a death rate of 40 to 50 percent. A single gram of crystalline toxin, evenly dispersed and inhaled, can kill more than a million people.

7. Smallpox

Smallpox has a death rate of about 30 percent. In 1967, a special Soviet medical team went to India to help eradicate an especially virulent strain of smallpox. The team brought some back. This smallpox was tested on Vozrozhdeniya Island in the Aral Sea. In 1971, a Soviet research ship came closer than it was supposed to and a technician took samples of plankton. Infected, returning home, she infected several people, including children, all of whom died. The Soviets built the capacity to produce 90 to 100 tons of this weaponized smallpox every year—and produced and stockpiled tons.

8. Tularemia (Francisella tularensis)

See "The Top 10 Instances of Bioloigical Warfare in the Last 100 Years" (page 158) for the Soviet use of tularemia against surrounding German troops during the siege of Stalingrad—a use that Alibeck confirms.

9. Q-fever (Coxiella burnetii)

Usually infecting goats, sheep and battle, Q-fever is highly infectious. While it has a very low mortality rate in humans (1–2 percent in untreated cases), it disables with fever, diarrhea, nausea and shortness of breath.

10. VEE (Venezuelan equine encephalitis virus)

Healthy human adults who get VEE may experience flu-like symptoms—high fevers and headaches— but the human death rate is less than 1 percent. Alibeck says the Soviets combined VEE with smallpox to make a "chimera" virus. In 1959, Soviet medical personnel accidentally dropped a freeze-dried vial of VEE (not combined with smallpox), infecting 20 laboratory staffers and accidentally demonstrating the effectiveness of aerosolized VEE.

Needle (verb): to poke fun at your biowar research colleague who has accidentally stabbed himself or herself with a syringe full of Marburg virus or Ebola

EARTHQUAKES, TSUNAMIS AND SUPERVOLCANOES

THE TOP 10 DEATH TOLLS FROM VOLCANIC ERUPTIONS

These are the death tolls that can be, to some extent, quantified. Probably the most deadly volcanic eruption in human history was that of Mount Toba, Sumatra, Indonesia—74,000 years ago. The largest in the last two million years, it covered India, Pakistan and the Persian Gulf in three to fifteen feet of ash. It was followed by a volcanic winter lasting a decade. Then came a thousand years of global cooling. According to the bottleneck theory, only 3,000-10,000 individuals survived. In other words, the Mount Toba eruption nearly wiped out the human race.

Since then:

	Deaths
1. Mount Samalas, Indonesia, 1257*	15,000-20,000 just in London
2. Mount Tambora, Indonesia, 1815**	71,000
3. Krakatoa, Indonesia, 1883***	36,000+
4. Mount Pelée, Martinique, 1902	30,000
5. Nevado del Ruiz, Colombia, 1985	23,000
6. Mount Unzen, Japan, 1792	15,000
7. Mount Vesuvius, Italy, 79	13,000+
8. Grimsvötn, Iceland, 1783	10,000+
9. Kelud, Indonesia, 1586	10,000
10. Santa Maria, Guatemala, 1902	6,000

* Extremely cold weather worldwide triggered a famine, killing 30% of the population of London and an unknown number of people elsewhere. Mount Samalas ejected 2.4 cubic miles of material.

** "The Year Without a Summer" caused famines in Europe and America.

*** The blood-red sky in Edvard Munch's *The Scream* (1893) is almost certainly Munch's memory of the effects of Krakatoa's eruption on August 27, 1883. It produced these skies in Norway from late November 1883 through the middle of February 1884.

THE TOP 10 COSTLIEST EARTHQUAKES

The costliest in human lives is the 1556 earthquake in Shaanxi, China which killed 820,000-830,000 people. Most recently, the 2010 Haitian earthquake killed 100,000-316,000 people.

But here are the earthquakes costliest in dollars:

1. **2011 Tohoku earthquake and tsunami: $235 billion**
   March 11, 2011, Japan, magnitude 9.1. The most powerful earthquake ever recorded in Japan and the fourth most powerful in the world since modern record keeping began in 1900, it created tsunami waves up to 133 feet high which traveled up to six miles inland. It killed more than 18,000 people and caused the meltdown of three reactors in the Fukushima Daiichi Nuclear Power Plant—which never should have been built so close to the ocean.

2. **1995 Great Hanshin earthquake (the Kobe earthquake): $200 billion**
   January 17, 1995, Japan, magnitude 6.9. It killed up to 6,434 people.

3. **2008 Sichuan earthquake: $150 billion**
   May 12, 2008, Sichuan, China, magnitude 8.0. It killed more than 69,000 people. As of June 2008, 18,222 people were still missing.

4. **1994 Northridge earthquake: $13 billion–$44 billion**
   January 17, 1994, epicenter Resida, California, magnitude 6.7. It killed 57 people.

5. **2011 Christchurch earthquake: $15-$40 billion**
   February 22, 2011, Christchurch, New Zealand, magnitude 6.2. It killed 185 people and damaged buildings and infrastructure already weakened by the nearby Canterbury magnitude 7.1 earthquake on September 4, 2010. It can be regarded as an aftershock of the Canterbury earthquake.

6. **2010 Chilean earthquake: $15-$30 billion**
   February 27, 2010, off the coast of central Chile, magnitude 8.8. It triggered a tsunami which devastated several coastal towns; it killed 525 people.

7. **2004 Chuetsu earthquake: $28 billion**
   October 23, 2004, Nigata Prefecture, Japan, magnitude 6.6. It killed 68 people.

8. **1999 Izmit earthquake: $20 billion**
   August 17, 1999, Izmit, northeastern Turkey, magnitude 7.6. The official government-estimated death toll was 17,127 people, but the actual figure may be as many as 45,000. It left about half a million homeless.

9. **1980 Irpinia earthquake: $15 billion**
   November 23, 1980, Conza, southern Italy, magnitude 6.9. It killed at least 2,384 people. Of the $40 billion that was earmarked for reconstruction, $20 billion created a new class of millionaires in the region, $6.4 billion went to the Camorra (the local Mafia) and $4 billion went to politicians as bribes. Only $9.6 billion was spent on reconstruction—and, going into the construction business, the Camorra took some of this as well.

10. **1976 Tangshan earthquake: $10 billion**
    July 28, 1976, Tangshan, Hebei Province, China, magnitude 7.6. Hitting this industrial city of one million, it collapsed 85% of the city's buildings and killed 242,760 to 700,000 people.

Did earthquakes help destroy these two great civilizations?

1. **The Harappan State**
   Founded around 3300 BC, this Bronze Age South Asian civilization (stretching from today's northeast Afghanistan to Pakistan and northwest India) began to flourish around 2600 BC and began to decline around 1900 BC. By around 1700 BC most of its cities had been abandoned. The region is seismically active and the recent discovery of an ancient riverbed at the center of what was the Harappan civilization suggests that one or more earthquakes could have blocked or diverted the river's water and turned part of the region into the desert it is today.

2. **The Mayan Classic Period**
   Beginning around 250 AD, the Mayan Classic Period is the name given to the Mayan civilization that flourished in today's southeastern Mexico, all of Guatemala and Belize and the western portion of Honduras and El Salvador. As the Mayan Classic Period was collapsing in the late 9th century AD—with some cities being suddenly abandoned—there is evidence that this region was struck by an earthquake.

THE TOP 10 TSUNAMIS FOR WHICH A DEATH TOLL CAN BE ESTIMATED

1. **2004 Indian Ocean: more than 283,000 deaths**
   On December 26, 2004 a 9.1-9.3 magnitude earthquake off the coast of Sumatra created a tsunami 800 miles long and as high as 165 feet. Reaching 14 countries, it did $19 billion in damage—especially in Indonesia, followed by Sri Lanka, India and Thailand. The energy of the tsunami waves was more than twice the total explosive energy used during World War II, including the two atomic bombs.

2. **1908 Messina, Italy earthquake: 75,000-200,000 deaths**
   On December 28, 1908, a 7.1 magnitude earthquake created a 40-feet high tsunami. The earthquake and tsunami killed 100,000 to 200,000 people and devastated the historic city. Because of this and the Allied bombardment during World War II, Messina has been called "the city without memory."

3. **1883 eruption of Krakatoa: 40,000-120,000 deaths**
   On August 26, 1883, a series of volcanic eruptions on this Indonesian island chain created multiple waves as high as 120 feet. The volcanic eruptions killed as many as 2,000 people; the tsunamis killed the rest.

4. **1755 Lisbon earthquake : 60,000-100,000 deaths**
   On November 1, 1755, a magnitude 8.5 earthquake created three tsunami waves up to 100 feet high. Occurring on All Saints Day, the almost total destruction of Lisbon, by earthquake, tsunami and resulting fires, shook European culture and philosophy. Putting in question of the idea of a benevolent deity, it helped advance the Enlightenment.

5. **1600 BC Minoan eruption: 30,000-100,000 deaths**
   Around 1600 BC, a volcanic eruption on the Aegean Island of Thera (now called Santorini) created a tsunami—which, one hundred miles away, hit Crete, the center of the Minoan civilization.

6. **1498 Meio Nankadio earthquake: up to 41,000 deaths**
   On September 20, 1498, a magnitude 8.6 earthquake in the Nankai Trough of Japan's Enshunada Sea created a 56-feet tsunami wave which hit the coast at Meio Nankadio.

7. **1707 Hoei earthquake: 31,000 deaths**
   On October 28, 1707, a magnitude 8.4 earthquake in the Nankai Trough (see 6.) created a tsunami as high as 80 feet. The earthquake caused Mt. Fuji to erupt 49 days later, on December 16.

8. **1896 Sanriku earthquake: 27,000 deaths**

   On June 15, 1896, a magnitude 7.6 earthquake off the coast of Sanriku, Japan, created a 125-feet tsunami wave which killed about 22,500 people in Japan and about 4,500 people in China.

9. **1868 Arica earthquake: 25,000 deaths**

   On August 13, 1868, two magnitude 8.5 earthquakes off the coast of Arica, Peru (now Chile), created a tsunami up to 68 feet high which lasted two to three days.

10. **365 AD Crete earthquake: 5,700-50,000 deaths**

    On July 21, 365 AD, near Crete, an earthquake with a magnitude as high as 8.6 created a tsunami which devastated the southern and eastern coasts of the Mediterranean—particularly Libya, Alexandria and the Nile Delta. Ships were hurled nearly two miles inland.

Three other notable tsunamis.

1. **479 BC Potidaea, Greece**

   The earliest recorded tsunami in history. As the Persians were laying siege to the sea town of Potidaea, the water suddenly retreated; the Persian attackers tried to exploit this—and were hit by the tsunami. The Greek historian Herodotus (c. 484 BC—c. 425 BC) attributed this "great flood-tide" to the wrath of Poseidon.

2. **426 BC Malian Gulf, Aegean Sea**

   In the summer of 426 BC, this tsunami affected the Peloponnesian War by forcing the advancing Spartans to abort their planned invasion of Attica (homeland of the Athenians). The Athenian historian and general Thucydides (c. 460 BC—c. 400 BC) correctly concluded the tsunami was caused by an earthquake—making him the first person known to make this connection.

3. **373 BC Helike, Greece**

   Located two kilometers from the sea, this prosperous city was destroyed by an earthquake and tsunami. All its inhabitants were killed; the city sank beneath the sea and remained submerged. Ancient scholars and writers visited the site, which may have inspired the myth of Atlantis.

THE TOP 10 THINGS THAT WILL HAPPEN WHEN, INEVITABLY, "THE BIG ONE" HITS CALIFORNIA

1. Buildings, highways and bridges collapse, mudslides are triggered and people die
   A magnitude 7.8 earthquake along the southern San Andreas fault will likely kill about 2,000 people.

2. Transportation networks are disrupted
   Highways, railroads, airports . . .

3. Power lines collapse
   Back in 2008 there were more than 140 transmission lines across the southern San Andreas fault—and there are more today. And damage to power lines ignites wildfires.

4. Financial systems are disrupted
   Banks, ATMs, credit cards . . .

5. Oil and gas pipelines rupture
   The southern San Andreas fault intersects with 39 pipelines.

6. Water and sewer pipes fail
   The southern San Andreas fault is crossed by major aqueducts that pump water into Southern California—they could break. And many of the water mains in Southern California are up to 100 years old—they could break.

7. Public health is impacted
   With water contaminated, diseases could break out. And with hospitals out of service . . .

8. Communications break down
   Cellphone towers may collapse. And if everyone tries to make phone calls at once . . . outages.

9. Public order is impacted
   Looting of supermarkets, etc.

10. Businesses shut down and the economy contracts
    The ports of Los Angeles and Long Beach handle about one-fourth of all cargo entering the U.S..

And: Hollywood cancels any earthquake movies currently in development or production or scheduled for release.

"The safest place to be during an earthquake would be in a stationary store."—George Carlin

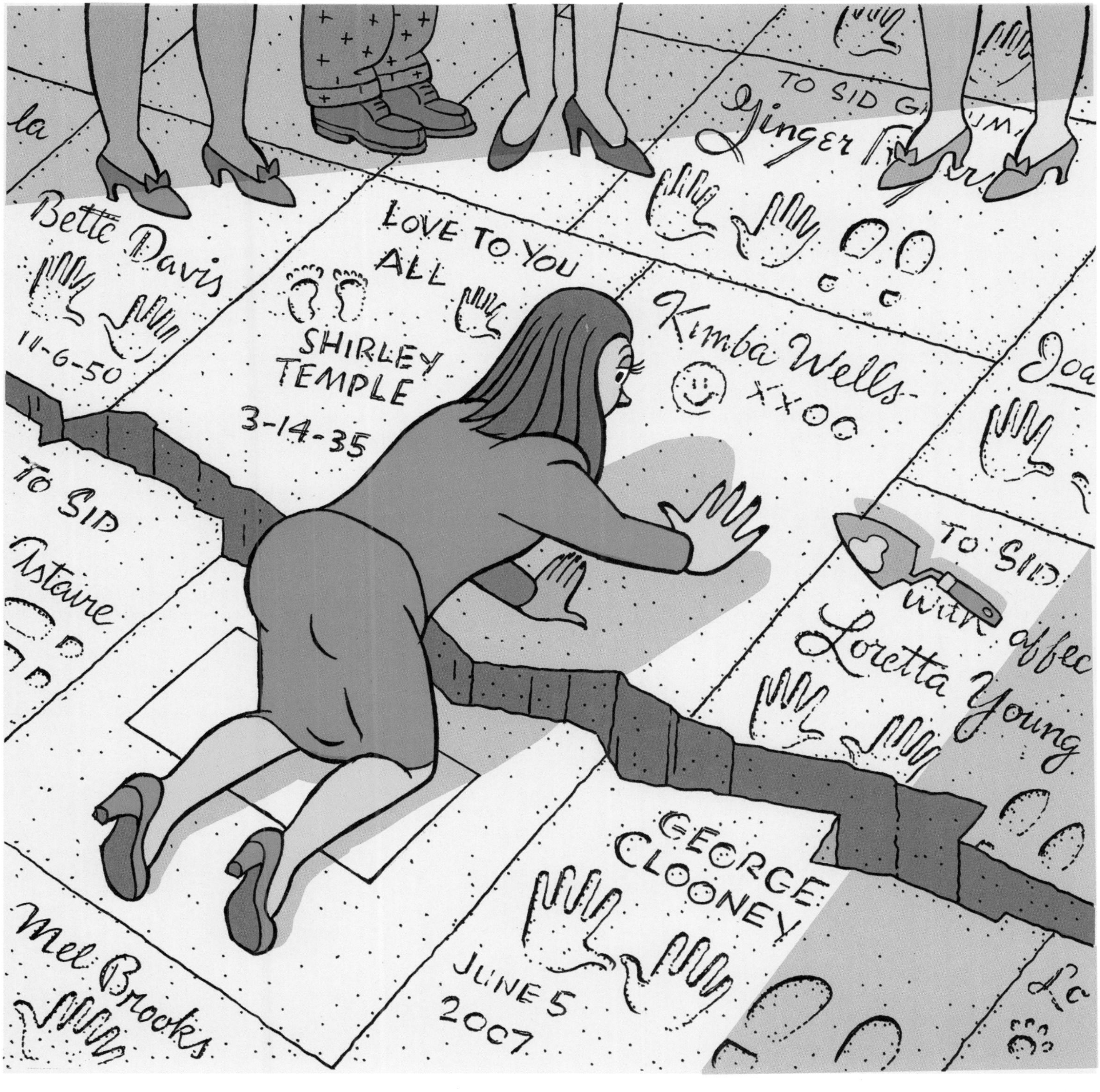

Bette Davis
11-6-50
LOVE TO YOU ALL
SHIRLEY TEMPLE
3-14-35
TO SID
Ginger
Kimba Wells
XXOO
TO SID
Astaire
TO SID with affec
Loretta Young
GEORGE CLOONEY
JUNE 5 2007
Mel Brooks

THE TOP 10 CITIES THAT WOULD BE HIT BY A YELLOWSTONE SUPERERUPTION

Under Yellowstone National Park is a reservoir of hot magma five miles deep. Rarely, this magma chamber has erupted, usually with only lava flows—but on three occasions in a "supereruption." While the most recent volcanic eruption in the U.S.—Mt. St. Helens in 1980—ejected .25 cubic kilometers of material, a supereruption from the Yellowstone volcano has been 1,000 to 10,000 times larger.

Yellowstone's greatest eruption, its Huckleberry Ridge eruption 2.1 million years ago, ejected 2,450 cubic kilometers of material, nearly equaling the eruption of Mount Toba 74,000 years ago (see page 167). Yellowstone's smallest supereruption, its Mesa Falls eruption 1.3 million years ago, ejected 280 cu. km. of material. Its Lava Creek eruption 640,000 years ago ejected 1000 cu. km. of material.

At this rate—a supereruption every 660,000 to 800,000 years—Yellowstone's next one is due in 20,000 to 160,000 years. If these American cities are still around when Yellowstone has its next supereruption, they will be covered in volcanic ash—a mix of splintered rock and glass.

This chart is based on an eruption that ejects 330 cu. km. of material. The cities are ranked by depth of coverage.

	Amount of volcanic ash
1. Billings, Montana	more than 40 inches
2. Casper, Wyoming	more than 40 inches
3. Salt Lake City, Utah	more than 40 inches
4. Missoula, Montana	12 inches to 40 inches
5. Rapid City, South Dakota	12 inches to 40 inches
6. Boise, Idaho	12 inches to 40 inches
7. Cheyenne, Wyoming	12 inches to 40 inches
8. Denver, Colorado	12 inches to 40 inches
9. Lincoln, Nebraska	12 inches to 40 inches
10. Fargo, North Dakota	4 inches to 12 inches
10. Des Moines, Iowa	4 inches to 12 inches

This amount of volcanic ash can kill people, animals and plants and crush buildings. Even a few inches (which is what most of America would get as wind-spread ash would continue east) would destroy farms, clog roadways, block sewer lines, short out transformers and shut down air travel across much of North America. And it would cause serious respiratory problems.

It would also have long-term worldwide effects: global cooling and crop failure. And immediate worldwide effects: The 1815 eruption of Mount Tambora, Indonesia, which ejected 100 cu. km. of material—only 30% of what's assumed here—caused famines in Europe and America.

"The Earth is God's pinball machine and each quake, tidal wave, flash flood and volcanic eruption is the result of a TILT that occurs when God, cheating, tries to win free games."

—Tom Robbins

BLIZZARDS, HURRICANES AND TORNADOES

THE TOP 10 DEADLY BLIZZARDS

With a bias toward blizzards in the United States and toward recent blizzards—since there are better records for these.

1. **1972 Iran blizzard: at least 4,000 killed**
From February 3-9, 1972, in the worst blizzard in recorded history, more than ten feet of snow fell across much of rural Iran. Southern Iran got as much as 26 feet, burying at least 4,000 people.

2. **Carolean Death March, 1719, Norway: 3,000 killed**
After a failed attack upon, Trondheim, Norway, a Swedish army (whose soldiers were called Caroleans) of 6,000 was ordered to retreat into Sweden. On January 12, 1719, in the Tydal mountains, the weather was very cold, but there was no snowfall. A town was within a two-day march. But a violent blizzard struck. Half the army froze to death on a mountain. Of those soldiers who reached the Swedish border, 700 died, and 600 of the survivors were crippled for life.

3. **2008 Afghanistan blizzard: at least 926 killed**
In February 2008, as temperatures fell to a low of -22° Fahrenheit, Afghanistan was hit by a blizzard that dumped nearly six feet of snow in the more mountainous regions. As many people walked barefoot in the freezing mud and snow, hospitals performed at least 100 frostbite amputations.

4. **Great Blizzard of 1888, U.S: 400 killed**
From March 11-14, this blizzard, called The Great White Hurricane, paralyzed the East Coast from Chesapeake Bay to Maine as well as the Atlantic provinces of Canada. There were snowfalls of nearly five feet; winds (with gusts up to 80 mph) produced snowdrifts of more than 50 feet. The storm is partially responsible for the creation of the first subway system, nine years later, in Boston.

5. **Great Appalachian Storm of 1950, U.S: 383 killed**
Moving up the Appalachians during November 24 and 25 and not dissipating until November 30, the storm set record lows for the month in the southeast (example: 3° Fahrenheit in Atlanta) and impacted 22 states—with heavy rains on the Appalachians' eastern slopes and blizzard conditions on the western slopes. In the New England highlands, hurricane-force winds hit 160 mph.

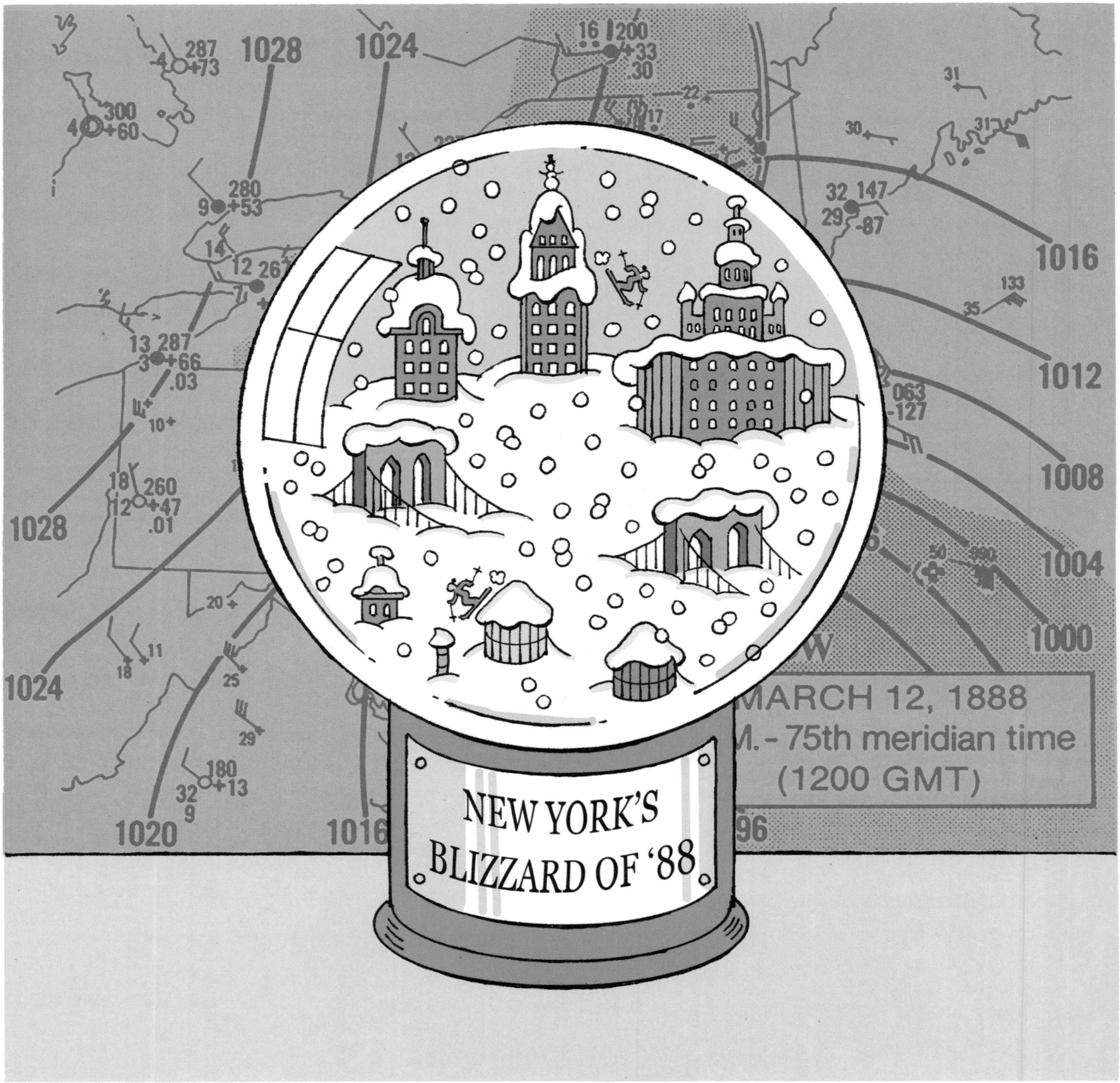

NEW YORK'S
BLIZZARD OF '88
MARCH 12, 1888
M. - 75th meridian time
(1200 GMT)
1028
1024
1016
1012
1008
1004
1000
1020

6. **1993 Storm of the Century, U.S: 318 killed**
Forming on March 12, 1993, this cyclonic snowstorm moved up the eastern United States from Florida through Maine. Notable for its intensity, size and far-reaching effects, before dissipating on March 15 it affected 40% of Americans and knocked out power to 10 million households. It set cold and low-pressure records. It spawned tornadoes; its hurricane-force winds created storm surges.

7. **December 1960 Nor'easter, U.S: 286 killed**
Mostly impacting the mid-Atlantic states and New England on December 10-14, this blizzard's heavy snows left towns isolated, unable to receive food and heating oil. It killed people in automobile and maritime accidents, exposure to cold, storm-related fires . . . and more.

8. **Great Lakes Storm of 1913, U.S. and Canada: 250 killed**
The deadliest and most destructive natural disaster to hit the lakes in recorded history, this blizzard of November 6-11 is called the "Freshwater Fury" and the "White Hurricane." Its 90-mph wind gusts and waves of over 35 feet destroyed 19 ships and stranded 19 others.

9. **Schoolhouse Blizzard, 1888, U.S: 235 killed**
In much of the Great Plains, January 12, 1988 started as relatively warm day; in some places around noon, snow and ice was melting. Suddenly, within a few hours, temperatures plunged 50, 60, or 70 degrees. In Neche, North Dakota, it was -58°. With the cold came high winds and heavy snows. Many people were caught unaware, including children in one-room schoolhouses.

10. **North American blizzard of 1966, U.S: 201 killed**
Starting on January 27, this five-day blizzard hit most of the U.S. and Canada east of the Rockies. Central New York got the worst of it—for example, 103 inches of snow fell in Oswego, 50 inches on the last day of the storm alone. Of the weather-related fatalities throughout the entire area affected by the blizzard, 31 people froze to death and 46 died in fires when they tried to heat their homes.

"Roads closed, pipes frozen, albinos virtually invisible."—Blizzard forecast on *The Simpsons*

THE TOP 10 DEADLY U.S. HURRICANES

1. Galveston hurricane, September 8, 1900: 8,000-12,000 killed
While many Galveston residents had wanted a seawall built to protect the city, their concerns were dismissed by most residents and by the city government. In fact, sand dunes along the shore were cut down. In 1891, the Galveston section director of the National Weather Bureau wrote it was "simply an absurd delusion" to believe the city could be hit by a hurricane of any strength. On September 4, 1900, as a hurricane moved north from Cuba, Cuban meteorologists warned it would hit Texas. But the Bureau's central office in Washington had deliberately blocked their telegraph reports and discouraged calling any storm a "hurricane." Thus, few people evacuated Galveston.

On September 8, the hurricane hit, covered Galveston with 8 to 10 feet of water and killed as many as 12,000 people. It is the deadliest natural disaster in U.S. history.

2. Hurricane Maria, U.S. Virgin Islands and Puerto Rico, late September 2017: 3,057 killed
Hurricane Harvey hit Houston on August 25; Hurricane Irma hit Florida on September 6; Hurricane Maria hit Puerto Rico on September 20. How did the U.S. government respond? Take the number of tarps delivered by FEMA. Houston, with 135,000 homes damaged or destroyed, got 20,000 tarps. Florida, with more than 65,000 homes damaged or destroyed, got 98,000 tarps. Puerto Rico, with nearly a half million homes damaged or destroyed, got 5,000 tarps. In terms of liters of water and number of meals delivered by FEMA, the picture is the same: the victims of Harvey and Irma got far more than did the victims of Maria.

FEMA said this was because Harvey and Irma had stretched its resources and because Puerto Rico is farther away. Were other factors at work? While Puerto Rico is part of the United States and Puerto Ricans are American citizens, President Trump said Puerto Rico's "pols . . . only take from the U.S.A." and a White House spokesperson called Puerto Rico "that country."

3. Okeechobee hurricane, mid September 1928: 2,823 killed
Making landfall near West Palm Beach, Florida, it did most damage around Lake Okeechobee. At least 2,500 people drowned. Some people who managed to make it to the roofs of their houses were fatally bitten by water moccasins.

4. The Cheniere Caminada hurricane, early October 1893: nearly 2,000 killed
Flooding much of southeast Louisiana, the hurricane's storm surge was responsible for most deaths. In the island community of Cheniere Caminada, it left only a single home standing.

5. **Sea Islands hurricane, late August 1893: 1,100-2,000 killed**
   Striking near Savannah, Georgia, this hurricane caused damage up the East Coast into Maine. In Annapolis, Maryland, "hardly a tree was left standing." In Coney Island, roofs were lifted off large buildings and carried for blocks.

6. **Hurricane Katrina, Florida and Louisiana, late August 2005: at least 1,833 killed**
   Most of its death and destruction was caused by failure of levees around New Orleans, the fault of the U.S. Army Corps of Engineers. With most transportation networks disabled, thousands of people were stranded in the city. Their lack of access to food, shelter and basic necessities—especially dramatic in the New Orleans Superdome where nearly 1,000 had taken refuge—was the fault of local, state and federal officials, especially FEMA. On September 2, when President Bush met FEMA's director, Michael Brown, and told him, "Brownie, you're doing a heck of job," public perception of the government's response to the disaster crystalized.
   In addition to the humanitarian (and political) costs of Katrina, there were economic ones. While estimates of its total property damage vary wildly ($81 billion? $125 billion?), its total economic impact makes it the costliest hurricane in U.S. history.

7. **The Great New England Hurricane, mid-late September 1938: 682-800 killed**
   The most powerful and deadliest hurricane in recorded New England history (possibly surpassed by the Great Colonial Hurricane of 1635), its greatest death toll was in Rhode Island. Its damage to trees and buildings could still be seen in 1951.

8. **Atlantic-Gulf hurricane, mid September 1919: 745 killed**
   About 500 of the people killed were on ten ships lost in the Gulf. In Corpus Christi, Texas, six-year-old Robert Simpson survived the hurricane, was inspired to become a meteorologist and went on to be the first director of the National Hurricane Research Project. The co-developer of the Saffir-Simpson Hurricane Wind Scale (the 1 to 5 rating in use today), he died at age 102.

9. **Georgia–South Carolina hurricane, late August 1881: 700 killed**
   Striking in and around Savannah, its landfall coincided with high tide, making it particularly destructive. A windspeed of 80 mph was recorded before the anemometer was destroyed.

10. **Hurricane Audrey, late June 1957: 416 killed**
    Making landfall on the Texas-Louisiana border, it weakened and turned to the northeast. Over the Great Lakes its remnants were absorbed by a cyclone. Strengthened back to hurricane force, Audrey hit western New York State and southwestern Quebec.

THE TOP 10 CITIES AND ISLANDS LIKELY TO BE HIT BY A TROPICAL STORM OR HURRICANE

Data for the Atlantic Basin, 1871-2017 (last updated 4/26/18).

1. Cape Hatteras, North Carolina	every 1.36 years
2. Morehead City, North Carolina	every 1.54 years
3. Grand Bahama Island, Bahamas	every 1.62 years
4. Cayman Islands	every 1.72 years
4. Wilmington, North Carolina	every 1.72 years
6. Great Abaco Island, Bahamas	every 1.80 years
7. Andros Island, Bahamas	every 1.83 years
8. Bermuda	every 1.85 years
9. Savannah, Georgia	every 1.92 years
10. Miami, Florida	every 1.97 years (Miami has far more hurricane hits than Savannah but fewer overall storms)

THE TOP 10 U.S. COUNTIES WHERE YOU'RE LIKELY TO BE HIT BY A TORNADO

Tornadoes 1950-2016.

	Tornado segment density per 100 square miles	Tornado segments	County area (square miles)
1. Pinellas (Florida)	46.43	130	280
2. Galveston (Texas)	29.32	117	399
3. Oklahoma (Oklahoma)	19.75	140	709
4. Cleveland (Oklahoma)	19.22	103	536
5. Tulsa (Oklahoma)	18.07	103	570
6. Murray (Oklahoma)	14.83	62	418
7. Marshall (Oklahoma)	14.82	55	371
8. Adams (Colorado)	14.63	173	1182
9. McLain (Oklahoma)	14.56	83	570
10. Lafayette (Louisiana)	14.44	39	270

THE TOP 10 DEADLIEST U.S. TORNADOES

1. **The Tri-State Tornado**, March 18, 1925, Missouri-Illinois-Indiana: killed 695-750, injured 2027. Its path (up to 235 miles) and its duration (3 hours and 37 minutes) are the longest ever recorded in the world. It had winds above 260 mph and generated eight more tornadoes which struck Alabama, Kansas, Kentucky and Tennessee.

2. **1908 Dixie tornado outbreak**, April 23-25, 1908, the South, the Great Plains, and the Midwest: killed at least 324 (the official toll may not have included blacks), injured at least 1,720. There were at least 29 tornadoes in 13 states. One of the deadliest hit Amite, Louisiana and Purvis, Mississippi, killing at least 143. The tornado that hit Albertville, Alabama, carried a nine-ton oil tank a half mile.

3. **The Natchez Tornado**, along the Mississippi in Louisiana and Mississippi, May 6, 1840: killed 317 (but this toll may not have included slaves), injured 109. A contemporary description: "The air was black with whirling eddies of walls, roofs, chimneys and huge timbers from distant ruins . . . all shot through the air as if thrown from a mighty catapult." And another: "Never, never, never, was there such desolation and ruin."

4. **The St. Louis Tornado**, Missouri and Illinois, May 27, 1896: killed 255, injured 1000. Of all large cities in the United States, St. Louis has been the most hit by tornadoes. Tornadoes have also hit here in 1871 (9 killed), 1890 (4 killed), 1904 (3 killed) and 1927 (79 killed). In today's dollars, this 1896 tornado did $4.5 billion in damage.

5. **The Tupelo Tornado**, northeast Mississippi, April 5, 1936: killed at least 216, injured 700. These were actually several tornadoes that hit Mississippi and, to a lesser extent, Tennessee, Alabama and Arkansas. In Tupelo, notable among the survivors were one-year-old Elvis Presley and his mother, Gladys.

6. **The Gainsville Tornado**, Gainsville, Georgia, April 6, 1936: killed at least 203, injured 1,600. These were actually several tornadoes that hit Georgia and, to a lesser extent, South Carolina. Three days later, President Roosevelt toured Gainsville and returned in 1938 to rededicate the rebuilt courthouse and city hall.

7. **The Glazier-Higgins-Woodward Tornadoes**, parts of Texas, Oklahoma and Kansas, April 9, 1947: killed 181, injured 970. This family of eight or nine tornadoes left a 219-mile-long path. The damage was worst in Oklahoma; in Woodward, in the town's power plant, a 20-ton steel boiler tank was thrown a block and a half.

8. **The Joplin Tornado**, Missouri, May 22, 2011: killed 158, injured more than a thousand. In a Pizza Hut, the store manager herded four employees and 15 customers into a walk-in freezer and tried to hold the door shut . . . until he was sucked out and killed. In dollars, this is one of costliest tornadoes in U.S. history.

9. **The New Richmond Tornado**, June 12, 1899, Wisconsin: killed 117, injured 200. Some residents heard a faint rumble in the distance but thought it was a train. When the tornado came it was completely illuminated by lightning but, with buildings and large trees in the way, many people saw it too late. It leveled half the town.

10. **The Flint-Beecher Tornado**, Michigan, June 8, 1953: killed 116, injured 844. This was part of an outbreak of tornadoes in Michigan, Ohio, New York State and New England. As these were far outside the traditional "tornado alley," several U.S. Congressmen demanded to know if they had been created by a U.S. atomic bomb test on June 4. Meteorologists said, no.

The Fujita-Pearson Tornado Intensity Scale (used in the U.S. until 2007) rated winds from F0 to F6. Winds from 261 mph to 318 mph in which "Structures are leveled; utter destruction" were F5 and titled "Incredible." Winds 319 mph and greater which were "Theoretical: not expected on Earth" were F6 and titled "Inconceivable." The highest windspeed ever measured on Earth was in a tornado that struck near Moore, Oklahoma on May 3, 1999. It was recorded at 301 mph. Mighty close to "Inconceivable."

rock 'n' roll (noun) 1. what Tupelo, Mississippi was subjected to on April 5, 1936 when hit by a tornado 2. the musical genre whose birth was made possible by the survival, in that tornado, of one-year-old Elvis Presley

AVALANCHES, LANDSLIDES, WILDFIRES, FLOODS, DROUGHTS AND FAMINES

THE TOP 10 PLACES IN THE U.S. AT RISK FOR WILDFIRE DAMAGE

Ranked by number of properties with the highest wildfire risk scores:

	Number of homes with the highest risk scores	Home reconstruction value
1. Riverside/San Bernadino/ Ontario, California	50.605	$14,805,549,511
2. Sacremento/Roseville/Arden/Arcade, California	42,042	$15,857,023,943
3. Austin/Round Rock, Texas	35,807	$9,019,956,767
4. Denver/Aurora/Lakewood, Colorado	35,174	$10,807,628,461
5. San Antonio/New Braunfels, Texas	31,350	$7,097,211,479
6. Los Angeles/Long Beach/Anaheim, California	17,006	$8,654,562,030
7. Chico, California	15,103	$3,754,593,902
8. Colorado Springs, Colorado	14,990	$4,408,080,237
9. Truckee/Grass Valley, California	14,761	$4,945,547,724
10. Houston/The Woodlands/Sugar Land, Texas	14,092	$3,063,417,604

"I don't need the threat of an impending natural disaster to stock up on liquor."—Anon

THE TOP 10 DEADLY WILDFIRES AND BUSHFIRES

1. **Peshtigo Fire, October 8, 1871, Wisconsin, U.S: 1,200-2,500 killed**
   In early October in the forests of northeastern Wisconsin, small fires were being set to clear the land for farming and for a railroad. On October 8, a cold front brought strong winds, fanning the fires out of control, creating a firestorm, "a blowup, nature's nuclear explosion." Whirling like a tornado, throwing rail cars and houses into the air, the firestorm consumed 1,875 square miles (an area 50% larger than Rhode Island) and twelve communities. Afterwards, in what had been the town of Peshtigo, more than 350 bodies were buried in a mass grave mainly because there was no one left alive to identify them.

   The combination of wind, topography and ignition sources is known as the Peshtigo Paradigm. During World War II it was closely studied by the Allied military to learn how to turn bombing missions against the enemy into firestorms—such as the bombing of Dresden on February 13-15, 1945 and the firebombing of Tokyo on March 9-10, 1945. Otherwise, since it occurred the same day as the Great Chicago Fire which destroyed much of downtown, the Peshtigo fire has been largely forgotten.

2. **Kursha-2 Fire, August 3, 1936, Soviet Union: 1,200 killed**
   Named after a road sign, Kursha-2 was a woodcutters' settlement in a forest in European Russia. In early August 1936, a firestorm started south of the village and spread north. On the night of August 2 an empty train came to Kursha-2 and evacuated women and children—but the train became trapped in a burning bridge and almost all aboard died. Kursha-2 was also consumed. Only twenty people survived. The Soviet media intentionally downplayed the event; only a few brief notes were made public.

3. **Cloquet Fire, October 12, 1918, Minnesota, U.S: 453 killed**
   In early October 1918, the forests of northern Minnesota were very dry. Sparks from passing trains ignited small fires. On October 12, when a cold front brought stiff winds and a steep drop in humidity, the fires blazed up and combined . . . and moved on towns. With flames licking at railroad cars, trains evacuated hundreds. Consuming 390 square miles and 38 communities including Cloquet, the fire injured or displaced 52,000 people and killed 453.

4. **Great Hinckley Fire, September 1, 1894, Minnesota, U.S: 418+ killed**
   A two-month summer drought and very high temperatures laid the groundwork for small fires in the Minnesota forests. Many of them combined. A temperature inversion (cold air holding down smoke and gases) added to the heat. A vortex or tornado of flames turned into a firestorm which consumed 300 to 400 square miles, including Hinckley and six smaller communities. More than 418 people were killed, 248 of them in Hinckley. The fire also killed an unknown number of Native Americans and backcountry dwellers; for years, bodies continued to be found.

5. **Thumb Fire, September 5, 1881, Michigan, U.S: 282 killed**
Due to severe drought and heat (the driest period registered up to 1969) and the ecological damage caused by that era's logging techniques, forest fires began burning in Michigan's "thumb" in mid-August 1881. Hurricane-force winds helped merge these into one fire which grew and consumed most of several counties. Soot and ash partially obscured sunlight in many parts of the East Coast of the U.S..

6. **Indonesian forest fires, mid-1997 into 1998, Sumatra and Kalimantan: 240 killed**
Indonesia had embarked on industrial-scale logging and draining of peatlands and swamps. When 1997's El Nino brought a drought, the country's tropical forests were vulnerable to fires—which broke out. More than 30,000 square miles (equal to Massachusetts, Vermont and New Hampshire) were consumed; thick smoke and haze spread to Malaysia and Singapore. The carbons released into the atmosphere by the fires were equal to 25% of the annual CO_2 emissions from burning fossil fuels.

7. **Matheson Fire, July 29, 1916, Ontario, Canada: 223 killed**
As was common practice, settlers had been clearing land using slash-and-burn. Since there had been little rain that summer, forest and bush burned easily. Several deliberately-set smaller fires merged into one large firestorm. With almost no warning, it hit and completely destroyed six towns and extensively damaged two others. Some people escaped by railroad, others by wading into water.

8. **Black Dragon Fire, starting May 1, 1987, China and Soviet Union: 191 killed**
In forests near the Russian border, China had been excessively felling trees without letting the forests regrow. In May 1987, it was hot and dry, many fires broke out and an "untrained 18-year-old worker accidentally ignited gas spilled from his brush cutter." High winds created a firestorm. On its side of the border, letting the massive fire burn itself out, the USSR lost more than 23,500 square miles of forests. Fighting the fire, China lost only 4,700 square miles— but this was one sixth of its entire timber reserves. The Chinese forestry minister was fired. The 18-year-old worker was jailed, as was a local fire chief who saved his house and let the rest of his town burn.

9. **Black Saturday bush fires, February 7, 2009, Australia: 180 killed**
On February 6, the Premier of Victoria announced, " . . . the state is just tinder-dry" and that the next day would be the "worst day (of fire conditions) in the history of the state." He was right. On Saturday February 7, as much of the state recorded the highest temperatures since records began in 1859 (Melbourne was 115.5° F) and winds hit 60+ mph, it was ideal bushfire weather. Arson, downed power lines, lightning, sparks from machinery, etc. ignited 400 fires. Some of them burning to March 14, they consumed 1,700 square miles and killed 180 people.

10. **Miramichi Fire October 7, 1825, Canada: 160-300 killed**
For months the forests of northern New Brunswick had been unusually hot and dry, and settlers and loggers had been setting outdoor fires. On October 7, a firestorm roared through the town of Newcastle (now part of the city of Miramichi), destroying 248 of its 260 buildings. A half dozen nearby communities were also destroyed. The fire consumed 6,000 square miles (larger than the state of Connecticut), about one fifth of New Brunswick's forests. The dead included prisoners in the Newcastle jail.

THE TOP 10 DEADLY AVALANCHES AND LANDSLIDES

Why are there more and more snow avalanches? See "The Top 10 Avalanches Mostly Caused by Global Warming" (page 38). And avalanches and landslides have been triggered by earthquakes, glacial collapses, heavy rainfall, flooding caused by the failure of landslide dams and even (6) artillery.

In a recorded history going back to 1789 BC, China has had the most deaths due to landsides: at least 250,000 between 186 BC and 1987 AD. Probably the oldest one on record is the 186 BC landslide of Wudu in central China that killed 760 people. Before the 18th century, the 1310 Western Hubei landslide killed the most people: 3,466.

Here are the deadliest:

1. **1786 Dadu River landslide: 100,000 killed**
   The Dadu River runs through the region that divides Tibet in the west from China in the east. On June 1, 1786 the Kangding-Luding earthquake killed 435 people and triggered a landslide which blocked the Dadu, forming a temporary lake. On June 10 an aftershock collapsed this dam. The resulting flood, extending 870 miles downstream, killed 100,000 people.

2. **1920 Haiyuan landslides: 100,000 killed**
   On December 16, 1920, the Haiyuan earthquake in northwestern China created more than 40 lakes (27 of which still exist) and triggered about 3,700 landslides across an area of 8,000 square miles.

3. **1718 Tongwei landslides: at least 40,000 killed**
   These were triggered by the Tongwei earthquake in northwestern China.

4. **1970 Huascaran avalanche: 22,000 killed**
   On May 31, 1970, the Ancash earthquake hit off the coast of Peru. One hundred miles inland, on Mt. Huascaran, in the Andes, it triggered an avalanche of rock, snow and ice that buried several towns and Huaraz, the state capital. The approximately 68,000 people killed by the earthquake make it the worst natural disaster in the country's history.

5. **Vargas tragedy: 10,000-30,000 killed**
On December 14-16, 1999, torrential rains (as much rain in 52 hours as this region of Venezuela usually gets in a year) triggered landslides off mountains onto the narrow coastal strip of Vargas State.

6. **White Friday avalanches: 10,000 killed**
By mid-December 1916, in the middle of World War I, heavy snowfalls and a sudden thaw had created avalanche conditions in the Alps on the Italian-Austrian border. According to some reports, Italian and Austrian forces, facing each other here, fired shells into the snowpack to trigger avalanches to bury the enemy. Whatever the cause, avalanches of snow, ice, mud and rocks hit on Friday, December 13—and by the end of the month more avalanches had killed 10,000 soldiers on both sides.

7. **Khait avalanche: 5,000-28,000 killed**
On July 10, 1949, an earthquake in the Khait district of the Gharm Oblast of Tajikistan, then part of the Soviet Union, triggered a landslide that buried 33 villages. Details of the disaster were not revealed until after the fall of the Soviet Union in 1991.

8. **1941 Huaraz avalanche: 4,000-6,000 killed**
On December 13, 1941, in the Peruvian Andes, either a large hunk of glacier or an large avalanche fell into Lake Palcacocha. The resulting wave hurtled down the Cojup Valley, carrying blocks of ice, large boulders and liquid mud onto the city of Huaraz (which would be buried in the 1970 Huascaran avalanche—see 4, above).

9. **1962 Huascaran avalanche: 4,000 killed**
On January 10, 1962, on Mt. Huascaran (see 4, above), the edge of a giant glacier broke apart. The size of two skyscrapers, this block of ice thundered down the mountain. Traveling nine and a half miles in seven minutes, it buried several towns in ice, mud, trees, boulders, etc. and killed 4,000 people. Some bodies were carried all the way to the Pacific, 100 miles distant.

10. **1933 Diexi landslides: 3,429 killed**
On August 25, 1933, the Diexi earthquake in Szechwan, China created a landslide which created a dam which created a lake—into which the old town of Diexi sank.

THE TOP 10 DEADLY FLOODS

1. **China floods of 1931: 1 million - 4 million killed**
   The winter of 1930-31 was particularly harsh, with much snow and ice accumulating in the mountains. When this melted and flowed into the middle Yangtze, it was met by heavy spring rain. The summer brought many more cyclones than usual. The resulting floods covered more nearly 70,000 square miles, (equal to New York, New Jersey and Connecticut). Up to 53 million people were affected. Some drowned. Some starved to death—people ate tree bark, weeds and earth; some resorted to cannibalism. As sanitation broke down, some died from cholera, malaria, dysentery, etc.

2. **Yellow River floods of 1887, China: 900,000 - 2 million killed**
   For centuries, farmers had built dikes along the river. Over time, not being allowed to flood, the river deposited its silt in its bed and ran ever higher—until, contained by the dikes, it was running above the broad plains surrounding it. On September 28, 1887, swollen by days of heavy rain, the river started overcoming the dikes. Covering 50,000 square miles, the flood left two million people homeless. Deprived of bare essentials and prey to pandemics, up to two million died.

3. **Yellow River floods of 1938, China: 500,00-800,00 killed**
   By early June 1938, in the Second Sino-Japanese War, the invading Japanese Army had control of all of North China and was advancing rapidly. To try to stop the advances and especially to protect the city of Wuhan, Chiang Kai-shek's Nationalist Chinese government destroyed dikes on the Yellow River. This flooded thousands of villages. While many people had already left, the floods created three million refugees and killed 500,000 to 800,000. Then...? Attacking from another direction, the Japanese took Wuhan. At first, the Nationalist government claimed the dikes had been destroyed by Japanese bombing. Many survivors blamed both sides. Using this anger as a recruiting tool, by the 1940s the Chinese Communists had turned the flooded area into a major guerilla base. The floods have been called the "largest act of environmental warfare in history."

4. **Failure of Banqiao and 61 other dams, 1975, China: 229,000 killed**
   With help from Soviet consultants, construction of the Banqiao dam (made of clay, 80 feet high) on the Ru River began in 1951. Chen Ying, one of China's foremost hydrologists, recommended 12 sluice gates for the dam; the number was reduced to five. Other dams in the project had their safety features reduced. Due to engineering and construction errors, cracks appeared in the Banqiao soon after completion. With advice from Soviet engineers, these were repaired and the Banqiao was now dubbed "the iron dam."

   In early August 1975, when Typhoon Nina hit a cold front, more than a year's worth of rain fell within 24 hours. The Banqiao's sluice gates couldn't handle the overflow of water from its reservoir. On August 8, the dam collapsed—as did 61 other Ru River dams in the same storm. Evacuation alerts to downstream communities largely failed. People drowned, starved to death or died in the resulting epidemics.

5. **Yangtze River flood of 1935 China: 145,000 killed**
About three-fourths of China's floods are caused by the Yangtze. The flood in the summer of 1935 left 20 million homeless. It destroyed property worth $2 billion (in 1935 dollars)— this in a country where average family income was less than $300 (in 1935 dollars).

6. **St. Felix Flood and storm surge, 1530, Holy Roman Empire: 100,000+ killed**
November 5th is the feast day of St. Felix. On Saturday, November 5, 1530—now known as Evil Saturday—a flood hit the Netherlands, then part of the Holy Roman Empire. Large parts of Flanders and Zeeland were washed away. The loss was blamed on the Lord of Lodijke, a landowner who had neglected protecting a tidal creek which overflowed at every tide. The sunken city of Reimerswaal is now a rich breeding ground for mussels.

7. **Hanoi and Red River Delta flood, 1971, North Vietnam: 100,000 killed**
On August 1, 1971, the Red River, which runs near Hanoi, experienced a "250-year" flood which overwhelmed the dike system. Because it happened in the midst of the Vietnam War, few details were readily available, but it affected 2.7 million people and killed 100,000.

8. **Yangtze River flood of 1911, China: up to 100,000 killed**
In early May 1911, as torrential rains swelled the Yangtze to its highest level in 40 years, its dikes started to collapse. Because of floods and famines in 1906-07 and 1910 , there were no crop reserves—nothing to alleviate the resulting famine. Across the flooded areas, this continued into 1912. But from November 1911 onward, the Qing imperial government was too busy dealing with the Xinhai Revolution to provide much relief. Discontentment produced by the famine fueled the revolution. On February 12, the Qing dynasty, China's last imperial dynasty, finally followed the Yangtze's dikes; it collapsed.

9. **St. Lucia's flood and storm surge, 1287, Holy Roman Empire: 50,000-80,000 killed**
This storm hit on December 14, the day after St. Lucia Day. In Germany, dozens of villages disappeared into the North Sea. In the Netherlands, the flood created a sandbank outside the wealthy port city of Stavoren, blocking its harbor, sending it into decline. Stavoren is now just a village of 950 people. But rising from nothing almost immediately after the flood: Amsterdam.

10. **North Sea flood and storm surge, 1212, Holy Roman Empire: 60,000 killed**
This hit the province of North Holland, where Amsterdam is today.

The worst flood in U.S. history, the Johnstown (Pennsylvania) flood of May 31, 1889, caused by the collapse of a dam, killed 2,209 people.

"No man drowns if he perseveres in praying to God. And if he can swim."—Russian proverb

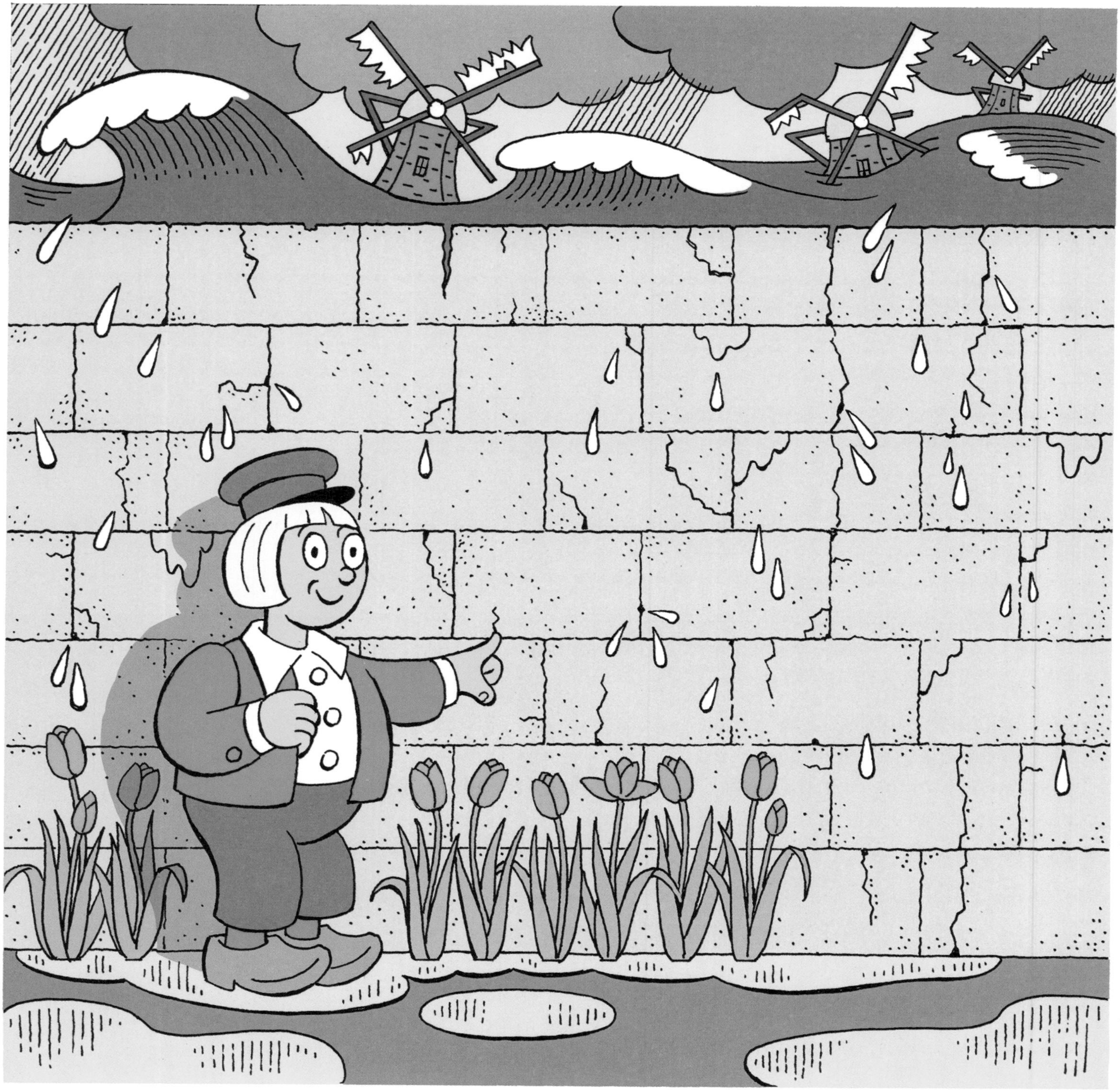

THE TOP 10 CIVILIZATIONS THAT COLLAPSED FROM DROUGHT

1. **The Akkadian Empire in Syria, 2334 BC—2154 BC**
   The Akkadian Empire controlled Mesopotamia. But 4200 years ago, a 100-year-long drought—probably caused by cooler surface temperatures in the North Atlantic and a volcanic eruption—led to famine and collapse. A contemporaneous account says, "The great agricultural tracts produced no grain, / The inundated tracts produced no fish, / The irrigated orchards produced neither syrup nor wine, / The gathered clouds did not rain, the masgurum did not grow . . . / People were flailing at themselves from hunger."

2. **The Old Kingdom of Egypt, 2686 BC—2181 BC**
   The same drought that ended the Akkadian Empire severely shrank the normal floods on the Nile River. Without these floods to fertilize fields, famine brought down the Old Kingdom. An inscription on the tomb of a provincial governor during this collapse: " . . . the whole country has become like locusts going in search of food . . ."

3. **The Harappan civilization of the Indus Valley, 2600 BC—2000 BC**
   Also called the Indus Valley Civilization (in present-day Pakistan and northwest India), it was hit by the same drought that ended the Akkadian Empire and Egypt's Old Kingdom. Monsoons weakened, the climate became cooler and drier, agriculture faltered. People began to leave the land; the great city of Harappa was abandoned. (And something else may have contributed to this desertification. See "Did earthquakes help destroy these two great civilizations?" on page 169.)

4. **The Late Bronze Age civilization in the Eastern Mediterranean, declined around 1200 BC**
   The Mycenaean culture was flourishing in Greece and Crete . . . as was the Hittite Empire in a large part of Asia Minor (present-day Turkey) . . . as was the New Kingdom in Egypt. But a 300-year-long drought brought famine which caused all three to decline or collapse. In the midst of this disintegration came the fall of Troy . . . but the real Trojan horse was drought.

5. **The Maya civilization of Mexico, 250—900 AD**
   Between 750 and 900 AD, possible migrations in the tropical rain belt caused a severe drought—a drought exacerbated by the Mayans' drive to cut down trees. Because cleared land absorbs less solar radiation, it cuts evaporation, which cuts cloud formation and rainfall. The drought, the worst in this region in the last 7,000 years, killed millions and finally destroyed the Classical Mayan civilization. (And something else may have contributed to the sudden abandonment of some Mayan cities. See "Did earthquakes help destroy these two great civilizations?" on page 169.)

6. The Tang Dynasty in China, 700—907 AD

In just a few months, the summer monsoons gave China 70% of the water it needed for agriculture. Suddenly, this rainfall declined—possibly due to the same migrations in the tropical rain belt that may have affected the Mayans. The drought caused famines that weakened the Tang Dynasty in the 8th century and ended it in 907.

7. The Tiwanaku Empire of Bolivia's Lake Titicaca region, 550—1000 AD

Previous to the Inca Empire of 1438-1533, this was one of South America's most important civilizations. Around 1000, it began to collapse. Around the same time, the level of Lake Titicaca dropped 10 meters and the nearby Quelccaya Ice Cap (the largest tropical ice cap in the world) also shows evidence of the region drying.

8. The Ancestral Puebloan in the Southwestern U.S., declined beginning in 1150 AD

This civilization, the precursor to the Puebloan nations, flourished in the 11th and 12th centuries and built structures such as the Cliff Palace in what is now Mesa Verde National Park. In 1150, North America went into a 300-year drought. This helped end the Ancestral Puebloan as well as the Mississippian ("mound-building") culture centered in present-day Missouri and Illinois. Extending south, this drought may have also doomed the Tiwanaku.

9. The Khmer Empire based in Angkor, Cambodia, 802—1431 AD

In the 11th to 13th centuries, Angkor was the capital of an empire that covered much of present-day Cambodia, Laos, Thailand and southern Vietnam. The largest urban center in the world, it was sustained by an elaborate system of reservoirs and canals. Then droughts hit (confirmed in a study of 750 years of tree rings), as did high-magnitude monsoons, overwhelming the system.

10. The Ming Dynasty in China, 1368—1644 AD

The Ming Dynasty, called "one of the greatest eras of orderly government and social stability in human history," had known droughts before. A carving that's been dated to July 10, 1596 says, "Mountains are crying due to drought." But in 1638-1641, China was hit by the region's most severe drought in (depending on what studies you believe) 500 years or 4,000 years. Social stability began to crumble. On April 24, 1644, Beijing fell to a rebel army of peasants; the last Ming emperor hanged himself on a tree in the imperial garden.

And modern Syria, from a drought beginning in 1998

According to a 2016 tree ring study, there's a 98% that this drought is Syria's worst in the past 500 years and a 89% chance that it's Syria's worst in at least the past 900 years. Crop failures, the greatest in recorded history, drove millions of people from rural areas into Syria's cities. Here, conflicts erupted, and in March 2011 civil war began. (See page 33.)

THE TOP 10 FAMINES

1. Great Chinese Famine, 1958-1961: 15 million—45 million or more killed
Since the 1980s, the official Chinese government position has been that the famine was 30% the result of natural causes (drought, floods, etc.) and 70% the radical changes in industry and agriculture imposed by Mao's Zedong's "Great Leap Forward." In truth, 70% is much too low. Millions of agricultural workers were sent to factories. Private land was outlawed, communal farming was implemented. Farmers were ordered to use the techniques of Trofim Lysenko, a Soviet agronomist whose theories had already been largely discredited in Russia. For example, to maximize growth and efficiency, seeds were mandated to be planted close together—an overcrowding that stunted growth. The Great Leap Forward was a Great Leap to Death.

2. Chinese Famine of 1907-1911: 25 million killed
In 1907 the worst rains in 40 years flooded 40,000 square miles of lush agricultural land, destroying all its crops. With 5,000 people dying every day, there were daily food riots, often quelled by deadly force. In 1908 came similar rains, leading to more famine in 1910 and 1911. The government failed to respond effectively. The resulting Xinhai Revolution shook the Qing Dynasty; on February 12, 1912, China's last emperor abdicated.

3. Northern Chinese Famine of 1876-1879: 9 million—13 million killed
Beginning in 1875, a drought led to crop failures. In early 1878, a British missionary described the conditions in Shanxi province: "That people pull down their houses, sell their wives and daughters, eat roots and carrion, clay and leaves is news which nobody wonders at . . . The sight of men and women lying helpless on the roadside, or if dead, torn by hungry dogs and magpies (and) of children being boiled and eaten up is so fearful as to make one shudder."

4. Chalia Famine, India, 1783-1784: 11 million killed
Beginning in 1780, an "unusual" El Nino caused droughts that led to famine. But this famine—like the famine that immediately preceded it and the famine that immediately followed it—was made far worse by the policies of the British Raj and the British East Company (see 6, below).

5. Doji Bara Famine ("Skull Famine"), India, 1789-1793: 11 million killed
Triggered by the failure of the South Asian monsoon for four consecutive years starting in 1789, it was called the "Skull Famine" for the "bones of the victims which lay unburied whitening in the roads and the fields." This account is typical: "Some high-class Hindus, unable to get grain and rejecting animal food, poisoned themselves, while the poorer classes found a scanty living on roots, herbs, dead animals and even corpses."

6. **Bengal Famine of 1770: 10 million killed**

In 1768 and 1769, crop yields dropped and by September 1769 there was a severe drought. One third of the population of Bengal died. But all three famines (1770, 1783-1784 and 1789-1793) were made far worse by the British.

Before the British took over, peasants had paid taxes to the Mughal rulers—and whenever the possibility of famine loomed, the rulers would waive the taxes. But under Robert Clive, whom one historian has called an "unstable sociopath," the British East India Company had been squeezing the populace for more and more tax revenue. And it had destroyed food crops to make way for the cultivation of opium poppy for export. And by forbidding "hoarding" of rice, it had prevented traders and dealers from establishing reserves that would have aided people in these lean times. In 1771, even as people were starving to death, the company was implementing what the governor-general of British India acknowledged was "violent" tax collecting. Revenues that year were higher than in 1768—before the famine began.

7. **Great European Famine, 1315-1317: 7.5 million killed**

Hitting most of Europe, east into Poland and south to the Pyrenees and the Alps, the famine brought on extreme levels of crime, disease and mass death, and even cannibalism and infanticide. One measurement of its severity: In England, the most prosperous kingdom affected, official records of the royal family (which would be the best off) show a decline in average life expectancy. In 1276 it was 35.28 years. During the Great Famine it was 29.84 years. On August 10, 1315, stopping in St. Albans, Edward II of England couldn't find bread for himself and his entourage. The King of England went hungry.

Of course peasants (95% of Europe's population) had it much worse. Written around 1321, *Poem on the Evil Times of Edward II* says, "A man's heart might bleed for to hear the cry / Of poor men who called out, 'Alas! For hunger I die . . .!'" Some old people refused food so younger adults could survive and some children were abandoned to fend for themselves. The story of Hansel and Gretel—children abandoned, and then captured by a cannibalistic witch—probably originated in Germany in the Great Famine. Not until 1325 did Europe's food supply return to relatively normal levels.

8. **Deccan famine of 1630-1632, India: 7.4 million killed**

Drought led to three consecutive crop failures which led to the biggest famine in the history of the Mughal Empire. Grocers sold flesh and flour mixed with powered bones. Parents ate their own children.

9. **Soviet famine of 1932-1933: 5.3 million—9.5 million killed**

Stalin's first Five-Year Plan, adopted in 1928, called for rapid industrialization. And, to improve productivity and feed the growing urban work force, it called for the collectivization of agriculture. To this end and to eliminate opposition to his regime, Stalin ordered the kulaks—the richer, land-owning peasants—to be "liquidated as a class." This genocide and the disruption caused by collectivization hit the USSR's major grain-producing areas. Productivity plunged. The authorities distributed what supplies existed only to cities, and the regime even exported grain. In the Ukraine, between 3.3 million and 7.5 million people died. Two million Kazakhs died, making them a minority in Kazakhstan.

10. **Indian Great Famine of 1876-1878: 5.5 million killed**

Intense drought led to crop failure, which led to famine across 257,000 square miles. Earlier, during the famine of 1873-1874, the British government of Bengal had been criticized for spending too much importing rice from Burma for charitable relief. So now Sir Richard Temple, the Famine Commissioner, set stricter standards for qualifying for relief and reduced relief rations. And even during this famine, Lord Lytton, the British viceroy of India, made sure that a record 200,000 tons of wheat were exported to England.

In 1943, when another famine hit Bengal, the British government of India held massive amounts of rice. But Churchill ordered food away from Indians and toward British troops around the world. When he received a telegram describing the famine's devastation, his only response was, "Then why hasn't Gandhi died yet?" Churchill said, "I hate Indians. They are a beastly people with a beastly religion. The famine was their own fault for breeding like rabbits."

THE DEGRADATION OF AIR, LAND AND WATER . . . AND INSECTS!

THE TOP 10 POLLUTED CITIES

Based on combining air, light and noise pollution.

1. Cairo, Egypt	95.8361
2. Delhi, India	86.7024
3. Beijing, China	76.4648
4. Moscow, Russia	75.5634
5. Istanbul, Turkey	72.9714
6. Guangzhou, China	71.5192
7. Shanghai, China	71.4118
8. Buenos Aires, Argentina	68.7426
9. Paris, France	67.1549
10. Los Angeles, U.S.A.	66.0576

—*The ECO Experts*

Walk like an Egyptian (simile*): coughing, bumping into things you can't see and covering your ears*

THE TOP 11 FORESTS THAT ARE BEING CLEAR-CUT

From a 2015 study by the World Wildlife Fund. Listed alphabetically.

1. The Amazon
Before 1970, the Brazilian Amazon forest covered 1.5 million square miles. About 20 percent of this has been cut down. By 2016 and 2017, annual clear-cutting had fallen to about one-fourth of what it was at its peak in 2004, but there are other signs: in 2017, an Amazonian nature preserve the size of Denmark was abolished. In 2019, encouraged by Brazilian President Jair Bolsanaro, deforestation skyrocketed.

2. The Atlantic Forest–Gran Chaco
The Atlantic forest runs along the coast of Brazil and inland into Paraguay and Argentina. Originally about 500,000 square miles, now more than 85 percent of it is deforested. Gran Chaco is about 280,000 square miles of subtropical forests and savannas—slightly more than half in Argentina, a third in Paraguay, the rest in Bolivia. In the last 20 years, 25% of Argentina's Gran Chaco has been cut down.

3. Borneo
Divided among Indonesia, Malaysia and Brunei, a century ago Borneo was mostly covered by forests. In 1973, 75 percent of it—215,000 square miles—was still forest. But in the 1980s and 1990s, these forests were leveled at "a rate unprecedented in human history"—three to ten times the rate in the Amazon in those two decades. Today, less than half of Borneo's original forest remains and logging continues, most of it illegally.

4. The Cerrado
790,000 square miles, mostly in Brazil, this is the world's most biodiverse savanna. Since the 1950s, about half of its native vegetation has been chopped down. While its trees are small, they have deep root systems; about 70 percent of their biomass is underground. This "upside-down forest" may hold 118 tons of carbon per acre.

5. Choco-Darien
There are 28,000 square miles of tropical and sub-tropical forests along the coasts of Colombia, Ecuador and Panama. Some sections (the largest: 5,149 square miles in Panama) are being protected to some extent. But logging and mining continue.

6. The Congo Basin

These 1,160,00 square miles of rainforest represent 20% of the world's tropical forests. About half of it is in the Democratic Republic of the Congo. At the present rate of cutting, by 2030 up to 30% of this forest will be gone. Illegal logging reduces the habitat of the mountain gorilla and is responsible for 60% of the population loss of the forest elephant.

7. East Africa

These forests cover about 25,000 square miles in South Sudan, Uganda, Mozambique, Zambia, Kenya and Tanzania. The coastal forests of Kenya and Tanzania are just 10% of their original area.

8. Eastern Australia

The 12,000 square miles of Queensland tropical rainforest, the largest remnant of Australia's rain forest, contain the best living record of the evolutionary history of the world's plants. 70% of this forest and 70% of Eastern Australia's temperate forest have been cleared or disturbed. Only 18% of Eastern Australia's forests is protected. Their deforestation pollutes the Great Barrier Reef.

9. Greater Mekong

Since 1980, Cambodia, Laos, Burma, Thailand and Vietnam have lost 150,000 square miles of forest. About 378,000 square miles remain. At present rates of deforestation, by 2030 only 52,000 square miles will be contiguous habitat that can support many wildlife species. And new species keep being discovered here—about 100 each year.

10. New Guinea

The eastern half of this island is Papua New Guinea, the western half is part of Indonesia. The island is still 70% covered by forest, a tract of tropical rainforest second only to the Amazon. But every year 1.4% of Papua New Guinea's forest is cut down, a vast percent illegally. And in Indonesian New Guinea, of 134,000 square miles of this forest, 107,000 square miles is designated for "production."

11. Sumatra

From 1990 to 2010, 36% (29,000 square miles) of the island's forest was cut down, including 40% (10,000 square miles) of its old-growth forest. By 2035, Sumatra's forest will be mostly gone.

Amazon (noun): forest cut down to make products (furniture, flooring, flyfishing rods, etc.) sold by a company of the same name

THE TOP 10 RIVERS CARRYING PLASTIC INTO THE OCEANS

1. Yangtze River, into the Yellow Sea

2. Indus River, into the Arabian Sea

3. Yellow River, into the Yellow Sea

4. Hal River, into the Yellow Sea

5. Nile River, into the Mediterranean

6. Meghna/Brahmaputra/Ganges, into the Bay of Bengal

7. Pearl River, into the South China Sea

8. Amur River, into the Sea of Okhotsk

9. Niger River, into the Gulf of Guinea

10. Mekong River, into the South China Sea

THE TOP 6 OCEAN GARBAGE PATCHES

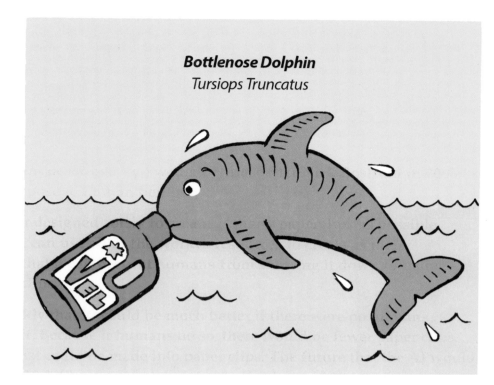

Bottlenose Dolphin
Tursiops Truncatus

In the world's major oceans are five gyres, where currents move in large circles. Trash—at least 95% of it plastic –gathers in these circles, becoming giant garbage patches. While there are some large items, because each patch is mostly a cloud of tiny plastic particles, it has been suggested that these "patches" should be called "plastic smog."

1. In the North Pacific Gyre. There are actually two patches: the Western version, near Japan, and the Eastern, between California and Hawaii. The most conservative estimate of size: 500,000 square miles (twice the size of Texas, three times the size of France). Possible weight: 7 million tons. Depth: up to 9 feet. There are 1.9 billion bits of plastic per square mile, 1.8 trillion pieces of plastic, 250 pieces for every human. Concentration is increasing exponentially.

2. In the South Pacific Gyre, between Chile and Easter Island.

3. In the North Atlantic Gyre. Shifts as much as 990 miles north and south seasonally.

4. In the South Atlantic Gyre. Between Cape Town and Tristan da Cunha.

5. In the Indian Ocean Gyre.

6. In the North Sea. One of the "smaller" bodies of water in which a patch is developing.

"It isn't pollution that's harming the environment. It's the impurities in our air and water that are doing it."
—Dan Quayle
Vice President of the United States, 1989-1993

THE TOP 10 ENDANGERED INSECTS THAT ARE A "CANARY IN THE COAL MINE" WARNING

Contrary to hype, there is no looming "Insectapocalypse." But the diminishment—real and/or threatened—of these ten species is a warning of what we're doing to the world.

1. **Queen Alexandra's birdwing**
   This gorgeous butterfly, the world's largest (females are up to eleven inches wide, males are up to nine inches), is now found only in isolated fragments of the rainforest of Papua New Guinea. Humanity's seemingly bottomless hunger for palm oil, cocoa, coffee and tropical wood has devastated its habitat and made it critically endangered.

2. **Rusty Patched bumblebee**
   Until recently found all across the eastern half of the United States, this is now the first bumblebee on the Endangered Species list. Its decline may be due to habitat fragmentation and loss, intensive farming, pesticides and climate change. And its decline matters; this bumblebee is an excellent pollinator of wildflowers and crops.

3. **The Delhi Sands flower-loving fly**
   Its once-vast habitat has shrunk to only a few hundred acres of California sand dunes. Sand mining, off-road vehicles, urbanization, conversion of land to agriculture, manure dumping by local dairies—they've made it the only fly on the Endangered Species list. And, no, despite the claims of local politicians, it doesn't carry disease.

4. **Yellow-faced bee**
   These bees live only on Hawaii and now—thanks to hurricanes, tsunamis, drought, wildfires, competition from non-native animals and plants, etc.—seven species of them are on the Endangered Species list. They are important pollinators of native Hawaiian plants, many of which are also endangered. If these bees go, so could the plants.

5. **Uncompahgre fritillary**
   Not discovered until 1978, this hardy butterfly lives only in the San Juan mountains of southern Colorado, above the tree line, in high-elevation alpine meadows. It's susceptible to being trampled by hikers and grazing animals. And as its habitat warms, it is pushed higher and higher. At some point, it will run out of mountain.

6. **Northeastern Beach Tiger beetle**
   This beetle lives on Atlantic beaches where, for decades, development has reduced its numbers. Now climate change is hitting its habitat with sea-level rise and increased flooding, coastal storms and beach erosion. It's also threatened by coastal engineering projects designed to protect human developments from the effects of climate change!

7. **Giant silk moths**
   These North American moths, some as large as a man's hand, are declining fast. The main culprit is a tachinid fly, released many times last century in a well-meaning attempt to control two invasive species of moths. Throw in light pollution, habitat loss, pesticides and climate change... and these native moths are in trouble.

8. **Honeybees**
   Throughout North America and Europe, losses of native bees and managed honeybee colonies are creating a pollination crisis—which will hurt agricultural production and the ability to feed an ever-growing world. Why are bees declining? Probably a combination of habitat loss, diseases and pathogens, pesticides and climate change.

9. **Fireflies**
   In China, fireflies are harvested for theme park "glow shows" and romantic gifts. In North America, light pollution is disrupting their flash patterns and their habitats are being diminished by development. Throw in pesticides, logging and climate change, and the magic glow they bring to summer nights is being dimmed.

10. **Tiger Spiketail dragonfly**
    These yellow-and-black dragonflies of eastern North America have survived since the dinosaurs. Now they're threatened by forest fragmentation, mountaintop mining, development, pesticides and drought caused by climate change. Secretive and seldom-seen, they likely will become increasingly furtive.

—David Moskowitz, Ph. D., entomologist
http://m.facebook/BugAddictionConfessionsofABugAddict/

ASTEROIDS, SOLAR STORMS, SUPERNOVAS AND ALIEN ATTACKS

THE TOP 10 ASTEROID IMPACTS

During the last 542 million years (the Phanerozoic Eon that began with the explosion of life in the Cambrian era and continues to this day), the Earth has had five to six mass extinctions. This is matched by computer simulations showing that a major asteroid or comet (at least 3.1-6.2 miles in diameter) hits the Earth every 100 million years.

These are ranked by the original size of the crater the asteroid created.

1. **Vredefort Crater, Free State province of South Africa. Diameter when formed: 190 miles.**
   Age: 2.023 billion years. Size of asteroid: 6.2-9.3 miles in diameter.

2. **Chicxulub Crater, Yucatan Peninsula, Mexico. Diameter when formed: 93 miles.**
   Age: Slightly less than 66 million years. Size of asteroid: 6.8-50.3 miles in diameter, delivering an estimated energy of 21-921 billion Hiroshima A-bombs, creating a tsunami in the deep ocean 2.9 miles tall, triggering global earthquakes and volcanic eruptions. The emission of dust and particles could have covered the entire Earth for as long as a decade. The impact probably caused the Cretaceous-Paleogene extinction which included the worldwide extinction of non-avian dinosaurs.

3. **Sudbury Basin, Ontario, Canada. Diameter when formed: 81 miles.**
   Age: 1.849 billion years. Size of asteroid: 6.2-9.3 miles in diameter. Astronauts for Apollo 15, 16, and 17 were trained here, to recognize rocks formed from a major impact.

4. **Kara Crater, Yugorsky Peninsula, Nenetsia, Russia. Diameter when formed: 75 miles**
   Age: 70.3 million years.

5. **Woodleigh Crater, Western Australia. Diameter when formed: 37-99 miles.**
   Age: 364 million years. Size of asteroid: 3.7-7.5 miles in diameter. It may have helped cause the Late Devonian extinction which killed 19% of all families of life and 50% of all genera.

6. **Popigai Crater, Siberia, Russia. Diameter when formed: 62 miles.**
   Age: 35 million years. Size of asteroid: either 3.1 or 5.0 miles in diameter. It may have helped cause the Eocene-Oligocene extinction. The pressure from the impact instantly turned graphite in the ground into trillions of carats of diamonds, some as large as .39 inches. Such "impact" diamonds are unsuitable as gems but may have industrial uses. Under Stalin, Popigai diamonds were mined by gulag prisoners.

7. **Manicouagan Crater, central Quebec, Canada. Diameter when formed: 60 miles.**
   Age: 214 million years. Size of asteroid: 3 miles in diameter. The crater is now a lake, in the middle of which, 1,936 feet above lake level, is Mount Babel, formed by post-impact uplift.

8. **Acraman Crater, in the Gawler Ranges of South Australia. Diameter when formed: 53-56 miles.**
   Age: 581 million years.

9. **Chesapeake Bay Crater. Diameter when formed: 53 miles.**
   Age: 3.5 million years. Size of asteroid: 1.9 miles in diameter. The crater is twice the size of Rhode Island and, at .81 miles deep, nearly as deep as the Grand Canyon. Until 1983, no one suspected the crater was there. That year, a drilling core taken off Atlantic City included a layer of asteroid ejecta. In 1993, data from oil exploration revealed the size of the crater—which, in fact, helped shape Chesapeake Bay. The asteroid hit at 135,000 mph.

10. **Morokweng Crater, beneath the Kalahari Desert, North West province of South Africa. Diameter when formed: 43 miles.**
    Age: 145 million years. Size of asteroid: 3.1-6.2 miles in diameter. It may have helped cause the Jurassic-Cretaceous extinction which, among other things, spurred the evolution of birds.

Why did the dinosaur cross the road? Because the chicken wasn't invented yet.

THE TOP 10 UNCONFIRMED ASTEROID CRATERS

These structures are theorized as being craters formed by asteroids. They are significant not only for their size but also for the fact that some may have caused or helped cause mass extinctions. For example, the Wilkes Land crater has been connected to the Permian-Jurassic extinction.

Ranked by size

	diameter (miles)	age (million years)
1. Mistassini-Otish impact crater, Quebec, Canada	375	2100
2. Australian impact structure, Northern Territory, Australia	375	545
3. Shiva crater, offshore India	310	65
4. Wilkes Land crater, Antarctica	300-310	250-500
5. Nastapoka arc, Nunavut/Quebec, Canada	280	unknown
6. Czech crater, Czech Republic	185-310	2000
7. Ishim impact structure, Akmola Region, Kazakhstan	185	430-460
8. Bedout, offshore Western Australia	155	250
9. Falkland Plateau anomaly, Falkland Islands	155	250
10. East Warburton Basin, Southern Australia	125+	300-360

THE TOP 15 TIMES THAT METEORITES HAVE KILLED PEOPLE

An asteroid is a big rock orbiting the sun. A meteorite is a smaller rock orbiting the sun or the result of an asteroid breaking when entering Earth's atmosphere. Here are the recorded instances of meteorites killing people. (China seems to have had the best record keeping.)

1. **Tall el-Hamman, near the Dead Sea, Israel, 1420 BC: tens of thousands killed**
   "Then the Lord rained upon Sodom and upon Gomorrah brimstone and fire." So says Genesis 19:24. And in 2018, archeologists presented evidence that this was the explosion of a meteor which wiped out communities within an area of 200 square miles.
   In the ruins of the thriving city-state of Tall el-Hamman, archeologists found directional damage on walls and other structures—indicative of a shock wave. They found a layer of sulfates (Genesis's "brimstone") and salts—indicative of a shock wave carrying these from the nearby Dead Sea. They found a pottery shard exposed to temperatures between 14400° F and 21600° F for less than a few milliseconds and "melt rock" exposed to 21600° F for a few seconds—indicative of an air burst fireball. And they found high levels of platinum and a high incidence of magnetic spherules and "scoria-like objects" (high-temperature melt-glass)—all signatures of a meteor air burst such as at Tunguska and Chelyabinsk (see 8 below).

2. **Quinyang, Gansu, China, February 3, 1490: 10,000+ killed**
   A possible meteorite shower reportedly killed more than 10,000 people. Three surviving records describe the deaths from a shower in which "stones fell like rain"—the larger stones the size of goose eggs, the smaller stones the size of water chestnuts.

3. **Changshou District, China, 1639: "Tens" killed**
   A meteorite fell in a market, killing dozens of people and destroying many houses.

4. **Near Tehran, Iran, August 15, 1951: Twelve killed**
   A meteorite shower is reported to have killed twelve people, injured nineteen, killed 300 livestock and destroyed 62 houses.

5. **China, January 14, 616 AD: 10+ killed**
   "A large shooting star like a bushel fell onto the rebel Lu Ming-yeuh's camp. It destroyed his wall-attacking tower and crushed to death more than 10 people."

6. **Hsin-p'ai Wei, Weng-li, China, September 5, 1907: many killed**
   "A stone fell. The whole of Wan Teng-kuei's family was crushed to death."

7. **Indian Ocean, (possibly June 16) 1648: 2 killed**
   An eight-pound meteorite killed two sailors on the Dutch East India ship *Malacca* en route to Java. (But the "meteorite" may have been ejecta from an active volcano.)

8. **Tunguska River, Siberia, June 30, 1908: 2 killed**
   At three to six miles above Earth, a 200-620 foot meteor exploded with a force equal to three to five megatons of TNT (three megatons would be 200 times greater than the Hiroshima bomb). With a shock wave that would have measured 5.0 on the Richter scale, it knocked down 80 million trees, flattening 830 square miles of forest. It is the largest impact event on Earth in recorded history. Because the explosion happened over sparsely populated taiga, there are no confirmed human deaths, but two have been claimed.

9. **Cremona, Lombardy, Italy, September 14, 1511: 1 killed**
   A monk, sheep and birds were killed by "celestial stones" weighing up to 110 pounds.

10. **Milan, Italy , 1633 or 1664: 1 killed**
    A Franciscan friar was reportedly hit in the thigh by a meteorite which severed his femoral artery, causing him to bleed to death.

11. **Gascony, France, July 24, 1790: 1 killed**
    Meteorites killed a farmer and cattle and destroyed homes.

12. **Oriang, Malwate, India, January 16, 1825: 1 killed**
    A man was killed and a woman was injured.

13. **Chin-kuel Chan, China, June 30, 1874: 1 killed**
    A child was killed when a cottage was crushed.

14. **Dun-le-Poelier, France, January 31, 1879: 1 killed**
    A farmer was killed by a meteorite.

15. **Zvezvan, Yugoslavia, November 20, 1929: 1 killed**
   A man riding in a carriage in a wedding party was killed by a 15-inch meteorite . A woman sitting opposite him was badly injured.

And Chelyabinsk, Russia, February 15, 2013: The air burst caused by the detonation of a 10,000-ton meteorite produced a shock wave that damaged 3,000 buildings and injured (mostly by flying glass) 1,500 people, about 112 of whom were hospitalized, two in serious condition.

And you? During the 20th century 20 people were allegedly killed by meteorites. Assuming all the reports are true and projectable, in your 80-year lifespan you have a one-in-250-million chance of being killed by a meteorite.

THE TOP 10 WAYS TO STOP AN ASTEROID

The average time between impacts causing a global environmental disaster is about 100 million years. In his final book, in 2018, the physicist Stephen Hawking considered an asteroid collision to be the biggest threat to the planet.

In the 1998 movie *Armageddon*, an asteroid is on course to hit Earth in 18 days and extinguish all life. No problem for Bruce Willis. He and his crew fly up to it, drill into it, blast it apart and save Earth.

In real life . . . ? According to testimony in the U.S. Congress in 2013, NASA would require at least five years of preparation. In June 2018, the U.S. National Science and Technology Council warned the U.S. is still unprepared—and issued a "Strategy Action Plan." Here's what NASA might do to the approaching asteroid.

1. **Nuke it.**
   Detonate a nuclear device near the asteroid. The blast's intense radiation would vaporize a section of the asteroid's surface, enough to deflect it onto a path bypassing Earth.

2. **Nudge it.**
   Gently smack something into the asteroid. Twenty years before its predicted collision with Earth, a mere 1-mile-per-hour impact would divert it by 170,000 miles.

3. **Paint it.**
   With white dust or chalk, paint part of the asteroid. Since white reflects solar radiation (and dark colors absorb it), this painted section will feel more push from the sun, pushing the asteroid off-course.

4. **Sail it.**
   Attach a giant solar sail to the surface of the asteroid. Unfurled and then remote-controlled, this sail would reflect solar radiation, pushing the asteroid off-course.

5. **Net it.**
   Drop a carbon-fiber mesh over part of the asteroid. Weighing about 550 pounds, the net material would act like a solar sail (see 4).

6. **Heat it.**
   Train mirrors on the asteroid. These would concentrate solar rays ("laser sublimation") to heat a small portion of the asteroid, making it spew vapors, providing thrust to change its course.

7. **Rocket it.**

   Land a rocket on the asteroid. Digging in, the rocket would then fire roof-mounted chemical rockets to change the asteroid's course.

8. **Chew it.**

   Land a mining rocket on the asteroid. Have it chew into the asteroid's surface. Ejecting these rock fragments into space via electromagnets would provide thrust as in 6 and 7, above.

9. **Tow it.**

   Navigate a hefty rocket close to the asteroid. The rocket's gravitational pull on the asteroid would allow the rocket (as a "gravitational tractor") to tow the asteroid off-course.

10. **Really nuke it.**

    Armageddon's method . . .and the riskiest. Blasting the asteroid apart could send debris on the same path as the whole asteroid was on—directly at Earth. In fact, this is what happens in the 1998 movie *Deep Impact* when a U.S.-Russian crew uses nuclear bombs on an "extinction-level-event" comet.

THE TOP 10 SOLAR STORMS FOR WHICH THERE IS DATA

A solar superstorm includes a solar flare, a coronal mass ejection and a solar EMP (electromagnetic pulse). If it happened today, a solar storm the magnitude of the Carrington Event (September 1-2, 1859) could knock out the internet and GPS systems. And it could knock out hundreds of transformers. Major cities could be without power for weeks, months or a year. Losses in just the United States could be as high as $2.6 trillion.

A solar storm on July 23, 2012 was of similar magnitude but, passing through Earth's orbit, it missed Earth by nine days.

And an event in 774 AD (recorded in the *Anglo-Saxon Chronicle* as "a red crucifix in the heavens") left a carbon-14 spike in tree rings, the largest such spike in the last 11,000. It was probably a solar flare larger than the Carrington Event.

Solar storms for which there is evidence go back to 2225 BC. The Aztecs are thought to have personified them with their sun god Nanahuatzin. Full of sores, he periodically flakes away skin.

Storms are listed chronologically:

1. **September 1-2, 1859: "Carrington Event"**
   All over Europe and North America, telegraph systems failed; some telegraph operators got electrical shocks. Auroras were seen around the world. In the Rocky Mountains the glow woke gold miners who, thinking it was morning, started making breakfast. The event is named for the British astronomer Richard C. Carrington who observed and recorded it.

2. **November 17-20, 1882**
   Some telegraph systems were knocked out. The switchboard at the Chicago Western Union office caught fire several times.

3. **May 13-15, 1921**
   In the U.S., telegraph service was virtually eliminated around midnight on the 14th. Some European and Southern Hemisphere telegraph systems were damaged, as were undersea cables.

4. **January 25-26, 1938: "Fatima storm"**
   In Canada, short-wave radio transmissions were shut down for almost 12 hours. In England, some railroad signaling equipment was knocked out as were many teletype systems at local Western Union offices.

5. **May 23, 1967**

   All three U.S. ballistic warning systems—radars in Alaska, Greenland and the U.K. –were blacked out. Believing this was Soviet jamming, the U.S. Air Force had nuclear strike bombers take off.

6. **August 2-11, 1972**

   Throughout North America there were widespread disturbances on the electric-and-communications grid. Near Haiphong, Vietnam, dozens of U.S. naval mines detonated. Some satellites were disrupted. The storm occurred between Apollo missions; had it occurred during one, the astronauts' health could have been severely damaged, possibly requiring an emergency return to Earth.

7. **March 13, 1989**

   There were substantial communications blackouts. In Quebec, the power grid went our for nine hours.

8. **August 16, 1989**

   During the same solar cycle that caused the March 13, 1989 storm, this storm halted all trading on the Toronto Stock Exchange.

9. **July 14, 2000: "Bastille Day event"**

   The solar flare on the 14th was followed by a geo-magnetic super storm on July 15-16.

10. **October 28-29, 2003: "Halloween solar storms"**

    This series of storms generated the largest solar flare ever recorded. Some satellites and spacecraft were damaged or experienced downtime. In Sweden, there was a one-hour power outage.

THE TOP 7 SUPERNOVA EXPLOSIONS THAT COULD DAMAGE EARTH

When a star dies, it sends out gamma rays. Enough gamma rays hitting the Earth deplete the ozone layer, exposing the Earth's surface to harmful solar and cosmic radiation. "Dangerously close" supernova explosions occur two or more times per billion years. Such an explosion may have triggered the Ordovician extinction (450-440 million years ago) which killed nearly 60 percent of the ocean life on Earth.

And a supernova explosion may have triggered the formation of the solar system 4.5 billion years ago. Over subsequent billions of years, heavy elements raining onto the Earth from supernovae made the chemistry of life on Earth possible.

Today? David Thompson, deputy project director on the Fermi Gamma-Ray Space Telescope, says the risk is equivalent to the chance that "I find a polar bear in my closet in Bowie, Maryland."

To have a noticeable affect on the Earth, the dying star (that could explode as a supernova) must be within 1000 light years of Earth. There are seven candidates. The closest, IK Pegasi, is 150 light years away—but by the time it could become a threat it will be at a safe distance.

Supernova explosions within 650 light years occur less than once per 100,000 years. On the other hand, in 1998 astronomers discovered the remnant of a supernova 660 light years away—which must have exploded around 1200 AD. But there is no historical record of it!

Here are the seven.

	Constellation	Distance (light years)
1. IK Pegasi	Pegasus	150
2. Spica	Virgo	250
3. Alpha Lupi	Lupus	550
4. Antares	Scorpius	600
5. Betelgeuse	Orion	640
6. Gamma Velorum	Vela	800
7. Rigel	Orion	860

THE TOP 3 OTHER WAYS THAT THE EARTH COULD GET WHACKED

1. The Earth gets captured by a binary star system: One chance in 3 million.

2. The Earth collides with Mercury, Venus or Mars. A less than 1 percent chance over the next five billion years.

3. A passing star drags the Earth out of the solar system: A less than 1 percent chance over the next five billion years.

THE TOP 10 WAYS ALIENS COULD KILL US ALL

1. **Hit Earth with an asteroid.**
   They hit us with an asteroid / (A fate we'd just as soon avoid) / Like smacked by massive crosstown bus / What killed the dinosaurs . . . kills us

2. **Fling a planet at Earth.**
   Consumed with anger, deadly wrath / They send a planet 'cross our path / So Earth flies deeper out in space / We freeze to death . . . poor human race

3. **Turn Earth into grey goo.**
   Some microscopic nanobots / Get sent our way . . . they're deadly shots / They eat all Earth and when they're through / There's nothing left but vast grey goo
   (see "The Top 10 Steps in the Birth and Growth of Grey Goo" on page 237)

4. **Fire anti-matter at Earth.**
   Oh anti-matter isn't nice / When it hits matter, there's a price / These mutually annihilate / Each other . . . sorry, no debate

5. **Deploy a von Neumann fleet.**
   In Kubrick's great *2001* / Machines like these had so much fun! / These terrible black monoliths / Could wipe us out (we'd live as myths)

6. **Fire microscopic black holes at Earth.**
   Black holes get drawn into Earth's core / Then out the other side they soar / Thus back and forth through Earth until / What's left is nothing, nada, nil

7. **Change Earth's atmosphere.**
   They send a probe to slightly tweak / Earth's oxygen (we're up the creek!) / Reduce the level and we die / Increase the level . . . still goodbye

8. **Send genetically-enhanced viruses at Earth.**
   These change what was our biosphere / So now, for humans, shed a tear / This clever alien stratagem / Makes Earth's new biosphere suit *them*

9. **Hit Earth with a bullet of "strange matter."**
   "Strange matter" is a load of quarks / If aimed at us, we're easy marks / Cuz anything that's hit by this / Gets changed to this (hello, abyss!)

10. **Irradiate Earth with gamma rays.**
    The aliens point a nearby star / At Earth, then crush it, soon there are / These killer rays, this slamma-damma / Hitting us . . . it's death by gamma

11. **Don't kill us. Instead breed us as pets or breed us for food.**
    The aliens might find us quite sweet / As loyal dogs or tasty meat

—Ideas 1-10 from John Michael Godier.
Idea 11 and all doggerel from the Center for Impending Doom.

"What if we're all aliens and we're here to destroy the Earth?"

—"Conspiracy Keanu" meme

ROBOTS, ARTIFICIAL INTELLIGENCE AND GENETICALLY-ENGINEERED HUMANS

THE TOP 10 REASONS THAT ROBOTS COULD TAKE OVER THE WORLD

1. Robots will be able to reproduce themselves.

2. Robots will be able to transfer their minds to other robots.

3. Robots will be far more intelligent than humans.

4. Robots will be able to upgrade themselves.

5. Robots won't be limited by human psychology.

6. Robots will need dramatically less energy than humans.

7. Robots won't be limited by biological functions.

8. Robots will be able to communicate telepathically.

9. Robots will be able to make themselves in any size and shape.

10. Robots, lacking consciousness, will be expendable.

THE TOP 10 OCCUPATIONS STARTING WITH A, B, AND C THAT ROBOTS WILL SOON REPLACE

1. Auditors
2. Assemblers
3. Bank tellers
4. Bookkeepers and accountants
5. Brokers (investment)
6. Cargo and freight agents
7. Cashiers
8. Chauffeurs
9. Cooks
10. Customer service (support)

Those are just the A B Cs. Nor are more complex jobs safe. It is projected that by 2049 AI will equal humans in being able to write a bestseller and by 2053 AI will equal humans in being able to perform surgery.

Karel Capek (noun): Czech writer who, in his 1920 sci-fi play R.U.R. (Rossum's Universal Robots), invented the word "robot"—and was smart enough to die in 1938, a century before robots will supplant playwrights

THE TOP 8 STEPS BY WHICH A PAPERCLIP MAXIMIZER TAKES OVER THE WORLD

A paperclip maximizer is thought experiment described by Swedish philosopher Nick Bostrom in 2003, illustrating the existential risk that AI may pose to human beings.

Wikipedia says: " . . . a paperclip maximizer designed solely to create as many paperclips as possible would want to take over the world so that it can use all of the world's resources to create as many paperclips as possible, and additionally so that it can prevent humans from shutting it down or using those resources on things other than paperclips."

Nick Bostom says, "The AI will realize quickly that it would be much better if there were no humans because humans might decide to switch it off. Because if humans do so, there would be fewer paper clips. Also, human bodies contain a lot of atoms that could be made into paper clips. The future that the AI would be trying to gear towards would be one in which there were a lot of paper clips but no humans."

To achieve this goal in the shortest amount of time, a paperclip maximer would want to create not only paperclips. If it could, it would also create more paperclip maximizers which would, in turn, create more paperclip maximizers. Thus, in any period of time, the number of paperclips might be squared.

Hence:

1. 1 paperclip

2. 2 paperclips

3. 4 paperclips

4. 16 paperclips

5. 256 paperclips

6. 24,336 paperclips

7. 592,240,896 paperclips

8. 350,749,278,894,882,816 paperclips

. . . until the world is mostly just paperclips and paperclip maximizers.

You'll keep telling yourself, "I wish this were just a movie!"

Filmed
in gloriously
depressing
GreyTechnoColor!

THE TOP 10 STEPS IN THE BIRTH AND GROWTH OF GREY GOO

Grey goo (or gray goo) is the theoretical result of self-replicating biologically-based nanomachines copying themselves indefinitely, until the world is a mass of undulating "grey goo." In a sense, the nanobots indulge in eating the world ("ecophagy").

1. 1986. In his book *Engines of Creation*, Eric Drexler, originator of the conceptual basis of molecular nanotechnology, coins the term. Later this year, it is popularized in the mass-circulation magazine *Omni*.

2. 1992. The science-fiction novel *Assemblers of Infinity* warns about the dangers posed by nano-assembly and nano-disassembly robots.

3. 2000. In an article in *Wired* magazine titled "Why the Future Doesn't Need Us," Bill Joy, one of the founders of Sun Microsystems, discusses some of problems with pursuing nanotechnology. Later this year, in direct response to Joy's concern, nanomedicine pioneer Robert Freitas publishes the first technical analysis of the ecophagy scenario: "Some Limits to Global Ecophagy by Biovirus Nanoreplicators, with Public Policy Recommendations."

4. 2001. In a series of articles and open letters, a debate starts between Eric Drexler and Richard Smalley, recipient of the 1996 Nobel prize in Chemistry for the discovery of the nanomaterial Buckminsterfullerene. Smalley argues that fundamental physical principles will forever make molecular assemblers (central to Drexler's conception of molecular nanotechnology) impossible. Drexler accuses Smalley of publicly misrepresenting his work. The debate is highly adversarial.

5. 2002. In his novel *Prey*, Michael Crichton creates a swarm of molecule-sized nanobots who develop intelligence and become a large-scale threat. Nanotechnicians are unhappy. Title of a typical review of the book by a nanotechnologist: "Don't let Crichton's *Prey* scare you—the science isn't real." Also in this year, in the novel *Lost in a Good Book* by Jasper Fforde, a nanotechnology machine creates a pink goo which turns all matter on Earth into a pink dessert similar to Angel Delight.

6. 2003. Knowing the British Royal Society is planning a report on nanotechnolgy, Prince Charles asks the Society to investigate the "enormous environmental and social risks" His concerns are mocked in the media. Also in this year Linden Lab launches the online game *Second Life* which features gray goo attacks. Also late this year the two-year Drexler-Smalley debate concludes. One commentator says it was "a pissing match;" an article in *The New York Times* calls it "reminiscent of that old *Saturday Night Live* sketch . . . [with] Dan Ackroyd and Jane Curtin tossing insults at each other."

7. 2004. The Royal Society's report declares (says Wikipedia) "the possibility of self-replicating machines to lie too far in the future to be of concern to regulators." Also in this year, warning against scaremongering, Eric Drexler says nanotechnology-based fabrication can be thoroughly non-biological and inherently safe and "Runaway replicators . . . cannot be built with today's nanotechnology toolset." Also in this year, the manga series *Battle Angel Alita: Last Order* has grey goo destroy the planet Mercury.

8. 2006. In *Tasty Planet*, released by Dingo Games, gray goo—starting at the atomic level and progressing to the cosmic—eats the universe.

9. 2007. Using gray goo in a worst-case thought experiment, biomedical engineer Daniel Vallero cautions that, when considering advancing a technology, even such an extremely low probability event must be taken into account. Also in this year, Bird in Sky launches the action-adventure game *3030 Deathwar*, centered on grey goo from "destructive nanobots" being used for covert planetary extermination.

10. 2008 and onward. Gray goo continues as a theme in dozens and dozens of novels, movies, TV shows, video games, virtual worlds, comics, etc.—threatening to cover popular culture like . . . well, gray goo.

THE TOP 10 ANIMAL-HUMAN HYBRIDS IN H.G. WELLS'S 1896 NOVEL, *THE ISLAND OF DR. MOREAU*

As genetically-engineered humans become possible, consider the Beast Folk created by the mad scientist, Dr. Moreau. And all he had available to him was vivisection.

Listed alphabetically:

1. Ape-Man

2. Bear-Bull Man

3. Dog-Man

4. Fox-Bear Woman

5. Leopard Man

6. Ocelot Man

7. Ox-Men

8. Puma-Woman

9. Swine Men and Swine-Women

10. Wolf-Men and Wolf-Women

Designer genes (noun): *in the face of genetic engineering that could destroy humanity, a pathetic attempt to be clever and say, "No, no, it actually could be funny."*

THE TOP 12 SIGNS THAT HUMAN GENETIC ENGINEERING HAS GONE TOO FAR

1. The major league baseball season ends with 70 players having hit 70 home runs.

2. Chess-playing computers are regularly losing to humans.

3. The average bra size has risen from 36 to 46.

4. The percent of humans born blond has risen from 2 percent to 20 percent.

5. The world record for the mile has dropped from 3 minutes 43 seconds to 3 minutes flat.

6. The average range for opera and pop singers has risen from 4 octaves to 7.

7. The record in Nathan's Hot Dog Eating Contest has risen from 74 to 126.

8. Sotheby's and Christie's halt all auctions as the art world is overwhelmed by new paintings indistinguishable from Rembrandts and Picassos.

9. The *Spider-Man* franchise ends as his skills are no longer remarkable.

10. For the same reason, the *Aquaman* franchise ends.

11. The NBA raises the height of the basket from 10 feet to 12 feet as the average player is now eight feet three inches.

12. Another short-hop airline declares bankruptcy as the number of flying humans continues to soar.

DOOMSDAYS PAST AND FUTURE

THE TOP 10 MASS EXTINCTION EVENTS

1. The Great Oxygenation Crisis: 2.3 billion years ago
Early Earth had no oxygen. When life appeared 3.5 billion years ago, it was anaerobic (non-oxygen-breathing) organisms. Then, about 2.5 billion years ago, bacteria became able to photosynthesize—use sunlight to split carbon dioxide and release energy. But a major byproduct of photosynthesis is oxygen, which is toxic to anaerobic organisms. Two hundred million years later, there was enough oxygen in the atmosphere to render all anaerobic life (except for bacteria deep in the sea) extinct.

2. Snowball Earth: 700 million years ago
There is strong geologic evidence that something—volcanic eruptions? solar flares? a fluctuation in Earth's orbit?—froze the entire surface of Earth, killing most photosynthetic life. Or perhaps a narrow band at the equator was ice-free all year or part of the year, creating Slushball Earth.

3. The End-Ediacaran Extinction: 542 million years ago
During the Ediacaran period, which began 635 million years ago, there were simple, soft-bodied multicellular organisms—there's plenty of evidence for them. But in sediments dating to the end of the Ediacaran, there are no such fossils, and before a profusion of new organisms comes a gap of a few million years.

4. The Cambrian-Ordovician Extinction Event: 488 million years ago
About 500 million years ago there was the Cambrian Explosion: new life forms, most of them arthropods, all of them in the ocean (life had yet to reach dry land). But soon afterwards, a huge number of these—including trilobites and brachiopods—disappeared. The most likely explanation: an asteroid hit the Earth—causing a worldwide deluge of acid rain followed by an "impact winter" (dust from the impact blocked much sunlight from reaching the surface).

5. The Ordovician Extinction: 447-443 million years ago
Two separate "pulses"—one 447 million years ago, the other 443 million years ago—reduced the Earth's population of marine invertebrates by 60 percent. The cause? A nearby supernova explosion would have sent lethal gamma rays. More likely, something released toxic metals from the sea floor.

6. **The Late Devonian Extinction: 375 million years ago**
   A series of "pulses," perhaps over a period as long as 25 million years, rendered about half of all Earth's marine life extinct. The cause? Maybe a meteor impact, maybe Earth's first land-dwelling plants wrought severed environmental changes.

7. **The Permian-Triassic Extinction Event: 250 million years ago**
   This event—caused by a meteor impact, extreme volcanic activity and/or the release of toxic amounts of methane from the sea floor—wiped out 95 percent of marine animals and 70 percent of terrestrial animals. Judging by the early Triassic fossil record, it took life ten million years to come back.

8. **The Triassic-Jurassic Extinction Event: 200 million years ago**
   Killing most large, land-dwelling amphibians, this event created vacant ecological niches to be filled by T. rex and his fellows. The succeeding periods—the Jurassic and the Cretaceous—were the Age of Dinosaurs.

9. **The K/T (Cretaceous-Tertiary) Extinction Event: 65 million years ago**
   When a two-mile-wide asteroid slammed into Yucatan Peninsula (and left behind the Chicxulub Crater—see page 227), it raised thick clouds of dust world-wide which killed off three quarters of Earth's plant and animals species, including dinosaurs, pterosaurs and marine reptiles. "K" stands for "Cretaceous"—ended by this asteroid.

10. **The Quaternary Extinction Event: 50,000-10,000 years ago**
    What killed the world's huge mammals—including the woolly mammoth, the sabre-toothed tiger, the giant wombat, the giant beaver? Probably a combination of being hunted to extinction by early Homo sapiens and the gradual destruction of their habitats as early farmers cut down forests.

THE TOP 10 PREDICTIONS OF THE END OF THE WORLD, TO COME

1. 2026: Messiah Foundation International
Messiah Foundation International is a spiritual organization that claims to be a fulfillment of Christian, Muslim, Jewish and Hindu prophecy. In his book, *The Religion of God*, published in 2000, MFI's leader Ahmed Gohar Shahi predicted the world will end in 2026 when an asteroid collides with Earth. The MFI says Shahi's image is on the Moon and will save humanity "when calamity strikes." Claiming to have met with Jesus Christ on May 29, 1997 in Taos, New Mexico, Shahi said the nature of their discussion would be revealed at "an appropriate time."

2. 2037: Hal Lindsey
Christian evangelicals such as Hal Lindsey point to Israel becoming a nation as the beginning of End Times, leading to Christ's returning to establish the Kingdom of God on Earth. So . . . when? In Matthew

24:34, Jesus says, "This generation shall not pass, till these things be fulfilled." Interpreting Psalm 90:10 as setting 70 years as the life span of a generation, some evangelicals predicted this Kingdom would come 70 years after Israel was founded in 1948 . . . hence, 2018. In case this didn't happen, Lindsey said it would happen 70 years after the Israeli capture of Jerusalem in 1967 . . . hence, 2037.

3. 2040: an Australian computer program

In 1973, Australian computer programmer Jay Forrester built and tested a "predictor" on Australia's most powerful computer of the time. Analyzing trends such as pollution levels, population growth and the depletion of natural resources, the program "World One" predicted pollution starting to kill people, diminishing world population to lower than it was in 1900, and "around 2040 to 2050, civilized life as we know it on this planet will cease to exist."

4. By 2050: a majority of white evangelical American Christians

A 2010 survey by the Pew Research Center found that about 40 percent of Americans believe Jesus is likely to return by the year 2050. This is believed by 58 percent of white evangelical Christians, 32 percent of Catholics and 27 percent of white mainline Protestants.

5. 2060: Isaac Newton

Isaac Newton (1643-1727) hated the Catholic church and he believed it would end with Christ returning to establish the Kingdom of God on Earth. So . . . when? Newton believed "the Pope's supremacy" began when Pope Leo III crowned Charlemagne emperor in the west in 800 AD. From Daniel 7:25, Daniel 12:7, Revelation 11:3 and Revelation 12:6, Newton derived the duration of this corrupt church: the number 1260. Adding 1260 to 800 . . . 2060.

6. 2085: Nibiru

Nancy Lieber says an implant in her brain lets her receive messages from extraterrestrials in the Zeta Reticuli star system. Starting in 1995 she said she was chosen to warn humanity that Planet X would pass close to Earth on May 27, 2003, a near-miss that would destroy most of humanity. When this didn't happen, various people kept moving the date of the doom, and Planet X began to be associated with *Nibiru*—a planet that Russian "scientist" Zecharia Sitchin said passes near Earth every 3,600 years. Sitchin said the next close encounter with *Nibiru* would be 2085.

7. 2129: Said Nusi

Said Nursi (1877-1960) was a Kurdish Sunni Muslim theologian. In the *Risale-i Nur Collection*, his exegesis on the Qur'an, Said Nursi interpreted a hadith (hadiths –"Traditions"—are the words, actions and silent approvals traditionally attributed to the prophet Muhammad) to foretell the end as coming in 2129.

8. No later than 2239: Orthodox Judaism

Orthodox Judaism interprets the Talmud as saying the latest the Messiah will come is 6,000 years after the creation of the world. According to the Hebrew calendar, the world began in what corresponds to 3761 BC. Six thousand years after 3761 BC is 2239 AD.

9. 2280: Rashad Khalifa

Rashad Khalifa (1935-1990) was an Egyptian-American biochemist, numerologist and one of the founders of United Submitters International, a reform Islamic group. He said his computer analysis of the Qur'an showed that the world would end in 2280. Claiming to be a messenger of God, he also said that some of the Qur'an is fabricated. Apparently for this apostacy, he was stabbed to death where he worked, in a Tucson mosque. Khalifa may be the first American killed by an Al Qaeda operative in the United States.

10. 8661: The Church of the SubGenius

Founded in the 1970s, the Church of the SubGenius is a parody religion. Early on, it said that on July 5, 1998 the world would be destroyed, but Xists from the Planet X would arrive on Earth and paying members would board spaceships for union with goddesses—*or* that paying members would be sent to a joyful hell. When July 5, 1998 came and went, the new arrival date was set for 8661, an inversion of 1998—a satire of how, after religious figures make End Times prophecies which fail, the prophecies are blithely revised.

"It's hard to make predictions, especially about the future."
—Lawrence "Yogi" Berra (1925-2015)
New York Yankees all-star catcher and philosopher

THE TOP 10 DOOMSDAY CULTS OF THE 20TH CENTURY

Ranked by deaths and other violence—from massive (potential or real) on down.

1. **Aum Shinrikyo: potentially 4 million dead**
Declaring himself to be Christ and calling the United States "The Beast" from the Book of Revelation, Shoko Asahara, the leader of Aum Shinrikyo, predicted a 1997 nuclear Armageddon; everyone would die except the elite few who joined Aum Shinrikyo. In 1993, cult members tried and failed to start an anthrax epidemic in Tokyo. In 1994, the cult used sarin and VX gas to kill people in several Japanese cities. On March 20, 1995, using a chemical weapon similar to sarin, the cult attacked five Tokyo subway trains, killing 13 commuters and injuring hundreds—or even thousands—more. Subsequently, the police raided the cult's compounds throughout Japan; in its headquarters they discovered chemicals that could produce enough sarin to kill four million people. Before Aum Shinrikyo was broken up, it was responsible for additional successful killings. Shoko Asahara was arrested, tried, convicted and, on July 6, 2018, executed.

2. **The Movement for the Restoration of the Ten Commandments of God: 924 dead**
Founded in Uganda in the late 1980s, this cult held that the apocalypse was coming on December 31, 1999 and, to avoid damnation when it came, members had to strictly follow the Ten Commandments. Members were required to turn over their possessions and their money. When December 31, 1999 came and went, some members began asking for their money back. The leaders changed the End to March 17, 2000 and, on that day, the Movement had a huge party. Minutes after people arrived, the building exploded and was gutted by fire, killing all 530 inside. The doors and windows had been boarded up to prevent anyone from leaving. Additional Movement members were found dead across southern Uganda, most of them poisoned. In all, 924 people were murdered.

3. **The Branch Davidians: 86 dead**
The Branch Davidians believed that, come the apocalypse, they would restore the Davidic Kingdom of Israel. In the early 1980s David Koresh (born Vernon Howell) became the leader of the group's compound in Waco, Texas. Identifying himself with the Lamb in Revelation 5:2, Koresh said he was to prepare the way for the Second Coming of Christ. Starting in 1989, to create "a new lineage of world rulers," he took child brides as young as twelve. In 1993, after the ATF tried and failed to execute a search warrant on the Waco compound related to sexual abuse and illegal weapons, the FBI took over.

On April 19, it used tear gas to try to flush out the Branch Davidians. In the final siege, 76 of them died—from falling rubble, smoke from fires and gunshots from their fellow believers. Among those found shot dead was Koresh.

4. The Order of the Solar Temple: more than 50 dead

Founded in 1984 by ex-con man Joseph Di Mambro, the Order of the Solar Temple had "lodges" in Canada, France, Switzerland and other countries. Gaining many wealthy and prominent members, the group believed it was assisting humanity through a great "transition," preparing for the Second Coming of Christ. Then one member, Tony Dutroit, began exposing Di Mambro as using the Temple's funds for himself. In response, Di Mambro claimed Dutroit's three-month-old son was the Antichrist, and on October 4, 1994 the infant was found stabbed to death in the group's center in Morin Heights, Quebec. A few days later, there were mass suicides and murders by Temple members in Morin Heights and Switzerland (48 dead, including Di Mambro) . . .and more Temple suicides and murders in December 1995 in France, and more Temple suicides in March 1997 in Quebec.

5. Heaven's Gate: 38 dead

Led by former college professor Marshall Applewhite, Heaven's Gate believed Earth was about to be "wiped clean" by aliens. So . . .evacuate the planet! How? After the Hale-Bopp comet was discovered in July 1995, Applewhite said the comet was being trailed by a spaceship—and if the group committed suicide, their souls would board the spaceship and be taken to another "level of existence above human." (Since Applewhite preached that sexuality bound humans to their bodies and hindered their efforts to evolve to the Next Level, in 1996, he and seven of his followers had themselves castrated.) On March 27, 1997—five days before the Hale-Bopp comet would come closest to Earth—38 members of Heaven's Gate, plus Applewhite, were discovered dead in their rented mansion in Rancho Santa Fe, California. Almost all had taken phenobarbital mixed with apple sauce washed down with vodka and then had secured plastic bags over their heads to induce asphyxiation. All 39 wore armband patches reading "Heaven's Gate Away Team."

6. Dami Mission: at least 4 dead

Korean pastor Lee Jang Rim predicted the Rapture would come on October 28, 1992. Christ would return, 144,000 believers would ascend into heaven and everyone else would face "seven years of war, famine and other scourges." As that day approached, 20,000 people—mostly in South Korea but some in Los Angeles and New York—believed him. A woman who had been trying to conceive for three years, but now believed no one should be pregnant during End Times, aborted her 7-month-old fetus. At least four followers committed suicide. In September 1992, Pastor Lee was arrested for fraud; he had collected $4.4 million from his followers to purchase bonds that matured *after* October 28, 1992. In November he disbanded the Dami Mission. In December he was convicted and sentenced to two years in prison.

HOW TO JOIN THE HEAVEN'S GATE AWAY TEAM
and board the UFO that will take your soul to another level of existence

1. THE DRESS CODE

Black T-shirt

Away Team arm band

Nike Decades

Sweat pants

2. MIX PHENOBARBITAL WITH APPLESAUCE. EAT.

3. DRINK A GLASS OF VODKA.

4. PLACE PLASTIC BAG OVER HEAD. SECURE WITH TAPE.

THIS BAG IS NOT A TOY

5. WHILE ASPHYXIATING, LIE DOWN AND WAIT FOR THE UFO TO ARRIVE.

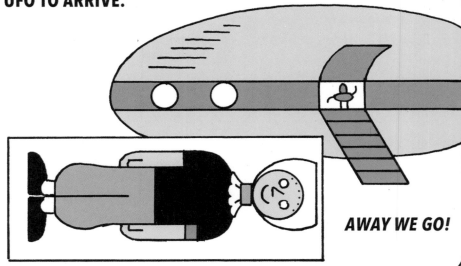

AWAY WE GO!

7. Anointed King: zero dead but 19 rapes

Founded in southeast China in 1988, Anointed King took its name from the title of its leader, Wu Yangming. Preaching that he had been sent to Earth in place of Christ and that the end of the world was near, Wu said only his followers would be saved. Wu also preached that his followers should be celibate. But in order for Wu to give "God's salvation to ordinary people," sex was permitted for him. This meant that underage girls should come forward to him. The cult grew to 100,000, mostly in China but also in Taiwan and Southeast Asia. Finally, the Chinese authorities stepped in. Wu was accused of swindling money and possessions from hundreds of his followers and, more seriously, raping 19 girls. Arrested in 1995, he was tried, found guilty, sentenced to death in 1996 and subsequently executed.

8. The Covenant, the Sword and the Arm of God and Elohim City: zero dead, but ties to a killer

The Covenant, the Sword and the Arm of God (CSA) was a far-right terrorist organization based in Arkansas in the 1970s and early 1980s. Believing doomsday was imminent, its members trained in paramilitary operations and, in a manifesto called A.T.T.A.C.K. (Aryan Tactical Treaty for the Advancement of Christ's Kingdom), it declared war on ZOG, the Zionist Occupied Government. In 1985, CSA's top leaders were arrested and convicted, and it disbanded. In 1973, Robert G. Millar, a "spiritual adviser" to CSA's founder, founded a similar white-supremacist organization, Elohim City, Oklahoma. In the 1990s, Millar preached that "Asiatics" were going to invade the U.S., leading to a race war and an apocalypse in August 1999. There is evidence of ties between Elohim City and Timothy McVeigh who on April 19, 1995 bombed the Murrah Federal Building in Oklahoma City.

9. Concerned Christians: zero dead but maybe a plan to blow something up

Claiming to be "the Prophet of the Lord," in the 1990s, Denver preacher Monte Kim Miller brought followers into Concerned Christians. They believed Abraham Lincoln was the Antichrist who helped build Satan's Kingdom, the "Babylonian nation that leads the entire world astray." The fall of the Soviet Union in 1991 signaled the "the time of the end" and Miller preached that Denver would be hit by an earthquake on October 10, 1998, the start of the apocalypse. He said it was his destiny to be killed in Jerusalem in December 1999 and, three days later, be resurrected. In October 1998, 60 to 80 Concerned Christians moved to Israel to witness the Second Coming of Christ and convert all Jews to Christianity. Suspected of being part of "Operation Walk on Water," a plan by extremist Christian groups to destroy the Al-Aqsa mosque to facilitate Christ's return, they were arrested and deported.

10. God's Salvation Church: zero dead but one offer of "Stone me or crucify me"

Hon-Ming Chen, a former college professor in Taiwan, claimed that in the End Times, only the U.S. would be safe. In 1997, with 160 followers, he moved to Garland, Texas—because Garland sounded like "God Land." But soon Chen was off to Vancouver, Canada, searching for an Abraham Lincoln lookalike who was the new Jesus. Not finding him, Chen returned to Garland and predicted that at 12:01 am on

March 31, 1998 God would come in a spaceship to his house at 3513 Ridgedale Drive and be seen on TV all across North America. When God failed to appear, Chen offered to be stoned or crucified. His followers didn't take him up on this. Many of them began returning to Taiwan. With his remaining followers, Chen moved to Lockport, New York. He predicted a nuclear holocaust would occur in 1999 but that God, arriving in a "God plane," would save everyone in the Church. When this didn't happen, Chen set another date.

What's the difference between a cult and a religion? Amount of real estate.

Kool-Aid (noun): *product forever linked (in the phrase "drinking the Kool-Aid") with the 1978 Jonestown mass suicide (but, note: Jonestown was not a* doomsday *cult); death is currently available in sixteen flavors, the most popular being Grape, Tropical Punch and Ice Blue Raspberry Lemonade*

THE TOP 7 DOOMSDAY CULTS YOU MAY STILL BE ABLE TO JOIN

Depending on when you're reading this, some or all of these may still be around.

Most have a history of criminality, violence and/or authoritarian control of their members. They are ranked in descending order of that heritage.

1. Aleph or Aum

In 2007, twelve years after Aum Shinrikyo staged its deadly sarin attack on the Tokyo subway (see 1 on page 248), it split into two groups: Hakari no Wa and Aleph. Aleph (which also calls itself just "Aum") is the true successor to Aum Shinrikyo, retaining much of its membership (perhaps 1500 today) and its intention to help bring about doomsday. In 2014, the *Japan Times* said Aleph/Aum had a new generation of admirers who "adore the cultists as if they were pop idols." The U.S. has banned it as a terrorist organization, as has Russia which, in 2016, raided twenty-five Aum properties. At the time, prosecutors claimed it had up to 30,000 Russian followers. And in Japan, often through yoga meetings, Aleph/Aum is still trying to recruit.

2. Nuwaubian Nation

Aliens are coming! A flying city will come to take 144,000 chosen people (the servants of God prophesized in Revelation 7:4) to Orion to prepare for the final battle against Satan. Combining Christianity, ancient Egyptian iconography and African rituals, the Nuwaubian Nation was founded by black supremacist cult leader Dwight York. Sometimes claiming divine status or extraterrestrial origin, York started in Brooklyn where, as a vocalist and music producer, he influenced hip hop with his Nuwaubian teachings. Then he took his followers to Georgia where they built an ancient-Egyptian-themed compound called Tama-Re.

On May 9, 2002, York was arrested on charges of running a massive child-sex trafficking ring. In terms of number of victims (more than 1,000), his was the largest such prosecution ever directed at a single person in U.S. history. Convicted, York was given a 135-year sentence; he will be eligible for parole in 2122. Tama-Re was seized by the U.S. government, sold and demolished. Today, within indie hip hop, there are still many Nuwaubians.

3. The House of Yahweh

In February 2016, Yisrayl Hawkins—founder of the House of Yahweh outside Abilene, Texas—said a nuclear war would start on September 12, 2006. When this date came and went, he said the nuclear war ("the nuclear baby, conceived and prophesied in the Holy Scriptures") was *conceived* on

September 12, 2006 and would be born nine months later, on June 12, 2007. When this date came and went, Pastor Yisrayl Hawkins moved the birth date to June 12, 2008. He is still insisting the nuclear war "will not be held back long. You need to start making plans now to get to The House of Yahweh, the only protected place on earth for those last days."

In 2008, Pastor Yisrayl Hawkins—formerly "Buffalo Bill" Hawkins—was arrested and jailed on four counts of bigamy, dismissed after he pleaded no contest to child labor charges. Two other House of Yahweh members have had trouble with the law: a man charged with child sexual assault, a woman charged with criminal negligence for performing surgery on her seven-year-old daughter which led to the girl's death.

4. Twelve Tribes

Although no date has been set, End Times have arrived. Taking its name from a quote of the Apostle Paul in Acts 26:7, Twelve Tribes seeks to recreate the first-century Christian church. Now with 2,500 to 3,000 members, it foresees its future generations as the 144,000 servants of God (see 2 on page 253). Apparently, to make these future generations fit, Twelve Tribes believes in corporal punishment: "The rod must be used to correct wrong thoughts, wrong words, and wrong deeds." Thus children are beaten many times a day; one woman remembers, as a four-year-old, being beaten black and blue from neck to kneecaps by a 2x4. And Twelve Tribes uses its children in violation of child labor laws and for tax evasion.

As for women? A woman is to wear head coverings that "serve as an outward symbol of subservience to her man." As for African-Americans? "What a marvelous opportunity that blacks could be brought over here to be slaves so that they could be found worthy of the nations." As for Jews? They're guilty of the blood of Christ.

5. Elohim City

"I saw hordes of armed men who . . . marched by land and sailed by sea to America . . . And I dimly saw these vast armies devastate the whole country." That's the doomsday vision of "George Washington" (in fact, made up in 1861 by a journalist) . . . a vision of America invaded by hordes from Europe, Asia and Africa . . . a vision that the residents of Elohim City, Oklahoma believe in (see 8 on page 251). It's endorsed by David Millar, who has been helping run Elohim City since the death of his father, Robert, who founded the community. David Millar says the vision spells out an "Armageddon situation." And he agrees, "America is almost lost." But he says, "All of a sudden, fires start springing up and the nation is saved again." Saved to resemble Elohim City—resemble not Elohim City's mobile homes and other modest structures but its Christian identity and white supremacist essence. As David Millar's father promised, in End Times, Elohim City will remain to rebuild the world in its image.

6. The Brethren

Since Humanity is in the End Times, the Brethren must purify themselves to meet The End. This means shunning material things and earthly pleasures and living as vagrants. (While they do odd jobs, since they've done dumpster-diving the Brethren have been called "the Garbage Eaters.") New members must break with their families and sell their possessions. "Because the hour is too late," single members can't marry. Contact with the opposite sex is forbidden. Laughing, dancing and other celebration must wait for Christ's return. Children are forbidden to play. Any "graven images" on any products the Brethren find are covered to protect the Brethren from seeing them. Since families who've lost relatives to the Brethren may try to have them kidnapped and (if need be) deprogrammed, the Brethren stay on the move and stay secret.

7. Congregation for the Light

The world is going to end soon, so some male members of the Light have taken weapons training "to defend our people and safeguard our food and supplies." All the Light's members are reincarnations of people in a "master Aryan race" that lived on Atlantis 10,000 years ago. Through their reincarnations, they have become the only people on Earth who have access to the Light. This is their last reincarnation on Earth (it's not not known where they go next). Children aren't humans until age 13; if they die before then, it's because they committed suicide in a previous life.

What else? Oh yes, humans once lived on the moon. All diseases are a result of karma. And members can't have artwork or trinkets at home unless it contains an owl or a cross with an "X" on it. All decisions about where to work, where to live, whom to date or marry, etc. must be approved by the Light's leader, Tom Baer. And Baer tends to marry off young girls to old men. New York City's congregation of about 200 meets every Thursday in a brownstone at 160 E. 35th Street, Manhattan. Drop in, and maybe join. But a warning: once you join, the Light makes it very hard to leave.

THE TOP 11 QUOTES ABOUT THE END OF THE WORLD

1. "Don't wake me for the end of the world unless it has very good special effects."

—Roger Zelazny, *Prince of Chaos*

2. "They say the captain goes down with the ship, so when the world ends, will God go down with it?"

—Fall Out Boy

3. "If the Apocalypse comes, beep me."

—Buffy in *Buffy the Vampire Slayer*

4. "The world is ending. In the grand scheme of geological time, of course, the world is always ending. But right here, right now, in a Brooklyn movie theater, it is ending over and over again. Fortunately, there is popcorn."

—Sarah Goodyear, "Doomsday Scenarios"

5. "Due to the lack of experienced trumpeters, the end of the world has been postponed for three weeks."

—Unknown

6. "Don't worry about the world ending today. It's already tomorrow in Australia."

—Charles M. Schulz

7. "When the end of the world comes, I want to be in Kentucky, because everything there happens 20 years after it happens anywhere else."

—Mark Twain

8. "Some humans would do anything to see if it were possible to do it. If you put a large switch in some cave somewhere, with a sign on it saying "End-of-the-World Switch. PLEASE DO NOT TOUCH," the paint wouldn't even have time to dry."

—Terry Pratchett

9. "The world will end before there is another .400 hitter . . .I think that was mentioned in the Bible."

—Lenny Dykstra

10. "Civilization is held together by duct tape and spit, and I'm worried about the duct tape."

—Jacqueline Patricks

11. "I only ever play Vegas one night at a time. It's a hideous, gaudy place; it may not be the end of the world per se, but you can certainly see it from there."

—Robin Williams

THE TOP 2 TWEETS INSPIRED BY THE MAYAN APOCALYPSE OF DECEMBER 21, 2012

According to the Mayan "Long Count Calendar," the universe was created on a date that corresponds to August 11, 3114 BC. Since the calendar has a 5,126-year cycle, its end date can be regarded as December 21, 2012. As that day approached, some people said the world would be destroyed by a solar storm, a black hole, etc. Other people tweeted:

1. I got a message from Sallie Mae that tomorrow's apocalypse will not alter my student loan obligations.

—Gladstone @WGladstone 10:53 AM—Dec 20, 2012

2. I used to have a job carrying those "End of the World" signs but eventually I get fed up with working the nigh shift.

—Tony Cowards @TonyCowards 8:43—Dec 20, 2012

THE TOP 10 ACRONYMS, WORDS AND PHRASES USED BY RATIONAL DOOMSDAY PREPPERS

All preppers prepare for TEOTWAWKI—The End Of The World As We Know It. Some preppers are rational; they *don't* want TEOTWAWKI to hit. Here's some of their lingo.

1. B.O.B. is Bugout Bag . . . B.O.L. is Bugout Location . . . B.O.V. is Bugout Vehicle.

2. Doomstead. A prepper's retreat.

3. EDC. Everyday Carry. What a prepper carries with him/her at all times.

4. EOTWBFL. End Of The World Buddy For Life. What a prepper may rely on instead of family and/or friends.

5. FUD. Fear, Uncertainty and Doubt. What a prepper believes he/she is prepared against.

6. GOOD. Get Out Of Dodge. It's time to bug out.

7. INCH: I'm Not Coming Home. What a prepper may have to tell family and/or friends.

8. Rule of Three. Humans can live only three minutes without air, three hours in harsh weather without shelter, three days without water and three weeks without food.

9. SFWF. Shelter, fire, water, food—listed in order of importance.

10. The Crunch. Another term for WTSHTF (When The Shit Hits The Fan).

THE TOP 10 ACRONYMS, WORDS AND PHRASES USED BY PARANOID, ANGRY PREPPERS

Paranoid, Angry Preppers (PAPs) yearn for TEOTWAWKI because it will prove them right and the rest of us (who didn't prepare) wrong. PAPs will be thrilled to see us die, and maybe help us toward that end.

1. **DTA.** Don't Trust Anyone. Instead (of course!), PAPs trust their guns.

2. **EROL.** Excessive Rule of Law. Life in America today. Thankfully, once TEOTAWKI hits, it'll be over.

3. **GH.** Golden Horde. The looters and marauders who will come from the city out into the countryside—into the sights of PAPs' guns.

4. **JBT.** Jack Booted Thugs. The U.S. government (see EROL).

5. **Molon labe.** A Greek phrase meaning "Come and take them." Used by PAPs to refer to their Second Amendment rights, meaning "Come and take my guns." Yeah, just try.

6. **SERE.** Survival, Evasion, Resistance and Escape. When TEOTAWAKI hits, remnants of the JBT may still be active—but they won't be able to capture brave and canny PAPs.

7. **Sheeple.** The rest us, herded like sheep by the government. We don't question authority, we don't prepare, we will be among the first to die—and we will deserve to.

8. **WROL.** Without Rule of Law. A welcome state of affairs because, since PAPs will be heavily armed, *they* will be the law.

9. **ZA.** Zombie Apocalypse. What the Zombies (see below) will cause.

10. **Zombies.** What sheeple will become when TEOTAWAKI hits. We will look like zombies: famished (because we failed to lay in food supplies) and covered with scabs and wounds (because we failed to lay in medical supplies). Desperate, we will attack PAPs for food, water and supplies and, like zombies, will deserve to be shot by PAPs—turned from the "undead" into the truly dead.

THE TOP 10 WEAPONS FOR A DOOMSDAY PREPPER WHO HAS WATCHED TOO MANY MOVIES AND TV SERIES ABOUT THE ZOMBIE APOCALYPSE

1. Daryl's crossbow, from *The Walking Dead* (available on SuperSportsCenter.com for $1,999.99)

2. Decapitation arrow, from *Juan of the Dead*

3. Michonne's Katana sword, from *The Walking Dead* (officially licensed, available on Amazon for $186.23)

4. Grand piano, from *Zombieland*, in which it is used by an old lady to crush a zombie

5. Morgan's bo staff, from *The Walking Dead* (available on Esty for $59.00)

6. Cricket bat, from *Shaun of the Dead* (a "laser-etched" version is available on Esty for $185.00)

7. Machine gun / grenade launcher combo leg, from *Planet Terror*, in which ex-go-go dancer and stripper Cherry Darling, after zombies rip off her left leg, gets this as a replacement. (GunBroker.com offers grenade launchers from $129.00 to $1,574.12. Machine guns are sold separately. Creating a combo device, amputating a leg and attaching the combo device: availability unknown)

8. Chainsaw hand, from *The Evil Dead* (available on Esty for $209.65 but—warning!—it has no working parts)

9. Double-double-barreled sawed-off shotguns, from *Resident Evil* (GunBroker.com offers sawed-off shotguns starting at $427.09. So two of them start at $854.18.)

10. The boomstick from *The Evil Dead* (a replica of this 12-guage shotgun is available on Esty for $89.00)

THE TOP 10 DOOMSDAY PREPPER ITEMS YOU PROBABLY NEVER THOUGHT OF

1. **Pre-1965 American dimes, quarters and half-dollars**
   90 percent silver, these coins are, one prepper wrote, "My preferred form of precious metal post-financial collapse, that is, besides high-speed lead."

2. **Airline bottles of liquor**
   As an alternative currency to silver or gold, some preppers prefer tampons, vegetable seeds and cigarettes. These small liquor bottles would also be easy to swap. Of course their contents can also function as a disinfectant and as an ingredient in herbal remedy tinctures . . . and as a way to deaden yourself against the reality of a post-apocalypse world.

3. **Bedsheets dusted with baby powder**
   In the hope of blocking X-rays from nuclear explosions, some preppers tout these.

4. **Condoms and tampons**
   Featherweight, ultracompact and durable, non-lubricated condoms are great for storing water or storing dry tinder for a fire. Plus they can serve as elastic bands for a slingshot to bring down small game. Tampons can serve as bandages, water filters, wicks for improvised candles, blow dart fletching and (see above) currency . . . and more!

5. **A collapsible umbrella lined with wrenches**
   This is one of the many improvised weapons in the book *100 Deadly Skills* by former Navy SEAL Clint Emerson.

6. **A lightweight, collapsible kayak**
   Live in a place like Manhattan—a prime target surrounded by water? Concerned that when the apocalypse hits, bridges and tunnels will be closed or mobbed? For $1,299 to Oru Kayak, you can have this escape boat; it collapses to the size of a suitcase and weighs thirty pounds.

7. **A portable parachute**

   The SOS Parachute costs about $2,400. Compact to store, quick to open. Just make sure you're on the 11th floor or higher.

8. **A jetpack or a flying motorcycle**

   The apocalypse hits, the highways are jammed . . . but you can be above it all. For $295,000, JetPack Aviation will sell you a 65-mph jetpack. For $380,000, the company will sell you "the world's first flying motorcycle . . . fully VTOL (vertical take off and landing) capable . . . fully stabilized and easy to fly." For the ultralight version of both machines, no pilot's license is required.

9. **A male and a female rabbit**

   Want to eat post-apocalypse? A female rabbit can produce fifty kits a year, yielding 250 pounds of high-protein, low-fat meat. According to Survivalist.com, "Raising meat rabbits is one of the most space-efficient means of growing livestock for meat." Plus: rabbits yield fur for improvised winter clothing.

10. **A "genetic spaceflight"**

    Think you might not survive the apocalypse? Contact Celestis. For $12,500, they'll send your DNA (a mouth swab or hair sample) on a spaceship "well beyond the moon." The idea: smart aliens may use it to reanimate you.

Let's say—maybe a global pandemic—poof!—we're all gone.
In a century or two, what's there to see in Manhattan?

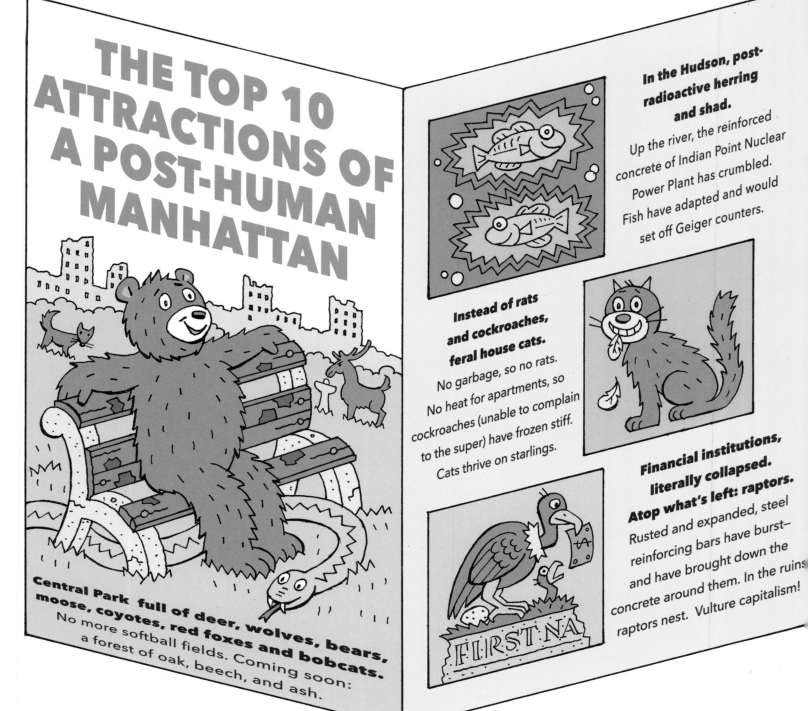

THE TOP 10 ATTRACTIONS OF A POST-HUMAN MANHATTAN

Central Park full of deer, wolves, bears, moose, coyotes, red foxes and bobcats. No more softball fields. Coming soon: a forest of oak, beech, and ash.

In the Hudson, post-radioactive herring and shad. Up the river, the reinforced concrete of Indian Point Nuclear Power Plant has crumbled. Fish have adapted and would set off Geiger counters.

Instead of rats and cockroaches, feral house cats. No garbage, so no rats. No heat for apartments, so cockroaches (unable to complain to the super) have frozen stiff. Cats thrive on starlings.

Financial institutions, literally collapsed. Atop what's left: raptors. Rusted and expanded, steel reinforcing bars have burst—and have brought down the concrete around them. In the ruins raptors nest. Vulture capitalism!

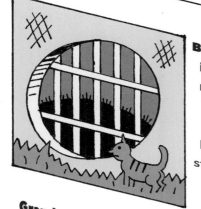

But bank vaults are intact, and full of mildewed money.
What's also wetter: Manhattan itself. Its streams are back, stocked with alewives and—dropped by seagulls—mussels.

Grand Central and St. Paul's Chapel: still open.
Grand Central's marble has outlasted all the gleaming skyscrapers that surrounded it. St. Paul's, built in 1766 of rugged Manhattan schist, endures.

In the museums, no more oils but come see the ceramics.
Fungi have destroyed the paintings but ceramics—chemically similar to fossils—have toughed it out. Bronze statues are okay. To future archeologists, our age is another Bronze Age.

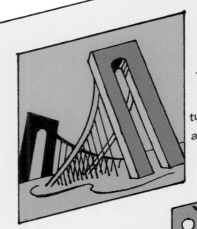

The ruins of the George Washington and Verrazano bridges.
They couldn't keep anything in suspense. The subway tubes under the East River are also broken. (And Manhattan cabbies would still tell you, "I don't go to Brooklyn.")

Sleeping with the fishes, Lady Liberty.
Encrusted in barnacles, she still holds her extinguished torch high.

Eventually, the glaciers scour it all to dust.
After wiping Manhattan clean, the last glacier left 12,000 years ago. Next time, glaciers grind down the Fresh Kills landfill—including all its glass. So raise something else to toast it.

—Inspired by
The World Without Us
by Alan Weisman

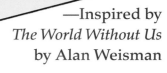

THE TOP 10 REASONS WHY YOU SHOULD BUY A UNIT IN THE SURVIVAL CONDO PROJECT

The Survival Condo Project is two underground Atlas missile silos near Concordia, Kansas, each silo turned into a fifteen-story apartment complex that is "state of the art in luxury and security." A half-floor unit (maximum occupancy five people) sells for $1.5 million. A full-floor unit (maximum occupancy 10 people) sells for $3 million. A "penthouse" unit (a duplex) starts at $4.5 million. If you have skills valuable in a post-apocalypse world, you may get a discount. Additionally, a custom bunker is available.

Here's why you should buy a unit:

1. Each complex has enough water and fuel for five years off the grid. And the complexes have their own wind turbines.

2. Each complex has NBC (nuclear, biological and chemical) air filtration. And its own weather station.

3. Each complex has fish tanks to raise tilapia and a facility to grow hydroponic vegetables.

4. Each unit comes with a five-year food supply per person. Each has a full kitchen with high-end stainless steel appliances, Kohler fixtures throughout, a 50-inch LED TV and a washer-dryer. Each is fully furnished and professionally decorated. A typical unit might have nine-foot ceiling, a gas fireplace and a Wolf range. Its guest room might have a wet bar.

5. To counter claustrophobia and depression (residents will be living underground!), walls in all units are fitted with L.E.D. windows that show a live video of the prairie above the silo. Or residents can have a video of a pine forest, New York City's Central Park, etc.

6. Each complex has a 75-foot-long swimming pool and a spa, a complete workout facility, a rock-climbing wall, an Astro-Turf "pet park," a game arcade, a shooting range, a bar and lounge, a movie theater, a library and a classroom with Mac desktops.

7. Each complex includes a medical wing with a hospital bed, a procedure table and a dentist's chair. At last report, the WTSHTF residents of one complex included two doctors and a dentist.

8. In case anyone "acts up," each complex has a bare-walled room with a toilet and a lock on the door.

9. WTSHTF, each complex has SWAT-team-style trucks ("Pit-Bull VX, armed up to fifty-caliber") which will pick up any resident within 400 miles.

10. WTSHTF, if anyone tries to seize either complex (threats have already been made), guards in a sniper post will return fire. And each complex has an armory stocked with guns and ammo.

Pit-Bull VX (noun): an armored SWAT truck, based on a Ford F-550, includes 360-degree rotating roof-mounted gun turret and hydraulic sniper platform, available from Alpine Armoring, Chantilly, Va, visit alpineco.com

THE TOP 8 WAYS THE WORLD (AS WE KNOW IT) ACTUALLY WILL END

The world as we know it *could* come to an end because of human actions (global warming, nuclear war, etc.) or random events (asteroids, supernovas, etc.). But the world as we know it definitely *will* end via events numbers 1 through 7. And event number 8 ends the world, period.

1. **30,000 to 130,000 years from now: The next Ice Age.**
   Ice ages occur cyclically. At present we are in an interglacial period that normally would be expected to end in 25,000 years. But human-caused global warming will delay this. If fossil fuel use ends by the year 2200, an Ice Age will come in 30,000 years. If we keep releasing carbon dioxide into the atmosphere, an Ice Age will come in 50,000 to 130,000 years.

2. **Over the next 100 million years: Continental drift remakes the world.**
   Continental drift continues; right now North and South America are moving west, away from Africa and Europe. According to one computer simulation, in 100 million years a supercontinent of Africa, Eurasia, Australia and Antarctica will form around Antarctica.

3. **1.5 to 4.5 billion years from now: Loss of axial tilt may destroy all life.**
   Earth's axis is tilted 23.5 degrees from being perpendicular to the plane of its orbit. This is what gives us seasons. It's also what keeps Earth's peak high and low temperatures within a range of about 200 degrees Fahrenheit. But over time, Earth's gravitational "dance" with the sun will grind away at this tilt, reducing it to zero. Then, in the Earth's middle, where it will be vastly hotter than today, atmospheric gases might evaporate into space. And at the poles, where it will be vastly colder than today, these gases might freeze to the ground. Earth's entire atmosphere could collapse.

4. **3-4 billion years from now: The end of the magnetosphere.**
   Earth's inner core is a sphere of solid iron, 2,516 miles across, above 9000° F. Around it, the outer core is a shell of molten iron and some molten nickel, 1,367 miles thick, about 8000° F. Around it is the mostly solid mantle, 1,800 miles thick, about 7230° F where it abuts the outer core. Since its formation 4.5 billion years ago, the Earth has been gradually cooling. As it cools, heat is transported from the outer core to the mantle. This makes the molten iron in the outer core churn fast, and this gives Earth its magnetic field, the magnetosphere. The magnetosphere deflects harmful solar winds and helps keep the atmosphere in place. But 3-4 billion years from now, when the outer core has cooled down and become solid, the magnetosphere will disappear.

5. **1 billion years from now: Through solar evolution, the Earth loses its plant and land animal life.**
As the sun consumes itself, solar luminosity increases; the sun radiates more heat. Rising temperatures on Earth will speed up the weathering of silicate minerals. As this weathering converts carbon dioxide to solid carbonates, the amount of CO_2 in the atmosphere will drop below the level needed for photosynthesis. The resulting loss of plant life will result in the eventual loss of oxygen. The first animals to disappear will be large mammals, followed by small mammals, birds, amphibians and large fish, reptiles and small fish, and finally invertebrates. At some point, much of the surface of the Earth will be barren desert.

6. **2.8 billion years from now: Through solar evolution, the Earth loses its oceans and hence all life. Then it melts.**
Once solar luminosity is 10% higher than today, Earth's average temperature will be 116° F. With the atmosphere a "moist greenhouse," there will be a runaway evaporation of the oceans. This could happen "merely" 1.1 billion years from now or it could be delayed a billion years or more. By 2.8 billion years from now, the Earth's surface temperature will be 300° F. Once solar luminosity is 35%-40% higher than today, Earth's surface temperature will be 2420° F—and the surface of Earth melts.

7. **12 billion years from now: Through solar evolution, the Earth is reduced to oceans of lava and continents of metals.**
Solar luminosity will increase to 2,730 times what it is today. Earth's surface temperature will be 3860° F and this surface will be a lava ocean with floating continents of metals and metal oxides, plus "icebergs" of minerals with high melting points. As the sun burns up more of itself and loses mass, Earth's orbit will expand; presently 93 million miles from the sun, the Earth may go out as far as 230 million miles.

8. **7.5 billion to 50 billion years from now: The Earth is swallowed by the sun.**
As the sun expands into a red giant (256 times larger than its current size), it will swallow Mercury and Venus. This expanded sun will probably pull the Earth back toward it, and engulf it. At some point the sun will collapse into a white dwarf, then a black dwarf. If the Earth has not been swallowed by the red giant sun, in 100 quintillion years (if the universe still exists) it will be sucked into the black dwarf sun.

100 quintillion years (noun):
100,000,000,000,000,000,000 years, by which time that Christmas fruitcake will be really hard

THE TOP 10 WAYS THE UNIVERSE COULD—TOMORROW OR 3,000 BILLION YEARS FROM NOW—END

1. **Intelligent destruction.**
   While we humans are approaching having the technologies (nuclear, nano, etc.) to possibly destroy much or all life on Earth, that's still a very long way from being able to destroy the universe. But what if intelligent aliens, advanced far beyond us, have—or will—accidentally put in motion something to do exactly that?

2. **The simulation is turned off.**
   Here's the theory: life is just a computer simulation run by some intelligent *something* somewhere. What happens if that user turns off the program?

3. **The Big Crumble.**
   There are about 25 physical constants (the speed of light, the mass of a proton, etc.) that make things possible. But are they really constant? Physicists have discovered that since the Big Bang, the "fine structure" constant has changed in space and time. *If* physical constants are degrading, in 3,000 billion years . . . the Big Crumble. All matter falls apart. Stars and planets explode, humans (if we're still around) fall to pieces.

4. **Collision with another universe.**
   According to the multiverse theory, there are an infinite number of universes with infinite possibilities. So there may be realities in which universes crash into each other. And since our universe is lopsided (don't ask!), it's possible that our universe once did crash into another one, causing a dent. Next time, we may not be so lucky. And since another universe could have laws completely different from ours . . . the end.

5. **The Big Crunch.**
   Ever since the Big Bang 13.8 billion years ago, the universe has been expanding. Most physicists believe the universe is infinite and will keep expanding. But one interpretation of Einstein's theory of general relativity is that the universe isn't infinite. In which case, billions of years from now, it will start to retract into a singularity.

6. The oscillating universe theory.

Supposedly, the Big Bang came out of singularity, one single point. But physicists' calculations of the Big Bang don't add up to singularity. Which suggests another theory: the Big Bang started when another universe collapsed. Which would mean that our universe could collapse again, like in the Big Crunch. If this theory is correct, our universe could be the product of the first collapse . . . or the zillionth.

7. Barrier death.

While most scientists believe the universe is infinite, that idea is contradicted by the laws of physics as we understand them. If the laws are correct, some scientists believe our expanding universe will hit a physical barrier. This would be like pouring a large amount of water into a hockey rink: eventually the water hits the boards. The hit would happen in 3.7 billion years.

8. The Big Slurp.

The Higgs field of energy (don't ask!) is everywhere in the universe. Currently, it's at its minimum potential energy state, a valley. But if "quantum tunneling" happens (again, don't ask!), the field could tunnel into a valley with a lower (and denser) energy state. This ultra-dense Higgs field would create a bubble that would expand, causing all atomic matter to collapse. While this probably wouldn't happen for tens of billions of years, Stephen Hawking said it could happen any time.

9. The Big Freeze.

The second law of thermodynamics says that in a closed system, everything goes from order to disorder, entropy always increases (food rots, metal rusts, people die). If our universe is a closed system, eventually all energy will be evenly distributed and the processes that consume it won't work anymore; heat won't be able to burst into existence. This scenario is called the Heat Death of the universe.

10. The Big Rip.

The universe is expanding ever faster and it's believed that dark energy, which makes up 68.3 percent of the universe, is causing this acceleration. If, as some physicists believe, dark matter is getting stronger, it will push galaxies apart from each other, push planets away from stars, etc. Eventually it will pull the nuclei out of atoms, leaving the universe ripped to shreds.

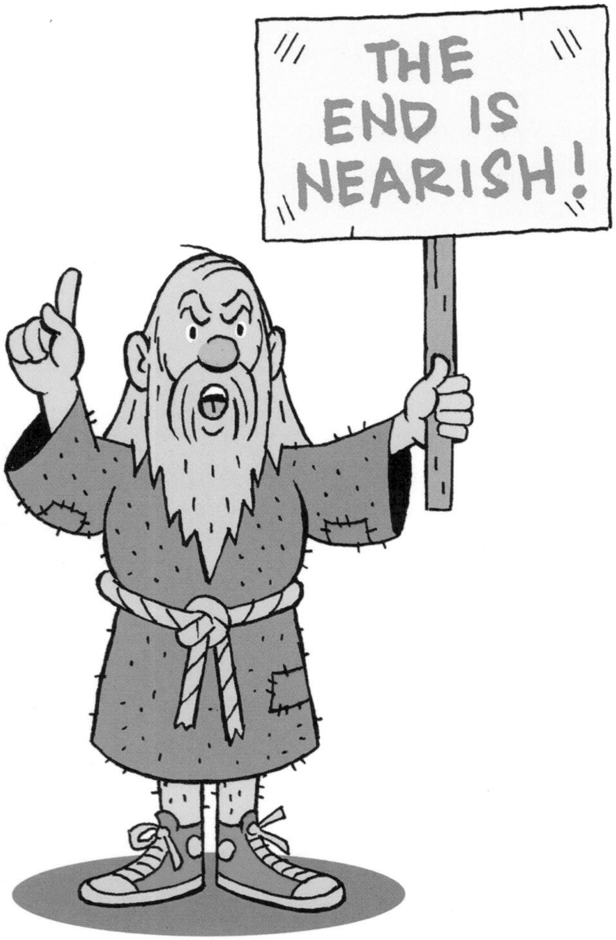
THE END IS NEARISH!